Senior Leadership Teams

LEADERSHIP FOR THE
COMMON GOOD

HARVARD BUSINESS SCHOOL PRESS

CENTER FOR PUBLIC LEADERSHIP
JOHN F. KENNEDY SCHOOL OF GOVERNMENT
HARVARD UNIVERSITY

The Leadership for the Common Good series represents a partnership between Harvard Business School Press and the Center for Public Leadership at Harvard University's John F. Kennedy School of Government. Books in the series aim to provoke conversations about the role of leaders in business, government, and society, to enrich leadership theory and enhance leadership practice, and to set the agenda for defining effective leadership in the future.

OTHER BOOKS IN THE SERIES

Changing Minds
by Howard Gardner

Predictable Surprises
by Max H. Bazerman and
Michael D. Watkins

Bad Leadership
by Barbara Kellerman

Many Unhappy Returns
by Charles O. Rossotti

Leading Through Conflict
by Mark Gerzon

Five Minds for the Future
by Howard Gardner

The Leaders We Need
by Michael Maccoby

Through the Labyrinth
by Alice H. Eagly and
Linda L. Carli

Senior Leadership Teams

WHAT IT TAKES TO MAKE THEM GREAT

Ruth Wageman

Debra A. Nunes

James A. Burruss

J. Richard Hackman

HARVARD BUSINESS SCHOOL PRESS

Boston, Massachusetts

15 14 13 12 11 10 9

Library of Congress Cataloging-in-Publication Data
Senior leadership teams: what it takes to make them great / Ruth Wageman . . . [et al.].
    p.   cm.
Includes bibliographical references and index
    ISBN 978-1-4221-0336-4
    1. Senior leadership teams. 2. Teams in the workplace—Management. 3. Group
problem solving. 4. Executive ability. I. Wageman, Ruth.
    HD66.7.S46 2007
    658.4'092—dc22

                                                                    2007028819

The paper used in this publication meets the requirements of the American National
Standard for Permanence of Paper for Publications and Documents in Libraries and
Archives Z39.48-1992.

Dedicated to the memory of
David C. McClelland

Contents

Preface

This book is about leadership teams. It is not about heroic leaders who personally transform entire organizations. Nor is it about senior management groups that efficiently dispatch the myriad tasks that float to the top of any organization.

We have heard many executives express the belief that there is something qualitatively different about what senior teams should be providing, something more than competent management. Often, they use the word *leadership* to capture what that is. That's what this book is about: senior team leadership. Specifically, it focuses on what it takes to lead teams whose members are themselves leaders—teams that chart the direction of an enterprise and then galvanize others' ideas and energy to sail that course.

Members of such teams have a dilemma. On the one hand, they are responsible for leading their own organizational units. On the other, they are expected to be fully engaged and committed members of the enterprise's senior team. It can feel like being caught in two powerful crosscurrents.

Given a choice about how to spend their time, most of the executives we have talked with do not hesitate: "Just let me focus on my *real* job," they say, "rather than waste all this time in endless meetings that accomplish nothing." For many overburdened executives, senior team meetings become obligatory appearances at events that have little to do with their leadership roles or the pressing organizational issues they face—and understandably, they would rather be somewhere else.

It doesn't have to be that way. This book was created to help senior executives identify the times and circumstances when senior leadership teams can be potent forces for enterprise effectiveness, and when they are not likely to add value. We show executives what is needed to create and sustain leadership teams whose members are invested in each other's success and who learn from one another as they work together to define and realize organizational objectives.

The Heroic CEO

To begin, here's a thought experiment: think of the best leadership team you have ever participated in or observed. Now think about the worst leadership team you can recall. What was the main difference between them? Why was one team so good, and the other so awful?

If you are like most of the people to whom we have posed this question, the first explanation that came to mind is the leader of the two teams. Indeed, "great leader" is almost always a central feature of the image we conjure when we think about a great team. An operating room team successfully executes a high-risk surgical procedure, and the lead surgeon emerges to receive the gratitude of the patient's family. An operational team sets a new plant production record, and the plant manager receives an award and a promotion. The senior leadership team of a multinational corporation charts a new and highly successful course for the business, and soon thereafter we see the CEO profiled in *Fortune* and a business school case written to help management students learn how they can do it.

The same thing happens for failures. The standard remedy for an organization's lackluster performance, for example, is to replace the chief executive. And it is not only bad decisions that draw notice. Inaction by a leader often is viewed as the main cause of what transpires and is reason enough for dismissal.

This pervasive human tendency to overemphasize one leader's personality or actions to explain organizational outcomes also dominates books on executive leadership. There are the "from the gut" autobiographical accounts by CEOs telling how they heroically turned around a failing or lackluster business. There are the "principles of leadership" books by consultants that distill the lessons they have learned into a set of injunctions about effective senior leadership. And there are academic tomes that identify the qualities that make for a great, or failing, chief executive. Almost all of these books share an unstated assumption: that everything depends on the person at the top, the heroic CEO.

But the demands on those who occupy the top roles of contemporary organizations are rapidly outdistancing the capabilities of any single person, no matter how talented. That is why a growing number of chief executives are turning to their direct reports—the senior managers of the enterprise—for help in meeting the leadership challenges they and their organizations face.

Senior leadership teams have great potential. They provide a rich pool of knowledge, talent, experience, and creativity for making enterprise-affecting decisions. Moreover, a team approach to executive leadership can provide the flexibility to transcend the traditional silo mentality that pervades many organizations and to effectively manage the important but often ambiguous white spaces that lie between those silos.

Yet chief executives often give insufficient thought to how they create, structure, and support their top teams, thereby unintentionally capping the potential of their teams' contributions to the enterprise. For example, CEOs commonly form their teams by simply convening the senior managers who already report to them and then test drive those teams for a while. If it seems necessary, they may bring in talented replacements for any members whose performance is shaky, surrounding themselves, as one executive noted, with "thoroughbreds."

At that point, unfortunately, chief executives often make a couple of bad assumptions. First, they assume that these high-powered executives will automatically work well together, even though thoroughbreds are notorious for not working together at all. Second, CEOs assume that their experienced and talented executives will clearly discern the right path for moving the organization forward and know what they have to do together to proceed wisely. But they don't, and they can't. Senior teams need to be properly set up and thoughtfully led.

The Core Idea

No CEO can make a leadership team great. What the CEO can do is put in place certain conditions that increase the chances that a group of senior executives will develop into a superb leadership team. But there is no guarantee. Human systems, be they schoolyard groups or executive teams, evolve in their own, often idiosyncratic ways. They are not like engineered mechanical systems in which pushing specific levers will lead to predictable effects.

This "increase the chances" way of thinking about teams may seem strange to some senior executives, especially those who rely on a dictum like that of former CEO and U.S. presidential candidate Ross Perot to "just get under the hood and fix it." In this book we show that the key to competent leadership of a senior team is to create and sustain six conditions that, when in place, dramatically increase the chances of senior team effectiveness. To repeat: you cannot make your leadership team great. But you can put in place conditions that increase the chances that it will become great.

This book draws on the conclusions from our multiyear research project on senior leadership teams to lay out those conditions and show you how to create them. The first three conditions are what we call the essentials. If you cannot establish these conditions (a real team rather than a team in name only, a compelling team purpose, and members who have the right capabilities), then it is better not to form a senior team at all. The second three are what we call the enablers. These conditions (a solid team structure, a supportive organizational context, and competent team coaching) smooth the road to senior team effectiveness.

At the most general level, the six conditions are easily understood and readily remembered. The challenge, and what this book is mainly about, comes when you implement those conditions in specific organizational circumstances. Our research shows that there is no single best way for a chief executive to create and sustain the six conditions, nor any fixed set of steps to follow in structuring, launching, and leading senior teams. Instead, we find that great leaders draw on their particular skills and preferences to create these conditions in ways that are tuned to the unique circumstances in which their teams operate.

Is This Book for You?

This book is intended for anyone who seeks an alternative lens through which to examine senior leadership teams: those who lead businesses, government agencies, educational and health care organizations, and non-profit enterprises of all kinds, as well as general readers who are curious about leadership at the top of an enterprise. It provides insights about why some senior leadership teams enter into a spiral of ever-increasing capability while others either struggle endlessly or crash and burn not long after being launched. We offer concrete and practical guidance, based on our years of experience as researchers and consultants, about how to capture and harness the real benefits of executive teams without falling victim to the problems and miscues that often derail them.

When you have finished the book, you will have answers to six questions that every chief executive who leads a team must deal with in one way or another. Busy leaders often answer these consequential questions implicitly, without much thought. This book helps you make your leadership choices explicitly, based both on your own aspirations for your team and on solid research findings about what it takes to make top teams great.

1. *Do I really need a leadership team?* This is perhaps the most important question that chief executives who are starting, have started, or have inherited a team should ask before they take another step. Unfortunately, it is a question that most executives either ignore or assume they've answered—until they begin to experience the frustration of a dysfunctional team. The best top teams are created by chief executives who have given careful thought to the functions the team will serve, who understand what it will take to create and sustain such a team, and who are prepared to spend the time and effort needed to structure and support it.

2. *How do I define the purpose of my team?* If you ask most leaders what the purpose of their top team is, at best they'll repeat the objectives of the enterprise. So it's not surprising that if you ask members of top teams what the team's purpose is you'll get a wide range of answers. The team members know

that the team should be playing an irreplaceable role in the organization. Just what that role is, however, is not clear. The best top teams are those whose leaders know exactly where they want to take the enterprise and have a strategy to get there, and who have articulated an explicit purpose for the team that focuses on the unique contribution it can make to realize that strategy.

3. *Do I have the right people on the team?* Chief executives often get caught in a chain of bad assumptions. First, if they inherit a top team, as many do, they assume that they need to maintain the status quo to build harmony and trust. Second, they assume that title equals membership: if you are a senior vice president, you're on the team, whether or not you add value. And third, they equate membership with status, and they worry that if they remove a member he or she will lose face and be offended. So they either freeze, making no changes in membership until the damage is done, or they become overly inclusive, adding more and more people to the membership roster. The best top teams have carefully chosen membership— people who have the specific knowledge, capabilities, and experience that are needed to achieve team purposes, and no members who are merely along for the ride.

4. *How should I structure the team?* Even teams that have a compelling purpose and the right members can get stuck or fall into a pattern of unproductive wheel-spinning. When this happens, it usually is because the team lacks the basic structures that are needed for members to work together efficiently and well. By "structure," we do not mean boxes and lines on the organization chart. Instead, we are talking about those few features of a team that most powerfully shape how members act and interact: the size and diversity of the membership, the way the team's concrete tasks are set up, and the core norms of conduct that guide members' interactions. The best top teams are created by leaders who know that basic structural features such as these can spell the difference between team success and failure, and they give careful attention to getting them right.

5. *What organizational support do I need to provide the team?* Another erroneous assumption often made by executive team leaders is that such teams are self-sufficient. After all, members are at the peak of organizational power, status, and expertise. But no matter how good the members are, senior teams can't do it all on their own. Just like front-line teams in the enterprise, senior teams need recognition and reinforcement when they perform well, trustworthy data to help members evaluate alternative courses of action, ready access to technical consultation for matters that lie beyond members' own expertise, and, of course, the mundane material resources that can spell the difference between frustrating and smooth teamwork. Leaders of the best top teams think explicitly about the kinds of organizational support their teams most need, and they exercise their own power to make sure the team gets that support.

6. *Who can coach a team of leaders, and when should he or she do it?* Superb senior leadership teams do not just happen; they develop slowly over time. And they need competent hands-on coaching along the way to help members resolve problems in how they are working together and also to alert them to opportunities for strengthening the team—opportunities that members might overlook. Although the chief executive sometimes takes personal responsibility for coaching the senior team, coaching may be better handled by another member or even by an outside consultant. And although coaching obviously is useful during times of trouble, some of the most helpful coaching occurs at other times in the team's life, especially when the team is taking on a new piece of work and again when it is time to reflect on the lessons learned from work just completed. Leaders of the best top teams recognize the value of team-focused coaching and make sure that it is readily available to the team.

Few chief executives find themselves entirely prepared to lead a team of senior organizational leaders. As we noted earlier, it is a challenging leadership task to harness a group of high-spirited, independent-minded thoroughbreds and then run them daily in the high-stakes horse race of the marketplace, with the owners (the board), bettors (investors), and even the institutional "bookies" (the analysts) all shouting advice and encouragement from the rail.

For most executives, as good as they are, leading a team of thoroughbreds is uncharted territory. Even though they may have been successful in previous high-profile organizational roles, they quickly learn that leading teams of leaders poses a new set of challenges. We hope that this book will be helpful to you in meeting those challenges.

Genesis of This Book

"Not another book about teams!" We enjoyed this remark from one of our anonymous reviewers (especially because this reader changed his or her mind after reading the book). But we understood the reaction: why, with a staggering number of books about teams out there, do we need another one?

We need one because senior leadership teams can be extraordinarily effective bodies—and we saw little guidance out there about what can be done to make that so. Two of the authors of this book (Nunes and Burruss) are veteran consultants with the Hay Group; the other two (Wageman and Hackman) are academics who study and teach about teams and leadership. This team of authors came together from a shared conviction that it is possible to have an effective senior leadership team, and we set out to explore that possibility.

Over the past decades, the two consultant authors have pondered with their clients the reasons that senior executive teams, although increasingly critical for organizational success, rarely work well. What, they wondered, were highly talented leaders doing wrong when they formed their teams? Many of the executives had created an informal group of staff who served as trusted advisers, whereas others had established large teams consisting of all their direct reports. Yet the results rarely were what the chief executives had hoped for. Worse, these two consultants heard many chief executives taking the skepticism about teams at the top— skepticism generated in the popular press—as permission to live with dysfunction or with resignation in the face of it. The consultants disagreed with the assumption, "It's always going to be like that when you bring together a group of thoroughbreds."

At the same time, but independently, the two university-based authors were conducting a series of research investigations aimed at identifying the organizational conditions and leadership behaviors that can increase the capability of any team to perform well. This research, much of which is summarized in Hackman's book *Leading Teams: Setting the Stage for Great Performances*, involved many types of teams, from musical ensembles to airline flight-deck crews to field service teams, but it did not focus specifically on the special demands and opportunities faced by senior executive teams. Yet the more the academic authors learned about the kinds of problems their consultant colleagues encountered with teams at the top, the more it seemed that those teams were struggling with the very kinds of design and leadership flaws that undermined teams in many other parts of organizations. How could these teams thrive, for example, when two members were competing for the top job and when all the members were rewarded exclusively for outstanding individual performance? How could they create alignment in the organization when they themselves had no shared purpose of any consequence?

A few years ago, the four of us discovered the commonalties and the complementarities in the work our two groups had been doing. We decided to pool our expertise and research capabilities to explore systematically what is required for senior leadership teams to perform superbly. We collected and analyzed systematic data from more than 120 top teams around the world, examining everything from organizational mission to the capabilities of individual team members. We observed these teams in action, conducted in-depth interviews of leaders and members, and collected quantitative and qualitative data about the teams using well-validated assessment tools. We also reviewed financial results, customer satisfaction, and other measures of performance for the teams we studied.

That research unearthed the six conditions that turned out to be key in composing, structuring, and leading executive teams. Moreover, the research provided numerous concrete examples of senior team leadership, some of which worked well and some of which did not. We draw heavily both on those examples and on our research findings in exploring what senior executives can do to strengthen their leadership teams.

Acknowledgments

We have had a great deal of help both in our research and in writing this book. We would like to thank Ruth Malloy and Signe Spencer for their invaluable assistance in collecting, organizing, and analyzing the data. We thank all our colleagues in the Hay Group who shared their insights and helped us with access and information about many leadership teams. We express our gratitude to early readers of the book for their astute observations and comments, including Nick Boulter, Murray Dalziel, Jan LaPierre, Patricia Marshall, Jeff Shiraki, and eight anonymous reviewers. We are grateful to all the chief executives and senior team members of the organizations around the world with whom we have worked and whose cooperation and candor helped us learn. We express our heartfelt thanks to our loved ones who supported us so much throughout this project. And, especially, we thank our partners in this venture, Mary Fontaine and Scott Spreier. Mary's conceptual contributions throughout this collaboration are everywhere in this book, and Scott's writing talents made the book possible.

1

The Fall of the Heroic
CEO and the Rise of the
Leadership Team

Diego Bevilacqua is an experienced executive, a respected leader, and a veteran of the usual corporate team-building exploits, including trekking through the steamy rain forests of Costa Rica. But nothing, including grinning crocodiles and howling monkeys, prepared him for the challenge he was handed at the end of 2000: to put together a leadership team that could, with few new resources or technology, rapidly build a successful business.

Bevilacqua talks about the food service business he took over after the merger of Bestfoods and Unilever as "a child with no family."[1] His challenge: to integrate Bestfoods' highly successful food service business with Unilever's much less effective counterpart. Although Bestfoods was the smaller entity, it had the stronger business. Bringing these two organizations together would be a politically charged process and an uphill battle against skeptics on both sides who believed that the merger would destroy rather than expand the food services business.

Bevilacqua inherited a set of leaders on both sides who knew the industry deeply and who had their own ideas about how the business should be run. But Patrick Cescau, then head of Unilever's Foods Division, now Group CEO, wanted Bevilacqua to take these two entities and create a business that "would be a 'formidable force in food service,'" says Bevilacqua. "The way I saw it, what I could do was give some leadership to this new group of people, this new business. And create a culture that would allow for the experts to openly challenge each other and actually co-create an agenda for the future."[2]

Bevilacqua and his key advisers developed a business model that had the new Foodsolutions—the two merged entities—operating primarily as a business independent of its parent. But it also would be interdependent with the rest of Unilever for back office support (including technology and R&D) and for collaborative relationships with the other high-value Unilever brands. "We saw that the retail business and food services had much in common," Bevilacqua says. "There was really no justification to create a separate superstructure. We wanted to create the focus, clarity, and independence needed to do what was right for that particular set of customers and market, but without creating costs that were not adding value." This "independent but interdependent" model represented a significant shift in the operations of the food services business, and it escalated the need for collaboration among the leaders of the new entity.

To foster greater unity of understanding and purpose, Bevilacqua brought together what we term an *alignment* team. This team consisted not only of his direct reports, the eleven people who made up his core leadership team, but also the next level—a total of forty-six executives. Bevilacqua spent a week with them clarifying and planning the implementation of the new strategic direction. "The challenge I put to them was as follows . . . 'Unilever has allowed us to be independent. So we've achieved independence, that's great. Tick. We are now accountable, though. So with independence comes accountability. And you are part of that. Help us define the future of the business. And how we are going to achieve it.'"

Bevilacqua knew he was surrounded by a team of experienced professionals, industry veterans who understood the business and their markets and were successful themselves. Together they would succeed.

But it wasn't that simple.

Within a few months it was clear that something was wrong. Although the team had what Bevilacqua believed was a solid business plan with specific marching orders, there was little unity among the members.

Only a few of them were fully on board. The rest either continued to operate as they always had or put their own unique spin on the new strategy. To call the group a "team" was, at best, a stretch. More accurately, it was a loose confederation of individual managers, all with their own agendas.

It wasn't long before the organizational chaos was reflected in lackluster business results, leaving Bevilacqua frustrated and angry. Why all the difficulty? Why couldn't a group of sophisticated, experienced business leaders come together to create a solid, strong-performing team? What was he, as their leader, doing wrong? "I knew we needed to create a team that was facing the same direction—that spoke the same language, talked about the same issues, focused on the same goals, and added real value to the rest of the organization," he recalls. "We tried a combination of tactics, pushing and pulling to get people to understand."

But little seemed to work. Bevilacqua knew that he had to take drastic action to stem the growing revolt and save the business. A clear sign that his leadership team was not working was that members repeatedly returned to the same issues—concerns that should have been addressed in a single meeting. Bevilacqua described a victim mentality taking hold of the group and a similar malaise affecting him. He began convincing himself that his ineffective and poorly united team was a problem he could not do much about. Like many other senior leaders, he began seeing the dysfunction at the top as inevitable in a group of thoroughbreds. "I thought, 'This is just nonsense. I can't manage a business in this fashion with every Tom, Dick, and Harry interfering at local, regional, and global levels. So if I am going to die, I would rather die of my own doing than because the world has interfered.'"

Leading in the Cauldron of Change and Competition

Bevilacqua is not the first experienced and talented executive to suddenly find himself and his organization in a dangerous tailspin. Nor will he be the last. A growing number of leaders are discovering that effectively running an organization, whether a business unit, a small company, a corporation, or a conglomerate, is harder than ever before.

It isn't that top leaders are less skilled or less experienced than leaders of the past. Nor are the teams they lead. The challenge is the change in roles of both leader and team member, roles that have been reshaped in the cauldron of intense competition and relentless change. Regionalization may have worked in the past. But today, with the emphasis on globalization and growth, it's all about scope, speed, and customer intimacy. Leadership teams must consistently ensure that clients' needs are met, and do it right now.

Consider Bevilacqua's challenge of developing a successful global food services business. What that meant was (1) combine the resources of two organizations having different values, cultures, processes, and leadership styles; (2) create a strategy for dozens of countries around the globe, each with its own culture, climate, and culinary demands; (3) do it all within twelve months, and (4) grow the business several percentage points that first year.

The difficulty is not always a factor of size and scale. Even leading a small organization has become more complex and challenging than it was a decade ago. Just ask people who head up a local not-for-profit. They will tell you about the increased public scrutiny, the ever-expanding list of regulations, and the elevated expectations of donors and recipients.

It is no wonder that, despite the lure of the executive suite, a growing number of senior leaders either are declining the top job or choosing to drop out. As one executive told us after taking himself out of consideration to head his conglomerate's fastest-growing division, "I know this job. It consumes your life. It's not what I want for me and my family."

Even if it is their goal to get to the top and they are fortunate enough to achieve that goal, many chief executives find tenure elusive. "Perform or perish" has become the rule. Study after study shows how tough and tenuous the top job is: in 1995, 72 percent of departing U.S. and U.K. CEOs either retired or died in office. By 2001 that group had dropped to 47 percent. During that same period, CEO turnover went up 53 percent.[3]

What such studies don't show is the struggle these executives go through long before they make their exit. These top players are not quitters by nature. They want to be successful. They will go through considerable pain to be successful. And so they continue to soldier on, realizing all the while that despite their best efforts, they are not reaching the results they need.

As leadership guru Warren Bennis puts it, "Our mythology refuses to catch up with us. And so we cling to the myth of the Lone Ranger, the romantic idea that great things are usually accomplished by a larger-than-life individual working alone. Despite evidence to the contrary—including the fact that Michelangelo worked with a group of 16 to paint the Sistine Chapel—we still tend to think of achievement in terms of the Great Man or the Great Woman, instead of the Great Group."[4]

The Heroic CEO Versus the Two-Heads-Are-Better-Than-One Approach

Going it alone is not just a romantic notion. It's human nature, at least in individualistic cultures. Despite all the talk of the importance of "the team" or "the organization" we still, in some parts of the world, celebrate the achievement of the individual leader in successfully maneuvering to the top of the organization. Just look at a cover of any popular business periodical. As often as not, the photo is of a single person, arms folded across the chest: the Lone Ranger, the Heroic CEO standing proudly atop the organization.

But this one-leader approach is starting to give way to the Great Group idea. In some countries, a division of leadership is legally mandated. In the United Kingdom, for example, regulatory bodies strongly recommend that the chairman and CEO roles be held by different individuals, and most publicly traded companies comply. In other places, including the United States, a few organizations have simply begun dividing the work of the CEO role among two or more coleaders, and others have taken a team approach in which senior executives work together to guide their organization.[5]

In many organizations the co-CEO option has met with limited success for a number of reasons, not the least of which is the inability of most leaders to share the top role no matter how good their intentions or persistent their efforts. Citicorp tried it following its merger with Travelers but quickly found that the structure did not work. Co-CEOs John Reed and Sandy Weill, who had cordially agreed to share the position after the merger, soon found themselves embroiled in a messy power struggle. In the end, Weill stayed, Reed left, and another board learned that as big as the CEO's role is, it's almost always too small for two strong leaders. Other high-profile attempts at corporate crown sharing, including Daimler-Chrysler, Kraft, and Time Warner, have met similar fates.

Actually, the poor track record of experiments with co-CEOs is nearly inevitable because of the way humans are wired. One product of our evolutionary heritage is the inevitability of hierarchies whenever groups form.[6] Organisms that win the competition for dominance have a better chance to reproduce and thereby pass their genes to successive generations, contributing to the long-term survival and strength of the species. This phenomenon is seen in creatures from ants to wolves.

It occurs even in insect groups such as swarms of wasps, a species that probably seems about as far from the top management suite as one can get. Female paper wasps quickly and definitively form a hierarchy when they come together, with consequences not only for their behavior but also for their physiology: dominant females become better able to reproduce, whereas subordinates become unable to do so.[7]

Despite the extraordinary ability of humans to transcend many of our evolutionary impulses, we also form ourselves into hierarchies whenever we come together, no matter what the purpose.

Those organizations that have succeeded with dual leaders typically have done so in title only. If you scratch the surface of the organizational chart you'll see that despite the same titles these co-CEOs actually have different roles. Frequently it is more of a CEO-COO kind of arrangement, with one leader externally focused and the other more internally or operationally focused. Until recently, for example, Bill Gates as chairman of Microsoft focused more on the firm's technology and external constituents while Steve Ballmer as CEO focused on the business side. True coleadership may be almost impossible in the executive suite. In the words of corporate governance expert Ram Charan, appointing co-CEOs is "not going to be the new best practice in business."[8]

The Senior Team as an Alternative Leadership Model

Evolution has wired us not merely to form dominance hierarchies but to work together when a vital task demands more than any single individual can accomplish alone. Organisms from ants to antelopes work closely together to fend off attacks from other groups, to capture resources that others enjoy, to cope with developing disasters, and to create structures that promote the collective well-being. Leading a complex organization is at least as demanding of coordinated collective work as is protecting territory, harvesting food, or constructing colonies. Might leadership teams offer a viable alternative to both the heroic leader and the co-CEO models?

The premise of this book is that teams are not only a feasible means of providing organizational leadership but that they are also increasingly necessary as the demands of top roles outdistance the capacities of any single person. That is why a growing number of chief executives are forming teams to help them lead their enterprises. This practice has a number of advantages, at least in theory. For one thing, leaders can avoid the messy coleader problem of who ultimately is in charge while at the same time sharing critical responsibilities and decision making. In addition, when a leadership team addresses strategic issues that cut across the enterprise, most of the people who will be responsible for implementing those decisions will be in the room.

Moreover, the chief executive can draw on the rich pool of knowledge, talent, experience, perspective, and creativity of the company's most accomplished leaders in making key organizational decisions. When harnessed, this creative energy can bridge boundaries, as the team deals with the opportunity-rich "white spaces" between areas where a lack of command and control must be replaced with collaboration.[9]

For many top leaders, increased reliance on a team for mission-critical issues has been a subtle and seemingly natural shift. After all, a group of senior leaders already exists. Why not simply lean more heavily on them for help and support? After all, isn't that why they're there?

Yes—and no. Certainly most top executives surround themselves with a cadre of top advisers, senior managers they trust to carry out the mission of the organization. But the members of this group also have specific leadership responsibilities that keep them working as individuals, each representing a function or business unit and not the enterprise—and this structure is at the center of the problem.

The Myth of the Spontaneous and Self-Sustaining Senior Team

In our work with chief executives around the world, we have seen the same scenario play out repeatedly. A new, talented executive—let's call her Julia—takes over the leadership of an enterprise, be it a business, a public service organization, or a foundation. Julia believes she has the lay of the land. She has done due diligence. She has reviewed the numbers. The financials and other fundamentals of the enterprise look sound.

Next she considers the leadership team. Due diligence here is a bit more difficult. There is less concrete information, less hard data. Perhaps she starts with the existing team and brings in some talented thorough-breds to counter the weaknesses.

With a supposedly strong team in place, Julia immediately turns to what she sees as the most critical enterprise issues. As a highly visible leader in a complex, fast-paced business environment she faces tremen-dous demands from many sources: governments, regulators, the stock market, the shareholders, the board, major customers, key suppliers, and employees. The list is huge, as is the pressure to perform—and perform quickly. In the rush to succeed, Julia ignores the crafting of her team, which is still little more than a loose federation of individual managers. Her assumption is that a team of experienced leaders will become a great leadership team without much help or direction (they are, after all, com-petent, experienced executives).

But they can't. Instead, each one has his or her own agenda and vision. There is no team focus, no shared direction, and, as a result, no traction. That is the challenge: how do you harness a group of high-performing, high-spirited thoroughbreds, in all probability the most talented individ-uals in your organization, so that they all run together and pull the orga-nization in the direction it should be headed? How do you create a real, effective, top leadership team?

Our Research: The Quest for Effective Senior Teams

As consultants and researchers, we understood the frustrations of chief executives when their teams floundered. When it came to the traditional organizational metrics, these leaders appeared to have all the bases cov-ered. For the most part, they had long track records as successful executives. Their team members also tended to be talented, experienced leaders in their own right. Many had created great teams within their own parts of the organization. And yet they were unable to operate as a great team themselves.

We wondered whether there wasn't a missing component—one that had to do with the unique structure and dynamics of senior leadership teams. What was special about these teams? Why did they seem so different from front-line teams in their own organizations? And why were some senior teams much more effective than others? It was at this point that we pooled our expertise and research capabilities and began exploring what is required for effective senior leadership teams.

The Teams We Studied

Since 1998 we have studied and analyzed data on more than 120 senior leadership teams from around the world. These teams lead entities ranging from small businesses to huge multinational conglomerates—and all kinds and sizes in between. Some lead not-for-profit and public sector leadership teams. Our sample represents a variety of industries, covers twelve nations, and includes organizations you have never heard of as well as many high-profile players, such as IBM, Philips Electronics, Reuters, Sainsbury, Shell, Standard & Poor's, and Unilever.

These leadership teams have joined in our research for a variety of reasons. Some are led by CEOs who explicitly sought help with a dysfunctional leadership team. Others have undertaken strategic and structural changes and wanted advice on the implications, if any, for the design and functioning of their senior teams. Although some of them were poor performers when we began studying them, others were fundamentally sound teams. We assessed the overall effectiveness of every team in providing effective leadership to their enterprises, and we explored a wide array of features of their purpose, structure, and leadership to understand what differentiated the superb from the struggling leadership teams.

Measuring the Effectiveness of Senior Leadership Teams

Unlike most of the research conducted on leadership teams in the past, which typically assesses *organizational* performance and calls that the performance of the senior team, we sought a more direct measure of team effectiveness, one that really could be attributed to the actions of the team itself and not to environmental forces or chance.[10] Because each of the teams we studied faced its own performance challenges, its own environment, its own clients, and its own purposes, we needed to craft a means of assessing their effectiveness that was both relevant to and comparable for all of them. So we sought reliable judgments of how well the teams performed *as teams* by drawing on the observations of expert individuals who worked closely with the teams and who had direct contact with the constituents these teams served.

First, we enlisted the help of about a dozen senior consultants who had been working with the teams and their organizations. In the course of their work, these consultants had collected extensive interviews, observations, and survey data on organizational climate, performance, and leadership effectiveness. We asked them to provide their ratings of each executive team on three effectiveness criteria.[11]

The first criterion was whether the performance of the team met or exceeded the standards of the people, both inside and outside the organization, who were most affected by the team's work. In our view, it is stakeholders' standards and assessments that count—stockholders, employees, customers, communities, whatever groups are most salient for a given team at a given time—and not those of the team itself or even of the chief executive. Rather than serve as evaluator or as a surrogate client, the chief executive is responsible first to help the team identify the standards that are used by its real clients, and then do whatever can be done to help the team meet those standards.

Our raters gathered information from the relevant range of sources for each team. They conducted conversations with board members, analyzed organizational climate data, assessed customer responses—whatever key constituencies the senior leadership team served. They then rated how well the team was doing in meeting the standards of those constituencies. Teams were scored on a scale ranging from 1 ("Numbers are overall very poor; multiple constituencies are seriously underserved by this team") to 5 ("In the eyes of all constituencies, these are winners. Customers, employees, shareholders, partners all are served well by this team"). All the teams in our sample judged as outstanding teams led strong and growing organizations.

Second, we assessed how well members worked together *now* to enhance—rather than undermine—their capability to work together *in the future*. Effective teams operate in ways that build shared commitment, collective skills, and smart work strategies, and not mutual antagonisms and trails of failure from which little is learned. They become adept at detecting and correcting errors before serious damage is done, and at noticing and exploiting emerging opportunities. And they periodically review how they have been operating, milking their experiences for whatever learning can be had. Our expert raters drew on the observations of those who worked directly with each team and provided an assessment on a scale ranging from 1 ("This team shows signs of falling apart completely") to 5 ("Significant positive trajectory—signs of increasing collaboration and learning").

Third, we evaluated whether the group experience, on balance, contributed positively to the learning and personal development of individual team members. Leadership teams have much to offer their members. They are, for example, wonderful avenues for learning—for expanding knowledge, acquiring new skills, and exploring fresh perspectives on the world. And, of course, collaborating with others on important work can spawn satisfying interpersonal relationships. Yet leadership teams also can stress their members, alienate them from one another, and undermine individuals' confidence in their own abilities. We count a senior team effective only when the team experience has a more positive than negative impact on members' personal learning and well-being. Our expert raters drew on the private interviews conducted with the team members to assess the degree to which members, on balance, experienced the team as a 1 ("Frustration dominates; members express a desire to get out of the team") up to a 5 ("Members are delighted to be part of this team and describe significant personal learning and growth from its collaborations").

We found that leadership teams that excel on all three of these dimensions are rare—but they exist. More common are leadership teams that fall short on at least one of these three criteria. Sadly, some fail them all. Most common are teams that are modestly successful. They are pleasing to some constituents but have not positioned the enterprise well for future challenges, and they show little sign of serious improvement in how members work together.

We also found that the vast majority of senior leadership teams that show signs of growing more capable in working together also contribute substantially to the development of individual members. That is, as teams become more robust, creative, and adaptive, their members become more deeply satisfied with their membership in the team, and their own leadership capabilities develop as well. For this reason, you will see that, throughout this book, we have combined these last two criteria (Is the team getting better as a team? Are the individuals becoming more capable?) when we present our findings. The same features that help a leadership team develop adaptive capabilities as a team also make the members themselves more capable as leaders.

Figure 1-1 shows the percentage of leadership teams in our sample that were outstanding (our experts rated them as at or near the top) in how well they perform, very poor (our experts rated them near the bottom), or mediocre (our experts place them in the middle of the pack). The figure also shows the percentage of leadership teams that exhibited outstanding signs of team and individual development versus those that were very poor or mediocre in how well the team and its members developed over time. As you can see, on each criterion one-quarter of the leadership teams were outstanding, a little more than one-third were mediocre, and well over one-third were quite poor.

Measuring the Conditions That Shape Senior Leadership Team Effectiveness

After identifying the outstanding, mediocre, and poor teams, we began exploring what had led to these differences in outcomes. We asked the chief executive to identify the members of the team to be sure we were really studying a senior team and not just a collection of the leader's direct reports, or the "upper echelon" of the organization.[12] As you will see in chapter 2, simply asking the CEO to give us a list of team members

FIGURE 1-1

Effectiveness of senior leadership teams we studied

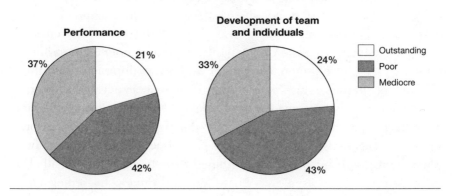

provided diagnostic data about how clear the boundaries of the team were (for example, when the CEO knew who was "on the team" but few members knew) and what chance it had of operating as a real team (not high if members did not know for sure who was on the team).

Once we knew who the members were, we asked each of them to complete an assessment that provided detailed descriptive data about the team's purpose, features of its structure and composition, the kinds of resources it had to work with, and the amount of hands-on coaching the leader provided—in other words, those aspects of the team's design or leadership that previous research has shown to strongly affect how, and how well, teams perform.[13] As you will see, these measures allowed us to array various features of a team's design and leadership on a scale ranging from 1 (poor) to 5 (excellent). We draw on these data to identify and discuss the most significant differences among outstanding, mediocre, and poor teams.

We also interviewed chief executives and team members intensively to assess their leadership capabilities, and we discuss the findings from those interviews in chapter 4.[14] We also explored the possibility that industry and other environmental differences were dominant in shaping the effectiveness of leadership teams, but those effects turned out to be small compared with the differences within industries. In other words, there were great and poor leadership teams in every industry we studied.

Next, we highlight the main findings of our research: the three essential and the three enabling conditions for leadership team effectiveness.

The Essential and the Enabling Conditions

The six conditions shown by our research to foster the effectiveness of senior leadership teams fall into two groups: three *essential* conditions, which are the basic prerequisites for good team performance, and three *enabling* conditions, which smooth the path to excellence and accelerate a team's movement down that path. Figure 1-2 shows an overview of these conditions. The essentials are just that: if organizational or personal circumstances prevent you from getting any one of them adequately in place, groups of senior leaders cannot collaborate effectively at all. The enablers, by contrast, serve to support the performance of senior teams

FIGURE 1-2

Six conditions for senior leadership team effectiveness

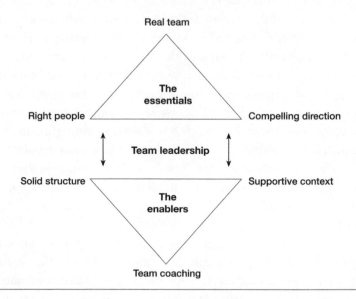

and enhance the ease and speed with which they develop into deft and ever-improving entities.

We devote one chapter to each of the six conditions (chapters 2 through 7). In each chapter, we explain what we have learned from our research about why that condition is critical for senior leadership teams. We describe our observations about the typical challenges that CEOs face in trying to get that condition in place for their teams, including stories and examples of the struggles of particular leaders. And for each condition, we offer examples that illustrate particular strategies leaders have used to overcome the challenges and to create and sustain each condition in their own senior leadership teams. These examples illustrate what chief executives can do to get the conditions in place in the unique organizational circumstances they face, using their particular styles and talents.

Throughout, we describe examples of actual leaders who have changed the design features of their teams; our aim is to provide alternative models and ideas for leaders who are considering strategies for creating these conditions in their own teams. The conditions we discuss in this book are valuable for any kind of task-performing team. However, we focus on the special challenges that senior leaders face in getting them in place for their groups of thoroughbreds, and our examples and advice throughout draw exclusively on the experiences of senior leadership teams.

Our research showed that the six conditions make a very big difference in the effectiveness of senior leadership teams. Indeed, nearly 50 percent of the variation in the performance of the teams we studied was accounted for by a team's standing on the conditions we assessed—that is, how well they were composed, structured, and supported. Merely knowing the standing of a team on the conditions dramatically boosts our ability to predict how well a senior leadership team will perform.[15]

The Essentials

Senior leaders establish the essential conditions for leadership teams by (1) creating a real team, rather than one that is a team in name only, (2) providing the team with a clear and compelling purpose, and (3) ensuring that the team consists of members who have the knowledge, skill, and experience that are required for the team's work. When these conditions are in place, the team has a solid foundation for carrying out its work and is positioned to set out on a course of increasingly competent teamwork.

When the essentials are not in place, however, members are likely to encounter chronic problems in working together, such as dysfunctional conflicts, uncertainty about how best to proceed with their work, continued focus on individual accountabilities at the expense of enterprisewide outcomes, cycling back through issues that have been resolved, and so on. Dealing with these problems diverts members' time and effort from the team's real work and, worse, may be an exercise in futility: problems that seem to have been resolved often reappear because they are rooted in a flawed basic design.

Therefore, if it is not possible to establish the essential conditions for a senior leadership team, usually it is better not to form the team at all. Suppose, for example, that the senior leadership of an organization is undergoing rapid change, with a number of current executives likely to

leave their posts soon and new senior managers about to arrive. Or suppose that the organization's strategy is so much in flux that it would be
impossible to formulate a meaningful statement of purpose for the senior
team. Or suppose that the leaders who would make up the team do not
have adequate knowledge and skill to lead at an enterprise level. In all
these cases it would be best to defer creating a senior leadership team
until it becomes possible to design it well.

It is not always possible to get all three of the essential conditions
fully in place when your team is launched. A chief executive must make a
judgment call about whether the conditions that *can* be established are
sufficient to get the team off to a good start, with plans to further
strengthen them as opportunities arise. The basic design of a senior leadership team does not have to be perfect from the start. But it does have to
be strong enough to provide a firm foundation for competent teamwork,
and it is the chief executive's job to assess whether that is so and, if not,
whether it can be made so.

A Real Team

Senior leaders have many accountabilities, including governance, building the capability of the organization, getting all members aligned with
collective purposes, crafting and implementing organizational strategy,
and managing day-to-day operations. Although all of these tasks are important, it is seldom appropriate for any single team to be responsible for
all of them (except perhaps in the case of a small, start-up enterprise). Yet
that often is what happens: a large group with an uncertain or constantly
shifting membership tries to address all these accountabilities but never
coalesces into a real team.

Real teams have clear boundaries. Everyone knows who is a member
and who is not. They have stability, and members have the time and opportunity to hone their ability to work together. And they are highly interdependent, with members drawing heavily on their colleagues' special
knowledge, skill, and experience in the work they do together.

You cannot create real teams by convening a set of people and calling
them a team. Instead, it takes careful thought and planning about the
work the team will do, its composition, and the way it will be launched
and developed. To have an effective senior team requires, first of all, that
it be a *real* team—and not a team in name only.

A Compelling Direction

Although any team needs to know where it's going, leaders of senior teams often struggle more than leaders of front-line teams when they try to turn the complex and often nebulous nature of executive responsibility into a clear team purpose. In the best leadership teams we have studied, we discovered that their leaders found a way to provide a crystal-clear sense of the team's unique added value in advancing the organization's strategy.

The team's purpose is not merely the sum of the individual members' contributions, nor is it the purpose of the organization. And it's not a broad, abstract, pie-in-the-sky phrase such as "serving customers" or "creating value for the firm." Rather, it is challenging, it is consequential, and, above all, it is clear. The team's purpose highlights the interdependencies among team members, and it orients the team toward its objective, helping members make intelligent judgments among alternatives as they lead the enterprise forward.

If you ask members of an effective senior team what their purpose is, they'll articulate those major strategic and tactical decisions that they are responsible for as a team. They also will tell you that even though this lens through which they see their team direction needs constant polishing, it is an effort that pays for itself many times over in better, faster decisions.

The Right People

The leaders at the top of an organization may not be classic "team players," but we have found that certain competencies spell the difference between collaboration and chaos in senior teams. In the most effective teams we've worked with and studied, members are selected by the team leader—it is, after all, the leader's team—based on what they bring to the table: do they add value to *this team* and its unique purpose?

Effective chief executives also are willing to replace members who are ineffective or, worse, dangerous—individuals who are armed with their own agendas and who can, sometimes covertly, derail the efforts of the rest of the team. At issue is whether an individual executive can handle both parts of the leadership job: the responsibilities of the position he or she holds *and* participation in a team that brings an enterprise perspective to every problem. If not, then you do not have the right person for the job—the whole job. The fact is, senior teams are exclusive. And membership is not a right or a privilege but depends on what the team needs to be successful.

The Enablers

The three enabling conditions are (1) a solid team structure, (2) a supportive organizational context, and (3) competent team coaching. These conditions enable a team to take full advantage of the solid foundation provided by the essentials. As with the essentials, the enabling conditions do not need to be fully present at the outset; they also can be strengthened as the team gains experience and maturity. Even so, it is always a good idea to review the enabling conditions when a team is launched to ensure that, at minimum, you do not put unnecessary obstacles in the team's path. Consider, for example, an organization where the following conditions are in place:

- Existing norms (a structural feature) encourage senior leaders to make the real decisions offline, in pairs or small groups of political allies.

- The reward system (a contextual feature) puts them into direct competition with each other for individual bonuses.

- The advice given to executives about managing their performance (an aspect of coaching) encourages them to focus exclusively on their line or functional responsibilities.

The prospects of a senior team succeeding in these circumstances are dim indeed. Although the main function of the enabling conditions is to help a team exploit its full potential, a wise chief executive takes steps to minimize such blatantly team-unfriendly features of the context. And, to the extent possible, the chief executive replaces them with the conditions described next, which foster rather than impede competent teamwork.

A Solid Team Structure

Even when a senior team has a clear purpose and well-established boundaries, the members often have trouble figuring out what to do together and how. Why? Because the team lacks the structure needed to ensure its success. It may be the wrong size, have poorly designed tasks, or develop team-unfriendly norms of conduct.

Most senior leadership teams are too large. We have seldom seen teams of more than eight or nine members operate as true decision-making leadership teams. When team membership gets into the double digits, the space needed for real interdependence, meaningful contribution, and team decision making tends to be squeezed out. Generally the best senior leadership teams we have seen have been among the smallest.

As with membership, so with team tasks: the fewer, the better. We have watched a depressing number of executives who are doomed to spend endless hours in unproductive meetings focused on laundry lists of small operational and administrative matters. The best chief executives design specific tasks for their senior teams, tasks that are whole and strategically important pieces of work, and then put those tasks—and only them—on the team agenda. The result, more often than not, is a team that digs in and gets down to work.

And then there is *how* they get down to work. In outstanding teams, members adhere to an established set of norms that govern their behavior both within and outside team meetings. These norms are not about being nice to each other. Instead, they bear directly on members' ability to work competently together on their collective tasks. For example, a team might have a norm that members will actively collaborate on key initiatives or that they will share all relevant information with one another. A team might agree that members will express disagreements openly in team meetings, or that they will listen especially carefully to contributions from people whose orientations differ from their own.

The chief executives of successful leadership teams make sure that members see the enterprise not through the lens of their line or functional role but rather as an executive responsible for the overall success of the company.

A Supportive Organizational Context

We were surprised to find that even in organizations where front-line teams get the information, the education, and the basic material resources they need—and are rewarded as a team when they excel—senior leadership teams often are seriously underresourced. The best-performing

leadership teams commandeer the resources they need. They are rewarded as a team beyond what they earn as individuals, underscoring the
reality that they are jointly accountable for the organization's success.
And they have ready access to the informational, consultative, and material resources they need for their work, including the *time* they need to
work effectively together.

The leaders of great leadership teams don't assume that it is an insult
to the ingenuity and expertise of the members to make sure they have access to all the resources they need to carry out their work at the highest
levels of excellence.

Competent Team Coaching

The best teams are continually being coached—and are coaching themselves—to evolve, learn, and grow. They learn from their leader, each
other, and their experiences. They discuss how best to approach various
kinds of problems and always review their actions and decisions to find
ways to improve how they operate as a team.

Even in the best teams we've worked with and studied, team growth
and development are largely informal and ongoing, so subtle that, at times,
an outsider might miss them. If you look closely you see the leader—and,
over time, the members—casually and quietly coaching one another both
in and out of meetings. They often end meetings by spending a few minutes discussing what worked and what didn't.

Indeed, we found that every CEO in our sample had a strong external focus, attending with great energy to matters outside the team and in
the broader environment, but it was only the leaders of outstanding leadership teams that had an equally strong internal focus—on the development of their teams.

Putting the Conditions in Place

The six conditions are helpful to any kind of team.[16] But the leadership
teams we studied were strikingly different from front-line production,
sales, or service teams in two important ways, as you will see throughout
this book. First, the features of good team design and leadership that are
hardest for chief executives to enact are often very different from the

ones that trip up leaders of front-line teams. Second, the actions it takes to implement those features often are more challenging for chief executives' preferred leadership styles and strategies than they are for the leaders of front-line teams.

The good news is that once you have the essential and enabling conditions in place, positive developments in the team happen very swiftly. You can begin tomorrow improving the design of your team, and within months you will see significant improvements in the team's effectiveness. The more challenging news is that getting the conditions in place takes an innovative, unconventional kind of senior leadership, one that is not practiced well by many seasoned, successful executives.

Diego Bevilacqua describes the development of his team as a difficult journey, and not without its share of pain and frustration. But he is the first to admit that, in the end, it was an important and satisfying one that not only helped him grow as a leader but also led to major growth within his team and ultimately the business. Indeed, had he not taken his team on such a journey, the business probably would still be a small and struggling piece of the Unilever portfolio.

If you are setting out on a similar venture, we offer you the chance to draw both on the lessons others have learned in building their senior teams and on the findings from our research. We hope to enable you to circumvent at least some of the trial-and-error learning that otherwise would be necessary. The chapters that follow provide the best road map that we have been able to construct for creating the conditions for senior team effectiveness. Throughout this book, we elaborate the tales of leadership teams that (ultimately) did especially well or that struggled severely to get the six conditions in place for their teams. We selected those teams on the basis of their initial standing on the six conditions, and we provide their stories as examples for how to—and how not to—create outstanding leadership teams. (In our case examples throughout this book, some names have been disguised for confidentiality.[17])

At the Starting Gate

It was Cescau who suggested that Bevilacqua pay more attention to building the right leadership team. It was excellent advice. With a year of strategic realignment work under his belt, Bevilacqua had a much clearer idea of the kind of executives he needed on his team: leaders who were forceful and determined, understood and were open to the new operating model but also willing to speak up—people who were not afraid to put their views on the table. Bevilacqua notes, "I wanted people who wanted to make it happen, who wanted to join something that was a bit unusual within Unilever, where they would have the freedom to operate as long as they were aligned with the rest of the business."

With a purpose for his leadership team clarifying in his mind, Bevilacqua began the difficult job of replacing members of his team—half of them within six months. Bevilacqua emphasizes that when he chose to let go of those six senior leaders in the organization, it was not because of poor delivery in their individual roles. "Each one of these guys was delivering," he says. "They were achieving their goals and targets. They were asked to leave, or eased out of the company, because they simply didn't work or didn't want to work together in an aligned manner."

Bevilacqua devoted significant time directly to the development of his team: an entire week away from the office, a meeting for Bevilacqua and his team members only. During that week his focus was on building this new group into a leadership team: they focused little on strategy or on building the business. They did not look at numbers, market shares, profits and losses. They focused exclusively on *what is this team for* that no other entity in the organization could accomplish.

The work Bevilacqua did on his team's membership and purpose had a quick and positive impact on performance. With a newfound unity, increased clarity, and accurate data with which to plan, the team saw the business begin to gain momentum. By the year's end, Foodsolutions reported growth of 5 percent. It was a respectable showing and outpaced market growth—and it was merely a precursor to the kind of growth and performance that ultimately made this team's business one of the top growth areas for Unilever as a whole. Patrick Cescau has pointed to Food-solutions as an example of what the larger organization can and must do to be successful in the future.

Given the hurdles that had to be overcome, the story of Diego Bevilacqua, his senior team, and the business they built might best be titled "Against All Odds." After all, it was a team and a business born from dif-

ferent cultures, different systems, different strategies, different structures, and certainly different leadership styles.

Yet in less than five years, Bevilacqua, his team, and the organization
they built became not only a highly successful part of the company but
also its model business. What is the secret of its success? Like many successful senior teams we've studied and worked with, Bevilacqua's team
addressed the components and conditions we've just outlined: Bevilacqua saw the need for a real team and created it. He selected the right
people, created a compelling purpose, established a structure and norms
that allowed the team to work effectively, and created processes to support their efforts.

Bevilacqua and his team are by no means unique. Many top leaders
we work with face similar challenges. With no clear road map to follow,
senior leaders must build their teams as much by intuition and luck as by
knowledge and experience. That is why we undertook our research and
share it in this book.

Successfully creating and leading a high-performing team will never
be easy. Our goal, in the chapters that follow, is to provide you with new
insights and information that—despite the challenges—will allow you to
make your senior leadership teams great.

PART I

THE ESSENTIALS

*C*hapters 2, 3, and 4 discuss the three conditions that together provide the foundation for great senior leadership teams: a real team
(chapter 2), a compelling direction (chapter 3), and the right people
(chapter 4)—what we call "the essentials."

All three conditions are necessary, as becomes clear when you imagine a
team with any one of them missing. For example, imagine a decision-making
team that has a compelling direction trying to function with members who
lack the capabilities needed to make key decisions. Or a real team with the
right people hamstrung by an unclear or unmotivating purpose. Or a set of
leaders who have the right skills to achieve a compelling purpose but who
are an unbounded swarm; they will never operate as a well-bounded group
whose members are ready and able to work together. Unless all three of the
essential conditions are present, a senior leadership team is almost certain to
struggle fruitlessly and ultimately to give up the struggle and stick to their
individual domains.

We have seen that as CEOs act to create an effective leadership team,
these three essential conditions are interrelated; taking action on one prompts
the need for changes in the others. As in Bevilacqua's case at Unilever (see
chapter 1), clarifying the boundaries around the team and defining the
members' interdependencies invite serious contemplation of whether the right
people are on the team. Reforming the team's membership can lead to a
readjustment of the team's shared purpose. The three essential conditions operate as connected threads. If you pull on one, you will find that you are tug-
ging the others into a different configuration.

The three essentials also are iterative. Defining the team's purpose, for
example, guides the team's direction well enough for you and the team to
move forward for now. But that direction will need your attention again
after the consequent changes in membership are settled.

27

These two ideas—that the three essential conditions are interrelated and iterative—played out clearly in Bevilacqua's launch of his leadership team at Unilever Foodsolutions. He began his leadership of a senior team with a broad definition of what the team was. He crafted a strategic direction for the organization and drew on the expertise of his alignment team—the large group of senior managers who led the operations of the business—to begin clarifying and implementing that strategy. The alignment team, its purpose, its membership, and its core interdependence—strategic clarity and implementation of immediate changes—served a particular purpose early in the life of the merger. Yet all three of these elements—the team's membership, purpose, and interdependencies—would change again, and radically, as Bevilacqua learned more from the continuing struggles of the new entity just what it needed from a leadership team.

Getting the Essentials in Place

You can put the essential conditions in place all at once or in any order that makes sense given your organizational and practical realities. Sometimes it may be advisable to define the main purposes of the team before you compose and launch it. At other times, as with Foodsolutions, it may be more effective to get the membership of your leadership team right and then convene the team before settling on the main purposes the team will be asked to achieve. The order in which you attend to the three conditions is of little consequence. What is important is that you establish all three conditions before you release the team to proceed with its work.

In the chapters that follow, we focus first on what we have learned about what is involved in creating a real team composed of the leaders at the top of your organization (chapter 2). We then turn to what our research has shown are the barriers against and the strategies that help to create a compelling team purpose (chapter 3). Finally, we explore what we have uncovered about the kinds of people who will make a lasting contribution to your team and those who are likely to derail it irreparably—and what you can do about it (chapter 4). The order of the chapters is arbitrary. As you take on any one of these essentials, you will find yourself acting on and adjusting the others as well.

2

First, Decide If You Need—
and Want—a Team

Frustrated with long meetings, infighting among his direct reports, and no real momentum in their work, Mike Waters, CEO of a large financial services firm, admitted that he was considering disbanding his senior leadership team. "Ours is too complex a business for a team to try to coordinate together," he said. "Maybe it would be more effective to scrap this committee chaos and work one-on-one with my individual direct reports. They are, after all, good leaders in their own areas."

Frank Forsythe, CEO of a global petroleum company, not only didn't think he needed a team but also was adamant that he didn't want one. A traditional executive who had grown up in an organization structured according to function, he saw his team as a distraction from and detriment to his own leadership. In his eyes, executives sitting together in a meeting were not doing the vital work of leading their own areas. And they were also more trouble for him. "I don't want my executives even talking to one another!"

Mike Waters didn't need a team. Frank Forsythe didn't want one. In our experience, neither executive was unusual except in his willingness to say out loud what many other leaders are thinking. Neither one, however, was asking the right questions in the right way. Try these: does this organization need a real team at the top? Given my company's strategy, given the operating model, given the changes we're making in how this organization operates, is it sufficient to have a collection of smart senior executives who focus on the performance of their own individual areas of responsibility? Or do we need something more? And one more question, the core of what you will be reflecting on in this chapter: are you up for leading a team of leaders?

The chapters that follow are mostly about the features of outstanding senior leadership teams and about the ways you can create and support one of your own. This chapter, however, is mainly about *you*—what kind of collaboration you want from your top leaders and what you are prepared to do to get it.

Do You Need a Team?

The first question is whether there is a vital business need that would be better met if you worked with a leadership team than with a loose collection of individual executives focusing on their own accountabilities. Is your organization engaged in rapid growth? Are you horizontally integrating your business, moving into new areas upstream or downstream, or both? Are you anticipating major capital expenditures? Is your firm moving into a new stage of its life cycle?

If you answer yes to any of these questions, it means that your business is operating at a high degree of complexity. You face a widening array of financial, technical, and human resources that need to be managed. Increasing complexity calls for debate, for broad knowledge, for synthesized ideas and creative plans, and for the deft orchestration of decisions. You very likely do need a team.

Bruce Campbell, CEO of Forward Air transportation company, was contemplating transforming his company from a terminal-to-terminal trucking operation into a full-service delivery company providing pickup and delivery of freight in key locations. Campbell recognized that this shift in business strategy would require a more complex operating model, an intensified focus on customer service, and more sophisticated information technology. Given the required high level of coordination among many moving parts, not only would his senior managers be doing work that was far more complex, but they also would be dramatically more interdependent.

Campbell's practice of having a weekly conference call with his senior leaders to share operational information did not provide an adequate forum for dealing with the issues that would arise from the planned expansion. Senior leaders would now need to come together face to face as a team for longer periods and would need to engage in serious debate when they met.

Campbell ultimately decided to create a senior leadership team, not because of his feelings about teams but based on a careful review of the new strategy and what it would take to implement it. In fact, he strongly preferred not to have a team. He summed up his feelings in one short sentence: "I hate meetings." But in the end, the clear need for a team trumped his reluctance to manage one.

Not every organization needs an integrated senior leadership team like this one. Indeed, if yours is in essence a holding company, if you are managing a number of highly independent and unrelated businesses, your senior leaders would gain very little from interacting, given the cost of bringing them together (or the opportunity costs of pulling them away from their individual accountabilities for the time it takes to conduct a good meeting).

Ric Andersen of IBM's Asia-Pacific region, for example, decided after careful consideration that a single leadership team did not fit in his highly diverse organization. In essence, he realized, he was leading a sort of "divisional holding company" within the larger corporation. The businesses he oversaw were highly autonomous and very different from one another. It wasn't that he didn't believe teams could be effective. He knew they could be, in the right situation and for the right purpose. Choosing not to create a leadership team was a reasoned decision about what his operations called for. If you make a similar reasoned decision that executing your operating model well demands no close interaction among your top executives, then we encourage you not to force-fit your senior leaders into a decision-making team.

Sometimes it is a close call. One of us has studied the senior leadership of professional symphony orchestras around the world.[1] Most major orchestras operate several businesses, often including educational offerings, community outreach activities, and special pops events in addition to mainstream concert programs. Might a senior leadership team be just what is needed to coordinate these diverse activities?

For many orchestras, a leadership team would be a fairly radical change. The long-standing tradition is that the three top leaders of an orchestra separately handle different aspects of the work: the music director is responsible for all artistic matters, the chair of the board is the link with the community and makes sure that the orchestra's financial footing is sound, and the executive director manages the enterprise. In most orchestras, these three leaders mostly stay out of their colleagues' domains. The board chair, for example, does not meddle in decisions about artistic matters, and the music director does not make financial decisions. It falls to the executive director, therefore, to integrate the three legs of what often is called the "three-legged stool" of orchestra management. That can be quite a challenge, involving extensive one-on-one negotiations with the other two senior leaders as well as with representatives of all the other constituencies that are involved with, and care deeply about, the orchestra.

Should the executive director form a senior leadership team consisting of at least the board chair and the music director, perhaps supplemented with a few of the orchestra's most senior functional leaders? It seems like a good idea: it could increase the alignment of senior leaders with overall orchestra purposes and could generate a level of coordination far beyond what occurs when each senior leader focuses on his or her own formal responsibilities. But how would you design such a team? How would you deal with the fact that the board chair is a volunteer who has many other obligations? Or that the music director may be a thoroughbred of the first order, unaccustomed to working in teams that he or she does not personally control? And what is to be done about the fact that the music director may be in town for only a dozen weeks a year (when rehearsing and performing with the orchestra)?

As we said, it's a judgment call. A well-functioning senior leadership team could generate a level of coordination and synergy rarely seen in the orchestral world. But history and traditional roles are so deeply rooted that it is by no means certain that the team could be designed well enough for members to work together effectively. The key to making a good choice, in this case as in many others, is to make that decision deliberately, to avoid being strongly swayed either by traditional management models or by fantasies of how wonderful it would be if all the orchestra's senior leaders were in the same harness pulling in the same direction.

Your own decision about whether you really need a senior leadership team—and whether you can design one that actually would work—is consequential for your organization and for those it serves, as well as for the quality of your own work life. The good news is that it does not have to be a one-time decision. Although your strategy and operating model may be better served right now by a loose confederation of individual leaders, whenever you contemplate a major change in how you do business you may need a leadership team. Members might come together as a team only temporarily to act as a sounding board and to advise you. They may remain as a team to manage a coherent and aligned transition. And they may or may not continue to operate as a team in leading the organization, depending on the ongoing interdependencies of the operation.

Campbell, for example, has chosen to create a team to do the highly interdependent work of leading the transition of Forward Air into an integrated service delivery company. The complexity of the task of designing the transition, its need for coordinated implementation, and the increasing interdependence among the various functions demand a leadership team. Campbell has yet to face the decision of whether he will continue to lead an interdependent senior team or whether, after the transition, he will refocus his senior leaders on their individual accountabilities and return to the once-a-week coordinating conference call.

What If You Need a Team but Don't Want One?

Do you hate the idea of leading a real team of your top executives? Some leaders, like Ric Andersen at IBM, truly don't need a senior leadership team, but many others fail to be impressed by the benefits of such a team even when their operating model begs for collectively managed processes in the pursuit of organizational opportunities.

Let's return to our two CEOs: Frank Forsythe and Mike Waters. Forsythe, it turns out, was not as tyrannical as he may have sounded; he was inexperienced with leadership teams. Teams had never been part of his organization's culture. Leaders, even at the top of his former company, had always been responsible for and entirely in authority over their specific functions. Like many executives, Forsythe could not get his head around the concept of a team that leads. Nor could he see how it would hurt his company not to have one. His reasons for not wanting a team were cognitive—difficulty envisioning what an interacting team of leaders could accomplish for his business. If you have a similar hesitancy, stay with us through this chapter and see whether the kinds of leadership teams we describe expand the options you consider.

Mike Waters, too, had to overcome negative perceptions about the value of a senior team. Waters was an aggressive, high-achieving executive, and facing the prospect of dealing with a group of equally aggressive, equally high-achieving almost-peers seemed like more trouble than it was worth. Unlike Forsythe, Waters had a more visceral distaste for the idea of a leadership team. Leading a team of leaders required him to spend what he perceived as far too much time dealing with team members and their personal agendas rather than important enterprise issues. And when his team finally focused on an important issue, members took forever to reach a consensus or decision. Debates were contentious and political. As one member wryly noted, "We spend all our time up in the air, flying around, but we seldom if ever are able to land the plane." Understandably, Waters had come to detest that sort of "teamwork."

There is no question that teams of senior leaders are tough, demanding, and often cantankerous. And many smart executives realize that combining their top leaders into a unified and powerful body is a direct threat to their own power, should the team's inclination turn that way. Like Waters, you may hesitate to take the risk of fueling such a potent force.

Both Forsythe and Waters were dubious of the value of senior leadership teams—Forsythe because he had no clear concept of what a leadership team could do, and Waters because he was reluctant to try to lead what he perceived to be a dangerous entity. But sometimes such doubts can generate costs as substantial as those incurred in creating a real leadership team. Organizations without teamwork at the top lose millions in missed and botched opportunities annually. Can you integrate an acquisition without the senior leaders of your functions collaborating? Can you implement an organization-wide change in your strategic focus without the understanding, commitment, and debates of the heads of your business units as you plan the changes in resource deployment, leadership succession, and shared services? Many leaders hope that the essential coordination somehow will happen without the need to create the senior team that can make it happen. And that hope, in most cases, is misplaced.

Let's look at one well-known example of how it can work. In the early 1990s, computer giant IBM appeared to be on a slippery and steeply declining slope. It was losing not only customers and revenue but also its way within the market. It lacked the integrated approach to leadership that Lou Gerstner would create a few years later, helping IBM reemerge as an industry leader.[2]

During Gerstner's tenure, IBM transformed itself from a lumbering behemoth into a faster, flatter, highly flexible, customer-facing powerhouse. The process included tearing down old silos that had become barriers to doing business effectively in a fast-paced global environment. Key to that process was the senior team Gerstner created.

He began by eliminating the long-standing and powerful six-member Management Committee, which had held sway over most major corporate decisions.

In contrast to the committee—which had long been a site where leaders from corporate staff and line units had come to rubber-stamp decisions already negotiated behind the scenes—Gerstner wanted a team that would engage with him in debating policy issues that cut across units. For that he created the Corporate Executive Committee. Operational problem solving and decision making, formerly under the authority of the Management Committee, was given to individual business units. The CEC, as it became known, was responsible for issues that cut across the enterprise. At the same time, to create communication and collaboration among the business units, the new CEO created a thirty-five-member Worldwide Management Council. That group was created to discuss results and companywide initiatives and to share ideas. It was an information-sharing executive team to complement the decision-making functions of the CEC.

Based on IBM's changing strategy, structure, and roles, Gerstner eliminated a traditional group that had outlived its usefulness and was impeding progress. In its place he created not one but two leadership teams, each with its own clear and distinct role in driving the new version of the organization forward.

Real Teams at the Top

To explore further the possibility of creating a real leadership team, let's examine a practical question: what would you do with such a team if you had one? In the earlier examples, you saw team members serving a variety of functions: exchanging complex information, advising their CEO about strategic changes, coordinating a transition of the operating model, engaging in robust debate, and making decisions that affect the enterprise.

Our research has identified four major types of senior leadership teams, each serving a distinct function. We call them informational teams, consultative teams, coordinative teams, and decision-making teams. In the sections that follow, we describe the kinds of work these teams do and raise a question: which type of team would best meet the leadership needs of your organization?

Informational Teams

Informational leadership teams exchange important information about various areas of the business and gather in one place external intelligence that may be useful to other parts of the organization. They also meet to hear about direction and initiatives from the CEO. Informational teams can create the shared point of view that is necessary for alignment among individuals and parts of the organization. The purpose of these teams is to make the individual leaders better informed, better aligned, and more able to do their jobs superbly.

For example, most CEOs bring together their direct reports to share critical information like production and sales data. You might have an informational team that does its teamwork in a "Monday morning call," in which senior managers with profit-and-loss accountabilities report in and functional heads provide updates to each other and to you. You might augment this practice by having periodic face-to-face meetings that include many of the senior leaders from the organization and that essentially follow the same format and expand the coverage of the discussion.

Ultimately, the purpose of a team that you use solely for informational face-to-face meetings is threefold: to hear from you, to brief you, and to inform other senior managers about important developments in the organization and its environment. Members of such teams are only loosely interdependent; they need each other for information but require little additional interaction to fulfill their responsibilities. Informational teams are the most basic kind of leadership team, and they necessitate no dramatic change in the interactions between you and your senior managers. The main conditions for them to be effective are for you to articulate a clear purpose for the team (see chapter 3) and to provide appropriate settings and structures for information exchange (see chapter 5).

Consultative Teams

To have a *consultative team* you might periodically bring together a team of senior leaders to discuss and advise you about key decisions you must make, such as responses to changes in the market, potential acquisitions, and other enterprisewide issues. Consultative teams do not make decisions. Rather, members provide necessary information, debate the relevant issues, and act as a sounding board before you make the call.

The purpose of a consultative team is to make the CEO better informed and better able to do the job effectively. CEOs often convene consultative teams immediately before board meetings, for example, or before analyst calls so that they are well briefed and can handle anticipated questions.

In contrast to informational teams, consultative teams actively debate key issues, giving members the chance to learn from one another and giving you the opportunity to obtain ideas and counsel from them. Consultative teams also promote information sharing among members and not just between them and you. Therefore, they can also serve the alignment function that is the main purpose of purely information-sharing teams. It's tougher to manage consultative teams than informational teams. In addition to needing a clear purpose, they require serious attention to who is on the team (chapter 4) and to how members work together (chapters 5, 6, and 7).

Coordinating Teams

You may want or need a *coordinating team,* whose members come together to coordinate their leadership activities as they execute strategically important initiatives. For example, a senior leadership team at an airline might meet to work through the launch of service to a new country. This kind of launch would require coordination across facilities, logistics, marketing, sales, partners, and government affairs—entities that usually operate relatively independently. Bruce Campbell, in managing the organizational transformation at Forward Air, assessed the growing interdependence and complexity of his new strategy and determined that he needed to craft a coordinating team to manage the transition of the company to one that would provide integrated services.

The function of a coordinating team is to manage the operational interdependencies of the enterprise. Members of coordinating teams are highly interdependent, have shared responsibilities, and must work together frequently and flexibly to accomplish their shared purpose.

Coordinating teams may also serve information-sharing and consultative purposes. Not all executives involved in coordination need serve as consultants to the CEO; you may choose a smaller and more select group for that purpose. You may also want to add larger groups of leaders beyond the core senior coordinating team for broader information-sharing meetings, typically held one to four times per year. But because of their intensive interaction, their need to learn from each other, and the robust discussions among members as complex initiatives are rolled out, coordinating teams require all the careful attention to team design and leadership that we describe in this book. It isn't sufficient to merely create an "overlay" team in hopes that it will bring order and efficiency to uncoordinated organizational units. It takes focused, competent leadership to create and support teams that can effectively coordinate organizational activities.

Decision-Making Teams

As their name implies, *decision-making teams* make the small number of critical decisions that are most consequential for the enterprise as a whole. Of all the teams we describe here, it is decision-making teams that result in the largest changes in the power dynamics among your senior leaders. A leadership team of this kind is not engaged in "leadership by committee." A decision-making team at the top is still your team, and it gets its authority over certain decisions directly from you.

When you're building a decision-making team, you must pay close attention to your leadership processes if you want to make the team outstanding, rather than one that struggles and fails to "land the plane." You need to articulate a compelling purpose for the team, and you need to get the right people on and the wrong people off. You need to create sound structures to support effective collaboration, and you must provide the contextual support and coaching that members need to perform superbly. An effective senior leadership team that makes enterprise-affecting decisions is the most complex—and potentially the most valuable—leadership team of all.

Creating the Right Kinds of Teams

The four types of teams are not mutually exclusive. Indeed, most organizations we have studied have more than one kind of leadership team operating simultaneously. One common configuration is a core decision-making team, which handles the highest-impact enterprise issues, along with a coordination team (which often includes members of the decision-making team) that oversees and manages major organizational initiatives. These two teams often are linked to lower-level operations teams to surface enterprisewide issues that require the attention of senior leaders. Moreover, their members may often be part of a larger group of leaders from around the organization who occasionally come together to create alignment across the enterprise. Forming a decision-making team, therefore, often involves creating additional teams, each with its own distinct but related purposes—and each with a specified conduit of information and coordination between teams.

For example, Brian Beamish, CEO of Anglo American Base Metals division chose to create three teams: a core decision-making team, a coordinating team, and a larger information-sharing team. This global mining division had a growth strategy to meet increasing demand—driven largely by growing metals consumption in India and China—for the metals it mined.

The Management Committee, as the top team was called, had ballooned to fourteen people, made up of four levels of management and representing operations, functions, and business units around the world. Nearly all the members saw this group as ineffective. Because of its size, there was little room for true debate among its members, and the group made few vital decisions.

Beamish's predecessor took steps to recraft this unwieldy body, but it was Beamish who finalized this work when he became CEO. Beamish divided senior management into three finely focused teams: the Executive

Committee, a four-person decision-making body that handled issues that cut across the enterprise; the Management Committee, which focused on coordinating operations and divisionwide initiatives; and the Alignment Team, composed of the top forty divisional managers, which engaged in information-sharing across the business. The Alignment Team included the members of the Executive and Management Committees as well as the leaders of key functions such as exploration and research and development. This information-sharing team convened about once every twelve to eighteen months. The Executive Committee members also serve as members of the Management Committee. This overlapping composition allowed members of the decision-making group to hear firsthand the input and concerns of the managers several layers below them. These three teams ran in parallel, each with a defined set of responsibilities and with the overlapping composition providing the necessary connection among the teams.

Of all the types of leadership teams we have studied, informational teams require the least attention and the least careful design. Define a clear purpose, create a little structure, and bring together your senior leaders to share the information that is necessary to create alignment of understanding throughout the organization. In chapter 1, you saw Diego Bevilacqua bring forty-six executives together in just that way. It took time and a good plan for the week, but it did not require agonizing over team membership or delineating all the members' interdependencies. These forty-six leaders engaged in serious and strategic discussions (although they did not make strategic decisions) that ultimately educated Bevilacqua and his core team and created the beginnings of a shared picture of the new strategy.

However, a serious word of warning. As Beamish had learned, a large, loosely bounded, unstable leadership team created for information-sharing purposes cannot be used for enterprise-level decision making without major redesign—in essence, creating a new team. If all you make of your senior leaders is an information-sharing team, then you have capped their potential for real interdependence in leading the organization.

By contrast, even though we have seen many senior leadership teams that are merely information-sharing teams, we have never observed teams that are *only* decision-making bodies. Decision-making teams tend to act at different times as any one of the four types of teams. If you opt to create a decision-making team, it also will serve as coordinator of core initiatives, as an advisory group for your own decisions, and as a vital source of information exchange and learning for the organization.

We are not suggesting that you'll give up your Monday morning call. Rather, when you create a decision-making team and do it well, you create a body that serves the organization in many ways. Once members make decisions together that affect the enterprise as a whole, they also become better at deciding when it makes sense for them to operate as a consultative team, to merely exchange information, to coordinate with each other, or not to operate as a team at all. But to have a leadership team that dexterous, you first must put in place the conditions needed to support an effective decision-making team.

There is nothing wrong with information-sharing, consultative, or co-ordinating senior leadership teams. All serve valuable purposes. But top organizational leaders often need and expect more from any such group. Yes, CEOs still need to obtain and share critical information and insights with the other senior executives, and often this is more easily done in a group setting. But CEOs also need help in solving critical problems, making key decisions, and creating and implementing strategy. In short, they need the dynamic force of a group of senior leaders using its collective intelligence to drive the organization forward. They need what we would describe as a *real team*.

Do you need a real team? See the self-test in figure 2-1.

FIGURE 2-1

Self-test: Do you need a leadership team?

Part 1: What's going on with your organization?	Part 2: What leadership functions need to be fulfilled collaboratively?
☐ Significant growth or retraction	☐ Information exchange among senior leaders that is essential for alignment
☐ Horizontal integration of semiautonomous units	☐ Consultation with you for strategic and complex decisions
☐ Major changes in capital or other resources	☐ Coordination of a key change initiative or interdependent operations
☐ Externally originated challenges to traditional ways of operating	☐ Decision making about critical enterprise issues
If none of the above are checked, you probably do not need a senior leadership team.	If two or fewer of the above are checked, you probably do not need an executive team.

Real Leadership Teams:
Senior Leaders Leading Together

In contemplating a real leadership team, you may be concerned that a collection of talented and opinionated people, once brought together, will run out of control. That is a risk, but it doesn't have to be that way. We are not inviting you to be dragged off by runaway horses. Indeed, if you decide that you need a team, we will show you what it takes to harness that entity and keep it from getting out of control.

Let's look at how a real leadership team can operate. A case example from our observations may help you see the positive potential of decision-making leadership teams. The example is a team that struggled a great deal at its beginning but became an outstanding leadership team over time. We pick up the team at about four months into its life.

For some issues, this leadership team could be described as informational. If you stuck your head into meeting, you would see members exchanging ideas and data. Occasionally you also would see members briefing the leader about an issue he had been asked to bring before the corporate executive committee. And the team moved into coordinating mode when it was time to launch a new initiative.

But this team did not merely exchange information; the members vigorously discussed key issues. Everyone was expected to participate on an equal footing. Members did not defer to the chief financial officer when it came to discussing the budget, or to the head of marketing on the strategy for a new product launch. Certainly members brought their own expertise and issues to the table. But the team drew on these member resources in the context of the division's larger strategy and business plan. Members' differences helped the team achieve depth in both its analyses of business challenges and in the advice it gave the CEO.

If a team member was absent, the other members did not see it as one fewer hurdle to overcome in reaching a decision or as one more opportunity to get their pet initiatives approved and funded, as was the case with many less-effective groups we observed. Rather, the members filled in for the missing member, discussing the subject at hand from his or her perspective as well as their own.

Discussion was only one part of the team's work. At some point, depending on the issue, the team—as a team—would come to agreement and make a decision. Often, a matter would be decided by the CEO after the team had discussed it. But other decisions were made by the team as a whole. For example, although individual members retained primary responsibility for developing priorities and strategies in their functions and areas, the team as a whole shared responsibility for approving them. Consequently, no single decision optimized one area of the business at the expense of the organization as a whole. Moreover, members shared responsibility for hitting the company's profit and growth targets. When this team made a decision, no matter how energetic the disagreements behind closed doors, it was a team decision. Outside that room you would never know who had held an opposing view. And because all the members were on board, the team's decisions got implemented.

There is one other telling difference between this team and other teams: the team did not cease to exist when the meeting was over. Subgroups were created to address specific issues, just as sand dunes form and reform in response to shifting winds. These subgroups came together to accomplish a specific subtask and then were absorbed back into the full team. The beauty of these executive sand dunes lies not only in their ability to rapidly address critical organizational issues with a broad range of leadership expertise but also in their power to cover critical but often neglected points of interdependence that lie outside the formal structure of the organization.

What Makes a Group of Executives a Real Team

The team we've just described became an outstanding senior leadership team. But some teams never come to act like real teams at all. If you're going to create any of the four types of teams, you need to set the stage for the kind of teamwork you want. Our research has shown that what makes the difference between a loose agglomeration and a real team is a leader who treats the team as an entity and puts in place three essential characteristics. Real senior leadership teams have interdependent work, they are clearly bounded, and they are reasonably stable over time.

- *Interdependent.* In real leadership teams, members share responsibility for achieving a collective purpose. They still are responsible for their individual roles, but they also work together, rely on one another, and use each other's experience, energy, and expertise to accomplish a collective, enterprise-affecting purpose.

- *Bounded.* Real senior leadership teams have clear boundaries. Team members as well as outside observers know who is on the team and who isn't.

- *Stable.* Real teams maintain a stable membership long enough for members to get to know one another's special strengths and limitations and to learn how to work together well as a team.

A team that is interdependent, bounded, and stable is a real team. Yes, the team leader—the chief executive—retains authority over the team for defining its purpose, creating and modeling its core norms, and other leadership functions. In this respect we diverge from the view of team expert Jon Katzenbach regarding what makes a group of leaders a real team. One of Katzenbach's rules of thumb is that if you peeked into the room where members were meeting you would not be able to tell who the team leader is.[3] We have not seen a senior leadership team operate that way. To the contrary, our work with senior leadership teams suggests that team members and leaders alike act in ways that preserve the distinct authority and leadership role of the CEO and that this pattern need not be an obstacle to the team's effectiveness. It's how a chief executive enacts the role of senior team leader that is important, and that we address in the rest of this book. The bottom line at the top: if your group of senior leaders is bounded, stable, and genuinely interdependent for enterprise-affecting work, then you have a real team.

These three characteristics are not only closely linked but also are critical prerequisites for putting in place the rest of the conditions that emerge from our research. Creating a real team is only the first step, the basic platform, in harnessing your team and getting it on a productive track. As you can see in figure 2-2, compared with their better-performing peers, the poorest teams in our study had little interdependence and were both underbounded and unstable in membership. Recall that we assessed each team on (1) how well it served its stakeholders and (2) how much the team and individuals were developing over time. The poorest teams failed their key constituencies and also showed little sign of improvement or learning—scores of 1 or 2 (on a 5-point scale) on both criteria.

FIGURE 2-2

Poorly performing senior leadership teams are not real teams

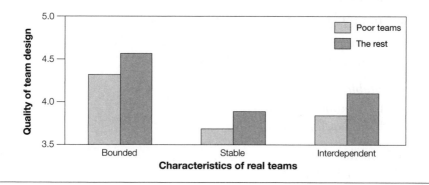

What most impaired the performance of these teams was the absence of the basic elements that would make them real teams. The work that they were asked to do involved no significant interchange of ideas and resources; mostly, members just listened to each other give presentations and updates. And membership in poor teams fluctuated constantly as people stepped in and out of leadership positions in the organization or on the team; when the senior team met, members had no clue as to who was really on the team and who was just visiting. Such entities, we found, cannot do well by their constituencies, nor can they develop as a team. In a nutshell, they are not real teams. We describe next what you can do to create one that is.

Interdependence: Insisting on Real Interchange

In interdependent teams, members work with one another to address issues, solve problems, provide advice, and make collective decisions. To create interdependence, you must insist that team members make decisions collectively on behalf of the entire enterprise rather than simply represent the interests of their own functions or areas. For example, you might obligate various regional, sector, and product-line heads to work together to determine which regions and business lines need the most investment. You would expect the individuals to care for their own areas, but you also would obligate them to consider the collective outcome. Ultimately, we have seen interdependent teams make decisions based on what is best for the overall organization, even if it costs their individual areas.

Interdependence does not come only from team members having a say in major decisions. Real teams also can be collectively oriented even when it comes to the straightforward tasks of daily communication and collaboration. You might ask your members, as did some leaders we have observed, not only to trade information at meetings but also to proactively volunteer information outside meetings that might be helpful to their colleagues. One payoff of this form of interdependence is that members gradually come to teach and coach one another, thereby making the individual leaders more capable and expanding the overall pool of knowledge and skill available to your team. Peer coaching, in turn, can be one of the most powerful influences of the effectiveness of teams whose work involves the acquisition, analysis, and application of knowledge and information to complex problems.[4]

An interdependent senior leadership team can provide a more powerful platform for managing the organization than does a collection of leaders that are a team in name only. By focusing on enterprise-level criteria, members elevate their own understanding of strategy and business goals, and they can collectively manage important tactical issues—such the completion and integration of a new acquisition—that require timely input from all members. These vital issues require that serious time be devoted to debate and interaction among senior leaders. Consequently, the best leadership teams that we have seen deal with items that are large in impact and few in number.

Of the three attributes of real teams, interdependence is perhaps the most difficult to create in a senior leadership team. Defining members' interdependencies is tightly linked with crafting a compelling team-level purpose. Often, one of the best ways to identify a senior leadership team's unique purpose is to explore where the real interdependencies lie and where they can be most fruitfully enacted. Articulating the team purpose can help the CEO and leadership team identify additional executive-level interdependencies, as well as remove from the agenda some items that might better be handled elsewhere in the organization. The process of establishing interdependence is iterative and is itself interdependent with the team's core purposes.

Boundedness: Who's on This Team, Anyway?

Almost every team we work with believes it has clear boundaries. Yet, amazingly, fewer than 7 percent of the teams we studied, when asked, agreed about who was on the team! So common is this discrepancy between perception and reality that it has become one of the first places we probe when working with a new team.

Our diagnostic question, posed to both the team's leader and its members, could not be simpler: "Who is on the senior leadership team?" The wide range of responses we get can be startling. At one organization, the answers ranged from ten names to more than thirty. Arturo Barahona, former CEO of AeroMexico, was stunned when told that his team believed there were eleven members. (There were actually nine.) "My God," he moaned, "if we can't get *this* right, how can we lead the whole business!"

To illustrate how common confusion is about the team's boundaries, we show in figure 2-3 reports from two teams we studied. For each team, we first asked the CEO for a list of people who were on the team. Then, on the survey instrument completed by all members of each team, we asked each person the CEO had named how many people were on the team. We also asked them to agree or disagree with a set of survey items assessing perceived boundedness of the team, such as, "Anyone who knows this team could accurately name all its members." Although virtually every team we studied said that the membership was clear (averaging

FIGURE 2-3

Two senior teams and their (un)boundedness

Team A	Team B
Actual team size (according to the CEO)	Actual team size (according to the CEO)
11	**5**
Estimates of team size (by individual members)	Estimates of team size (by individual members)
13, 12, 11, 11, 7, 12, 12, 24, 11, 15, 84	**5, 5, 7, 8, 9**

These examples are not unusual in our research. Only eleven teams we studied were in perfect agreement about who were members of the senior team.

4.83 on our 5-point scale), their estimates of the numbers of team members looked like the ones in figure 2-3—all over the map. Senior leadership teams are delusional about how bounded they are. They're certain that they know who's on the team—but they don't know at all.

Such confusion is a result of common executive processes. Like many leaders, Barahona's predecessor at AeroMexico, for example, had two internal advisers who regularly sat in on the senior team meeting. Because of their continued presence, many members assumed that they were part of the team. Why wouldn't they? The team leader never said otherwise.

As Barahona soon discovered, a porous and ambiguous senior team creates more problems than mere differences in perception. Although it was a tough decision, he wisely told both individuals that they were no longer needed in the meetings, quickly clarifying the boundaries for his team.

If you do not establish clear boundaries, your team cannot develop the collective identity that it needs to interact as a unit with external constituencies. The type of team you have and the work it will be able to do—to make decisions or merely to consult and inform—will become defined by who is in the room. When that changes, so will the work of the team and members' understanding of its purpose.

Two of us relearned this lesson recently as members of a small leadership team charged with defining a unique research and teaching focus for an institution of higher education. At the first group meeting, members came up with a way of framing that focus that left us energized: it was concise, and it had sharp edges. At the next meeting, however, two new group members showed up and two of the original members were absent. The new members suggested additions and qualifications to the emerging statement. At the third meeting, the group composition changed yet again, as did the draft of the statement.

Eventually the group created a product that was acceptable to everyone. It was, however, far less crisp—and took far longer in the making—than it would have been if the group's boundaries had not been constantly in flux. This example illustrates why creating a well-bounded team is high on our list of imperatives: if team membership is unclear or constantly changing, it is virtually impossible to create and sustain a real leadership team that can sharply define its purpose, coordinate members' work, or make decisions.

Note that if you use your team exclusively for consultation or information sharing, it can tolerate loose boundaries. In those cases, the purpose of the team is to contribute to the effectiveness of the individuals—the team leader and the team members. The group of people you choose to convene to consult to you, or to exchange information with one another, can fluctuate in response to circumstances without serious harm to the team's ability to achieve those purposes. With a clearly defined purpose and a few sound structures, consultative and information-sharing teams can survive underboundedness and still provide good advice and information. But if you convene your leadership team for coordination or decision-making purposes, then it must have clear boundaries if it is to develop the identity and sense of shared purpose that are needed for intense collaborative work. If the team needs additional advice or resources, then inviting a guest—clearly defined as a guest who is there temporarily in the service of a particular agenda item—will serve.

Ironically, team boundary problems often begin with a CEO who has the best of intentions toward his senior executives. The leader, not wanting to be viewed as ruthless, inaccessible, or capricious, errs on the side of inclusion. The senior team is a high-status assignment, so why hurt feelings unnecessarily? But unfortunately, clarifying the team boundaries often involves some pain and some difficult conversations about who is and is not on the team.

CEOs also often make the mistake of treating an organizational title as a ticket to senior team membership. They define their teams by the formal organizational structure—who is at the top of the hierarchy, one level (or worse, two levels) below the CEO? That's the team. But team membership is not about status, hierarchy, or inclusiveness. Nor should it be an entitlement based on role or tenure. Instead, you should select the best, most appropriate members for the team purpose you have in mind.

So ask yourself, Who is on your team? Do you think you would get the same answer if you asked those people on your list the same question? Our evidence suggests you would not. You may need to clarify the membership boundary as you launch (or relaunch) your team.

Stability: Time to Learn How to Work Together

Groups of people cannot become teams without stable membership for a reasonable period. They need enough time to accomplish significant work together and, crucially, to learn how to work together effectively.

Long-term stability in senior leadership teams, where performance is often measured in quarters and executive tenure sometimes in months, is rare. In the United States, for example, a team member may have only two or three years on a divisional team before being promoted or moved to another business unit. CEO tenure also continues to decline in many U.S. industries. Although stability may be greater in other countries and cultures—in Asia and parts of Europe, for example, teams often remain intact for years—even there it is threatened by the explosion of multinational organizations poaching talent.

The leaders of outstanding senior teams recognize these forces and use their power and political acumen to minimize their disruptive effects. Executives understand the costs of tinkering with the membership of a stable senior team whose members have learned how to work well together. They recognize that swapping members in and out can be just as disruptive for a leadership team as it often is for a professional sports team, especially when the change involves bringing on a new star.

We have seen, for example, a chief executive who deferred a needed shift of responsibilities for a team member until the leadership team had completed coordinating the acquisition of a new entity. Another CEO temporarily held off on a team member's well-deserved move to the leadership of a freestanding business unit until the team was ready to bring on that person's replacement. These executives realized that there always is tension between the needs and opportunities of individual members and the needs of the leadership team. They understood that sometimes the latter must temporarily trump the former.

When true stability is impossible, managing your leadership team's inherent instability may be the best you can do. Our research showed that competent attention to the membership cycle, from selection to socialization to departure, can attenuate to some extent the disruptions to a team's development caused by constant membership churn.

Planned exit and planned entry, we learned, are not the same as chronic instability, and there are ways to manage planned changes so that they contribute positively to a team's development. One of our colleagues uses the term "tea ceremonies" to describe the kinds of rituals for a member's departure that can help a team adapt to changes in its composition. And carefully managing the entry of a new member, often called *onboarding*, can significantly reduce the time needed to socialize a new member into the ways of the team, thereby allowing the team to benefit from the new-comers' fresh perspectives much sooner than otherwise would be the case.

Better Performance, Better Behavior

What can you expect if you do not create interdependencies, if you leave team boundaries fuzzy, or if you allow team membership to change unpredictably each time the team convenes? It's easy to see the effects of inattention to these three elements. When they are missing, members tend to view team meetings as extraneous work—boring, burdensome sessions that they avoid by sending a substitute or by skipping. As meetings drag on, some participants are transformed into agreeable robots—silently nodding in unison, bored to distraction, wishing the meeting would end, and surreptitiously checking their BlackBerries for an early flight home.

Because members of these teams-in-name-only typically go their own way, they focus on their individual roles between meetings, although occasionally they may collude to exhibit bad team behavior. We have seen, for example, more than one senior team in which members conspire in advance of the meeting to coordinate leave-early strategies so that no one will be the only member leaving before the meeting's scheduled end. The leader of such a group is often the lone integrator or, sadly, the enforcer.

If you observe a real team closely, you'll see quite different behavior. Figure 2-4 shows a snapshot of what it feels like to be a member of a real senior leadership team. Which one does your team feel like? In a real time, certainly you'll witness heated debate and passionate dialogue. But you'll also see much less of the angry, argumentative antics that keep less-effective teams from landing their plane. The bored but agreeable robot, too, is a rarity here. Members see their meetings as real, value-adding work, and they make every attempt to attend them. If they have to miss a meeting, they don't worry about sending a substitute (which isn't permitted, anyway) because they know that their concerns will be fairly represented by the other members. That sense of interdependence doesn't fade when the meeting ends. The leader and the members continue working together, seeking one another's advice and support and holding one another accountable.

FIGURE 2-4

To the team: Which type of team is more like yours?

	Team in name only	Real leadership team
Team meetings	• This is a distraction from your real work.	• This is vital work.
	• You "should" attend.	• You *want* to attend.
	• You look for ways to send a substitute.	• If you can't be there, you trust the team members to represent your concerns.
	• You can't wait for it to end.	• You feel productive and energized.
Between meetings	• Your peers feel irrelevant.	• You solve problems jointly with peers.
	• You avoid your peers or collude.	• You manage team accountabilities with peers.
	• You rely on the leader to integrate.	• You integrate yourselves.

Are You Ready to Lead a Team of Leaders?

If you're still exploring leadership teams with us, we assume that you be-lieve you might need a team. It's worth asking again: do you really *want* a team to help you lead your organization?

Yes, there are serious costs to not having a team if you need one. But there are costs to having one, and they are easy to see. Leading a real team of the organization's top leaders is very different from leading them one-on-one using the traditional hub-and-spokes model of paired conversa-tions between you and each of them. Your real team members will make tough decisions together after considerable and lengthy debate. Mem-bers will have to stretch their own well-learned habits of self-interest to consider the entire enterprise and not just their own areas of responsibility.

All this is excellent news for the organization—but be aware that it dramatically changes the power dynamics in the executive suite. When you are the hub of every conversation among your top leaders, you wield considerable direct control over them and their actions. Interacting with a team is a very different experience. The team members confront you, early and often. Indeed, if you set up the team properly and lead it in a way that allows members to evolve into a real team, you will have to be willing to encourage them to confront you. When you cannot see how your actions are undermining the performance of your organization, it will be their job to tell you. When you are missing opportunities to get the best out of your leaders by insisting they operate interdependently, it will be their obligation to point that out. Are you up for that?

Most top leaders who avoid developing or leveraging the power of a real top management team do so out of ignorance. Most have never experienced the powerful upside of a team of leaders. They don't know how to conceptualize, charge, or manage a leadership team. Recall Mike Waters, the CEO who believed that his organization was "too complex" for a team approach. That very complexity is the reason he needed a real team. And when we interviewed Waters's senior leaders, their perspective was not the same as his. They told us that the problem wasn't the team or the lack of opportunities for interdependence and collective decision making; rather, it was the leader. "We're not a team because Mike won't see us as a team," they told us. "That's the only limitation."

Neither Waters nor his team had ever seen or experienced a real leadership team. They didn't know what a real team at the top should look like, and they couldn't imagine how one would work. For this reason, we offer throughout this book multiple examples of leadership teams— their struggles and their accomplishments. We hope that these stories will expand and deepen your understanding of real leadership teams, and do so in a way that makes your choice to create one (or not) well informed and evidence based.

The Waters team story, as it happens, has a happy ending. Through intensive discussion among his top leaders of what they could achieve that otherwise would not get done, through restructuring, recomposing, and relaunching the team, through intensive team and individual development, and through many detours and refinements, this group of frustrated individuals gelled into a solid, high-performing leadership team. Waters and his direct reports took it on because the business needed it— and because he became convinced of the need for a real team even though he did not yet have a clear picture of how such a team would operate. And, like many executives, members of this team now say that they'd never settle for anything less.

Finally, we offer from our observations a word of advice that applies to the early stages of crafting your team. If you want and need a senior leadership team, you usually will have to prepare the ground to get the people and the organization ready for what will be a significant change in how leadership is exercised in your enterprise. Recall Bruce Campbell at Forward Air, who created a real team despite his dislike of meetings. Creating a space for his group of executives to meet and discuss and debate was a necessary first step, but it was not the only requisite change. The senior managers themselves also needed to change. To a person, they were excellent managers, well versed in the transportation industry. However, the new businesses they were entering required new ways of thinking and acting. They needed to change their focus from their own regions to the success of the entire enterprise. The purpose of the team would have to clearly specify that new focus to point all those thoroughbreds in the same direction. And, finally, the team would need resources to support it, as well as intensive and expert coaching to help it develop constructive working processes.

Are you ready and able to lead a real team? Are you willing to change your own behavior to make the team effective? Can you commit the time and energy needed to make your team great?

Here are some points to remember as you contemplate these questions:

1. Ask yourself if you need a team. Your reflexive answer may not adequately address the real issue that should inform it: are there vital organizational reasons that you need the senior leaders to collaborate in leading the enterprise?

2. Decide what kind of team, or teams, you want. Ultimately, it is your call what you want to ask the team members to take on as part of their leadership roles. If you want your leaders to coordinate major initiatives or to make highly consequential decisions together, then you must clarify team membership, define collective responsibilities, and keep your team reasonably stable so that members can learn how to work effectively together. They will not be capable of decision making and coordination unless you take the steps to make them into a real team.

3. Create clear boundaries for your leadership team, and specify how it will relate to other teams in your organization. Like many chief executives, you may discover that you need more than one leadership team serving more than one function. Your core decision-making team, which will be stable and exclusively composed, will handle enterprisewide decisions. Your broader

information-sharing team may be a larger body with more fluid boundaries; any high-level manager may, at some time, partici-pate. Coordinating teams that you create may vary in composition and design for different kinds of organizational initiatives. For each of these types of teams, being crystal clear about team boundaries and responsibilities—and about the relationships among the teams—is an essential first step if they are to develop the capability to fulfill their functions well.

We end this chapter by reiterating the core lesson of the essentials: it never is wise to rush ahead if you doubt that you can do a first-rate job of forming a real team, of articulating a compelling purpose for the team, and of choosing members with care and keeping them together so that they can learn. You may want and need a team—but you should take it on only if you can design, support, and lead it well.

3

Create a Compelling Purpose
for Your Leadership Team

An exasperated Arturo Barahona sat in his executive office on the
top floor of the AeroMexico headquarters in downtown Mexico
City, lamenting the struggle he was facing in moving the airline
from state ownership to privatization. Time, the young CEO knew, was
critical. To make the transition successful, he and his team had to transform AeroMexico rapidly into a competitive, market-driven, and customer-
focused organization.

Barahona turned in his chair to face an impressive wall of bookshelves, barren except for a row of thick McKinsey binders left there by
his predecessors. "That's our strategy," he said, pointing to the once shiny
volumes, now collecting dust. "All we have to do is get it off those pages
and into the organization."

Under the previous leadership the organization had spent valuable
time and a lot of money to develop a new strategy. Now, Barahona and his
team were left with the struggle to bring it to life. His leadership team
grasped the general direction of the company, but members lacked a
clear picture of how they could drive it forward.

Every member of Barahona's team had a slightly different take, based
on individual roles and experience, on what the issues were and what to

do about them. Compounding the problem, each member had his own perspective on the role of the leadership team in implementing the new strategy. Most of the members thought they should focus primarily on that piece of the strategy that most directly affected their areas of responsibility or expertise. The head of marketing focused on how the airline should shift its marketing strategy, but without considering operations, whose head was focused on the expansion of routes but had little understanding of the impact on human resources, which would be responsible for hiring and training the new staff. Instead of one agenda, there were many.

Had you asked any of the nine members of the AeroMexico senior leadership team what was in those tomes on Barahona's bookshelves, you would have gotten nine different answers. Most would have agreed that during the next five years the airline had to double its revenue and triple its profitability. Most might have mentioned that service had to improve, they had to find new sources of revenue, and the airline needed an infusion of new talent given its path toward privatization. But how the organization would achieve those goals was another matter, as was the team's role in making it happen.

Members had no clarity about why they were being asked to work as a leadership team and what they were expected to accomplish together. Although the team continually met and discussed a variety of issues—some obviously important, others minor—they gained little traction and experienced almost no progress. Indeed, the only things emerging from the top team's work were frustration and growing concern.

The frustration was heightened by the fact that Barahona and his team were experienced and talented executives. They knew things weren't working. They could see they weren't making the progress that was needed to build the business. But they couldn't figure out how to gain momentum.

What Barahona didn't yet realize was that he had just flown squarely into one of the toughest mountains faced by chief executives: the need to establish a compelling purpose for the leadership team.

Getting the Team Purpose Right

We've talked about the four types of senior teams: one that exchanges information only, one that advises you, one that coordinates the implementation of strategic initiatives, and one that makes enterprise-level decisions. Let's assume for the moment that you want a decision-making team. Just what decisions will it make? What defines the domain of what your team will accomplish together? How will you explain that to your team in a way that orients, focuses, and engages their energies? Deciding the kind of team you want does not in itself provide adequate direction to them about their purpose as a leadership team.

To get it right, chief executives must articulate to their teams a purpose that is *consequential, challenging*, and *clear*. These three ideas are straightforward, but they must be brought to life in unique ways for every leadership team.

The team purpose must be challenging enough but not impossible: what is this team of leaders up for at this point in its life? Early on, when leaders are first learning how to lead as a team, the level of challenge they can handle may be lower than when they have matured. A team purpose also must be consequential: what actions are crucial enough to be treated as the main job of the leaders and not a side job when their individual roles are done? And, finally, a team purpose must be clear: what are the critical few things that only this team of senior leaders, of all the people in this organization, can accomplish? What are these critical few now, and what are they in the long run?

A Purpose That Is Consequential and Challenging

Teams at other levels of the organization—front-line sales and service teams, quality teams, or teams of lower-level managers—often suffer from a lack of consequentiality in their purposes. For such teams, often the work they do has been inadequately connected by organizational leaders to larger, meaningful purposes, to the work of others, or to the organization as a whole.[1] Not so with senior leadership teams. They all perceive that what the top team does is highly consequential for both the short-term and the long-term performance of the organization.

In our research with these leadership teams, we have seen that a sense of consequentiality in the teams' purpose emerges naturally. Indeed, the teams in our sample scored an average of 4.8 on our 5-point scale assessing how consequential the team's purpose is. That's about as high as possible. Our observations suggest that this high score is less a function of brilliant direction setting by chief executives than it is a function of circular thinking: "We're the top leaders of the organization. Our purpose must be important for the enterprise." Nevertheless, members see that the work of a leadership team has a major impact not only on the lives and work of others—for better or for worse—but also on the viability of the enterprise.

It's the "for worse" part that creates stress. Although it's easy to establish consequentiality, chief executives often run up against hard walls in trying to get the team challenged to the right degree, and above all in getting the clarity right. In this chapter, we describe why getting the purpose right for a leadership team can be a daunting hurdle, something we illustrate through the tales of teams that struggled with a poorly articulated purpose. We then tell the stories of outstanding leadership teams to show you how it can be done well.

Getting the Challenge Right

What gets in the way of getting the level of challenge right for your leadership team? Assuming that your team members are strong, committed performers, they're used to running hard. They need some rein, or they will bolt in many directions. But they also need freedom to move. If you continually hold them in with a stream of insignificant meetings and trivial decisions, they will eventually balk or, worse, bolt. They are at their best when they are continually challenged and are providing real value to the organization.

Our research uncovered two intriguing patterns. First, leaders frequently overchallenged individual members but underchallenged the team. They sometimes demanded too much from senior executives in their individual leadership roles, holding them to the highest performance standards and constantly raising the bar to test individual capabilities. But they demanded too little from their leadership team.

Why challenge the individuals but restrict the team to trivia? Some executive leaders test their executives because they believe that by creating a culture of competition among team members, these senior players will remain well honed. Other leaders, although few admit it, also like keeping their team members so busy and focused on individual issues (and on one another) that they have no time to challenge their leader. Challenging a team, by contrast, can strengthen it enough that it becomes a threat to an insecure leader's power.

Consequently, the work of the team inevitably feels less important than the work of the individual members, and they wander away to focus on what they see as the most important of their accountabilities. To us, saddest of all are the executive teams that are brought together at the leader's convenience only to provide information about members' own areas. They never get to hear why they are convened and why nothing more is asked of them than reports. In such situations any sense of purpose evaporates. Members soon perceive their team interactions as a waste of time, and they give little time and energy to them.

The purpose of the team will be challenging only if the members are asked to exchange strategic information, coordinate enterprisewide initiatives, or make vital decisions on behalf of the organization. The team's purpose will seem trivial when the hard stuff is all in the individual jobs, relegated to the business units, or disaggregated and assigned to individuals, with members asked at meetings merely to report what's new in their areas.

On such teams, it's not surprising to see members choosing instead to spend their time in the field seeing important customers. The machinations used by members to avoid team meetings without spending political capital can be entertaining. One team we studied had a norm of not missing meetings—unless you had a meeting with a "strategic client." Strategic clients were so crucial to the business that a member could be excused from other obligations if that relationship needed attention. One of our team members was amazed by how often strategic clients could meet only on the day of the top team meeting.

On the best teams, though, the opposite occurs. Members experience the work of the team as being at least as important as their individual work. They sometimes may feel as if they have two full-time jobs, but members invariably bring to the team, and use to achieve its purpose, the full range of their expertise and experience.

Our second finding about getting the level of challenge right is this: *challenge without clarity hurts performance*. Figure 3-1 illustrates this finding. Poor teams are the ones that meet few of their constituencies' needs (those of customers, shareholders, boards, employees, etc.) and show few signs of becoming stronger over time. Mediocre teams do well by some, but not all, of their constituencies and show only modest signs of improvement in their ability to work and learn together. Certainly, members of each of these two groups feel somewhat challenged by their

FIGURE 3-1

The clarity–challenge balance in senior leadership team purpose

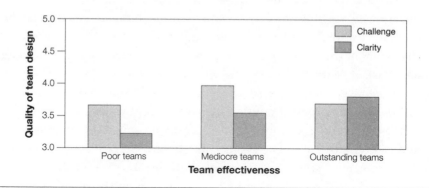

purposes, but both groups feel more challenged than clear about their work as a team.

The main lesson about the clarity–challenge relationship comes from the outstanding teams—those that serve all their constituents superbly even as they become better over time. Only the leaders of the outstanding teams got the team purpose right; they articulated team purposes that were at least as clear as they were challenging. More clarity is better than less. More challenge is better than less—to a point. But the two together have a powerful influence on the performance of leadership teams.

Too little clarity coupled with a daunting challenge means that members will be stressed, fragmented, and unable to move together to achieve a common purpose. Leaders of outstanding teams challenged their teams, but, above all, they made sure that their teams' purposes also were sharp and clear. Clarity of purpose makes the extraordinarily challenging and consequential work of senior leadership teams feel possible. It orients the team in a way that allows it to pull together toward the same end, rather than pull—diligently if frustratingly—in different directions.

We witnessed the importance of a clear and challenging direction recently in working with a major division of Millennium Chemicals, a global firm whose business strategy was to grow substantially, both organically and through acquisition. When we began studying the team, there was no clarity about how it was supposed to contribute to making this strategy come alive. In the two years before our involvement, not only had the firm not made a single acquisition, but it had not even identified any potential targets.

New CEO Bob Lee recognized that his senior leaders needed help in understanding their purpose as a leadership team. So Lee relaunched the team. Relaunching is a technique a leader can use when the team is on a poor trajectory that stems from multiple flaws in its setup. As with Lee's team, a *relaunch* involves bringing the team members together for the purpose of refocusing on the team: its purpose, its boundaries, and its rules of engagement (relaunching is addressed in detail in chapter 5).

Before Lee brought the team together for its relaunch, he realized that revisiting the team purpose also meant contemplating changes in its membership. Lee's relaunch included reducing the size of his decision-making team from fourteen to six. The larger, fourteen-person entity became a separate alignment team—the information-sharing body at the top of the enterprise. This change of the team purpose required that Lee have hard conversations in advance with more than half his direct reports about not including them in the decision-making team.

Some of his direct reports resisted, but for others, such as the chief scientist, it was a relief not to be obligated to listen to what he viewed as endless irrelevancies. Lee reported that after this conversation he felt as if he had handed the chief scientist a gift. To help smooth the transition for his senior leaders, the CEO kept the name of his larger information-sharing team as the Management Committee and kept its membership intact. He also gave a new name to the group of six: the Operational Team. (The second name was somewhat misleading, because this team actually dealt with the firm's most strategic and mission-critical issues.) These name changes helped with the transition to clarity of purpose for both teams.

Lee then told his decision-making team that its purpose was to make the decisions that would result in significant growth, including identifying at least two high-quality acquisition targets immediately. With the challenge and clarity pitched to the right level, the Operational Team quickly established a subteam to analyze potential acquisitions and began focusing the team's efforts on reviewing those analyses. Within eighteen months the firm had made successful acquisitions in Europe and South America. Having the right combination of clarity and challenge in enacting the division strategy enabled the team to focus its collective energy and accomplish its growth objectives.

Clarity Above All

Of the three qualities of a great leadership team purpose—consequentiality, challenge, and clarity—establishing clarity is the hardest. One executive aptly described the typical state of things: "Our team purpose is extremely important and extremely challenging . . . if only we knew what it was."

Gilles Waire, one member of a leadership team we studied, described when, for the first time in his experience, the divisional leadership team on which he served suddenly had clarity. Under the leadership of company president Ben O'Mara, the team had turned around the division. Now the team had the compelling job of spinning it off and taking it public. For the first time, members had a clear and challenging purpose as a team. "It galvanized us," Waire said. "We had a war room, we worked at it like you wouldn't believe, I barely saw my wife and children, it was exhilarating." He described it as "one of the highlights of my career." Sad to say, that clarity was created by the temporary circumstances of a clear outcome that all members could see. Once the spin-off was accomplished, Waire reports regretfully, O'Mara never again brought the members of the team together for any clear purpose, and as the team floundered, so did the company. Circumstances, as we have said, sometimes create moments of clarity. But can you imagine having that kind of clarity of focus, that energized alignment, in your leadership team all the time?

Real clarity can, indeed, create moments of exhilaration. Why is it so hard to establish ongoing clarity for a leadership team? Our research suggests that there are three common threats to clarity of team purpose.

First, many chief executives make the mistake of assuming that if the team members know the organization's mission statement, then they understand the team's purpose. When asked to identify their top team's purpose, many CEOs reiterate the organization's overall mission and then add, "Their purpose is to accomplish that." If you inspect the behavioral implications for your team of adopting the organization's mission statement as the team's purpose, you immediately see why it can't work. The two things are not the same. The organization's mission does not provide guidance about what the leadership team members do as a group.

One health care provider we studied, for example, had as its mission statement (paraphrased to protect anonymity), "To keep people comfortable, healthy, and safe." The chief executive asserted that knowing this mission statement was adequate to orient his team to what its responsibilities and actions should be. So, we asked, what would the team do to make people "comfortable, healthy, and safe"? Provide them with cozy chairs, blankets, and nutritious food? That would be absurd, of course, and that's the point: the behavioral implications of simply adopting the organization's purpose as that of the leadership team often are absurd. The team needs a purpose that is about its own special leadership responsibilities and opportunities in contributing to the organization's success.

The second common threat to senior leadership teams' clarity of purpose is the absence of a shared understanding of the organization's *strategy*, by which we mean the organization's distinctive approach to establishing sustainable performance.[2] Organizational researchers have emphasized the importance of senior team members having well-calibrated mental models of their organization's strategy. A lack of shared understanding of strategy arises when team members are not given the chance to calibrate their understanding of how the words in their strategy documents translate into organizational action.[3] It is not adequate to assume that having heard the strategy—or even being able to recite it in the same words—members have a shared understanding of what it will look like in practice or what their role is in implementing it. Our observations suggest that members must talk about the strategy as a team and play out its implications in direct conversation with one another.

The AeroMexico team described at the beginning of this chapter needed precisely this opportunity to grapple with what the company's competitive strategy meant for the business before they could draw out its implications for their own team. Barahona saw this need in members' unfocused conversations and interactions, and he took explicit action. But most leaders of executive teams assume that there is ample understanding and alignment about strategy if the team members do not explicitly challenge it and they use the same language to describe it.

If that is your assumption, you may be in for an unpleasant surprise. When we ask senior team members to describe their organization's strategy, their responses are very similar, often echoing key phrases in the mission statement or from the chief executive's charge to the team. But when they are asked how they will execute the strategy, the real story emerges.

Responses scatter widely, revealing a lack of calibration hidden by the use of similar words.

Len Stanton was a new CEO brought in to turn around a large conglomerate that his predecessor had run exclusively as a holding company. Early in his tenure, Stanton stated that he had a new strategy and the team would have a new purpose. The team would curtail acquisitions and focus instead on operational excellence and on becoming "a world-class operating company."

The functional heads took this to mean that *all* key processes were to be centralized. To meet Stanton's charge, they quickly ramped up corporate staff from twenty-five to more than five hundred, with no end in sight. Divisional presidents, by contrast, took Stanton's statement to mean that they now had resources at corporate to draw from as *they* managed change processes. Soon Stanton's leadership team was at war over who controlled key processes and initiatives, with the functional heads on one side and the division leaders on the other. When the actions of his direct reports became known to him, Stanton was shocked to see how misaligned they were. "I hadn't meant *all* our processes should be centralized!" Stanton reported ruefully. "I couldn't believe it when I realized just how little clarity I'd managed to create the first time around."

In a highly charged meeting, Stanton clarified to his team that what he meant was that the company would centralize a limited number of key processes and that the rest would remain with the divisions. The team was then able to spend its time working through what those key processes should be, and which should remain in the divisions. The previous lack of understanding among team members had not only slowed the execution of the other planks of the strategy but also had consumed a great deal of the CEO's time as he dealt with the divisive conflicts among his direct reports. It was only after he clarified the strategy that the purpose of the team could be addressed and clarified.

The third threat to clarity of purpose for a leadership team is the level of emotional courage that it takes to achieve—and sustain—clarity. Articulating a clear purpose can portend all kinds of emotion-laden troubles.[4] We have seen, for example, that some leaders have difficulty asserting a clear purpose because doing so precludes other purposes preferred by powerful or close direct reports. The threat to relationships of ruling out others' views is sometimes too painful even for highly experienced chief executives.

Moreover, some leaders have trouble keeping themselves focused on the team purpose when short-term demands become dramatic. For example, one divisional leader we studied suddenly focused her whole team on a new year-end revenue target she unexpectedly had received from corporate, thereby implicitly abandoning the longer-term growth objectives that she previously had set as her team's main purpose. All the impassioned conversations the team had had about putting growth at the center were forgotten in the face of one looming number and the potential displeasure of corporate if they did not make it.

We also have seen CEOs back away from articulating compelling team purposes because doing so surfaces genuine disagreements among key organizational leaders about where they believe the enterprise should be headed. Well-intentioned, passionate, and capable executives can disagree strongly about organizational direction. Make no mistake—these differences exist and will come out in one way or another, even though keeping team purposes ambiguous can allow the chief executive to keep them off the team's table for a while. Even so, those differences will be enacted behind the scenes as senior executives make independent choices that reflect only their own perceptions and preferences about collective directions. That state of affairs is inherently unstable. Sooner or later the disagreements will burst out, but the longer they are put off, the less likely it is that the team will be able to deal with them competently.

The temptation to put the team purpose second to the individual leaders' accountabilities is especially acute when one or more of them are superb at hitting their numbers and disinclined to cede decision-making authority to their colleagues. Chief executives may see the trouble coming and worry about it: what if their vitally needed star performers balk or become unhappy enough to think about leaving?

All these conflicts raise understandable anxiety in even seasoned chief executives. It can take fortitude to live with that discomfort. It takes courage to give the team the clarity it needs to function as a team despite the risks of what that clarity will reveal—and what the leader will need to confront—when members really understand what it means. And it takes high-level cognitive talent to conceptualize a team-level purpose that genuinely captures the full range of decisions and actions that you want for your team.

Some leaders begin the conceptual work of crafting a compelling team direction by simply laying out a set of discrete tasks—concrete pieces of work, or specific decisions—that members must perform as a team. Moving the team purpose from such concrete tasks to a higher-level purpose can be a difficult exercise. You therefore may be inclined to start at the opposite end of the spectrum. You may frame the team purpose in terms of a higher calling and then struggle to move from that level of abstraction to the practical things you must get done. Finding the right balance—blending the abstract, higher-order purpose with the tactical detail—requires great conceptual dexterity.

To get clarity of team purpose, ultimately you must use your authority as leader to articulate to the team what you want it for. To be sure, that purpose should be informed by the existing interdependencies among parts of the business. But it also must be informed by what you want to do alone and what you want your team to do. We turn next to strategies you can use to overcome these threats and to define and articulate a compelling team purpose that orients, energizes, and engages senior team members.

Getting to Clarity

So far we have emphasized threats to clarity of purpose for senior leadership teams, and the struggles leaders face in establishing clarity. But adequate clarity of purpose *is* possible; indeed, all the outstanding teams in our sample achieved it. We turn now to the lessons from those teams—and the ones that struggled but eventually got there—about how you can establish clarity of purpose for your team.

The set of actions involved is a short list, and we address each item in turn:

1. Identify the interdependencies among your team members that move the strategy forward. What leadership functions require that all the leaders be at the table?

2. Create a short list of decisions and actions that you want your team to achieve. What are the mission-critical things that can be done only by this team?

3. Raise that list to a thematic and compelling level so that it guides team decisions and actions.

4. Use your authority to articulate that purpose to the team. Only you can establish the purpose. Others can help refine it, but ultimately it is yours.

Identify the Interdependencies

If you want your team to make enterprisewide decisions or to coordinate strategic initiatives, you need to tell it that. But more is needed: the team needs to know which decisions fall into its portfolio and what initiatives it will coordinate. A good place to start is with a set of questions that helps identify those aspects of the business that require close interaction and joint decision making. A common misconception of executive team purpose is that all the items on the list must be strategic. Not so. Tactical items belong there, too, as long as they are mission critical and can be done only at the top. If they can be handled just as well elsewhere, that's where they should go.

It often helps for leaders to identify a handful of *must-win battles*—the actions the leadership team must get right if the enterprise is to achieve its strategic goals. Barahona's team, for example, agreed that to compete as a private entity in the marketplace required differentiating AeroMexico as an airline that provided superb service. For that and for its other must-win battles, the team developed a simple but specific matrix for creating shared understanding of what was meant. They asked, How would we explain this to our employees? What measures would tell us we were successful? What do we see as the obstacles to winning this battle? By generating a list of its must-win battles (one of which is reproduced in figure 3-2) and then working through their meaning together, Barahona's team established a clarity of purpose that went deeper than merely using similar language.

Teams facing must-win battles experience moments of spontaneous interdependence that can teach members and their leaders a great deal about which kinds of issues are truly interdependent and appropriate for the top team. These moments often take place at a time of organizational crisis, such as a focused threat from a key competitor.

For example, when the New Zealand government deregulated the fuels industry, Mobil Oil New Zealand identified a major opportunity to acquire a group of service stations that the leadership team knew its main competitor, British Petroleum, also would be avid to buy. The opportunity galvanized the team. Mobil New Zealand's CEO acted quickly, charging

FIGURE 3-2

AeroMexico: Must-win battles and senior leadership team purpose

Must-win battles	How would you describe this to a front-line employee?	What does success look like?	Key challenges and concerns
• Differentiate us through superior service. • Significantly improve customer service. • Develop brand identity. • Become the most technologically advanced airline. • Marketing—understanding customers.	• Maintain consistency of service. • Show friendliness and hospitality to customers. • Maintain punctuality. • Demonstrate efficiency. • Understand what the customer expects. • Surpass customer expectations—more of what customers want. • Provide the best possible experience. • Understand how specific jobs contribute to customer satisfaction.	• Customers prefer us. • High repeat business. • Low complaints. • Improved customer satisfaction. • Improved employee satisfaction. • Share gap minimized. • Reinvestment of margin in service.	• How to relate to unions to improve customer service (unions challenge management, unions provide conflicting information to employees). • Communication. • How to implement a service culture. • How to convince people this is the right way to go. • Not having enough customer satisfaction revenue or profit to invest in service.

Source: Arturo Barahona, personal interviews, 2001.

his team to identify those stations that they believed were strategically critical and, even before the stations went on the market, pursuing the needed government and legal approvals and preparing strategies for approaching the sellers. The moment the stations went on the market, the company moved, acquiring every station targeted—in one weekend! The speed of its action greatly damaged the competitor's market position. Mobil New Zealand's team members, who dubbed the campaign "the BP Wars," were so elated by their own teamwork and convinced of their ability to achieve great things together that they began working that way regularly.

The challenge is to translate such experiences of momentary interdependence into ongoing team purposes. To identify the core interdependencies of your team, we have found these questions helpful:

- What do we need each other for?

- What are the most critical challenges facing the business?

- Does the team have a collective strategy for addressing those challenges?

- How well is our strategy working?

Or try these: if I look at certain responsibilities that are owned by one function or by one region, or one business unit, do I see signs that there would be a greater benefit to the organization if we managed those things together? What's slipping through the cracks?[5]

Recruitment, allocation, and development of senior professional talent, for example, are often much better handled as interdependent activities throughout an organization than relegated to separate business units or to the human resource function. Especially when the pool of mission-critical talent is small and highly competitive—as, increasingly, it is throughout the world—you are far better served by having the top team manage decisions about whom to recruit, where to place them in the organization, and how to develop and retain their talents.[6]

The best solutions to questions about interdependencies often emerge in conversations among top leaders rather than wholly inside a CEO's head. Reg Smythe, chief executive officer of a retail financial services firm we studied, began by insisting that he didn't need a team; he thought his group of direct reports were a team merely as an artifact of the organization's structure. Team members disagreed with him. They noted, for example, that being kept from making decisions as a team had prevented them from establishing a brand or an image to be presented across all their clients. To a person, when told Smythe felt he didn't need a team, they cited a specific meeting in which they had collectively devised the business strategy they were executing. Yes, Smythe admitted, that was a great meeting. The firm clearly was better off as a result of that intensive collaboration.

That realization prompted Smythe to invite his team to join him in exploring what the team members, working together, could add to the business that would not be accomplished otherwise. It turned out that different issues were best handled in different ways. Sometimes Smythe identified specific goals that would be best met if assigned to the team rather than to any one area or function. Several times he reconvened the top leaders to test his ideas with them. With this back-and-forth combination of team conversation and his own conceptualizing skill, Smythe identified the full range of interdependencies that served as a starting point for articulating the purpose of his leadership team.

Here's another example. Franz LeGuin, CEO of a computer chip company we worked with, found traction for his team's purpose in a different set of questions. This company had three main businesses: automotive chips, cell phones, and networks. These businesses operated largely independently of each other. Moreover, a core strategic initiative for this organization was entry into the Chinese market—as it was for all its competitors. LeGuin asked, "What is slipping through the cracks between the businesses? What goals might be better served by leadership team responsibility?" LeGuin and his team judged that talent recruitment was being seriously underserved because those decisions were located strictly within human resources. Asked whether talent management would be better accomplished if line managers worked with the head of HR in making strategic decisions about talent, the team answered yes. Like Smythe, LeGuin found that hearing his top leaders' thoughts on key interdependencies sparked him to consider new ideas about what he wanted his team to accomplish.

Create a Short List

These examples are meant to help you find a process to identify the full range of interdependencies possible for your team. The answers to the leaders' questions are not, in and of themselves, statements of team purpose. Rather, they are the first step in getting to a purpose. Conversations between leaders and teams about the answers generate a long list. It's the leader's job to make that into the short list.

Our research shows that most leaders of outstanding teams craft a short list of major, enterprise-affecting decisions for their teams to engage. These decisions include what business to be in, which resources to deploy where, how to implement those choices, how to develop new leaders for the future, and how to reinforce those aspects of the organization's culture and values that contribute to its success. They also include important tactical issues such as dealing with immediate financial crises, moving into major new markets, making acquisitions (such as Mobil's gas station sweep), and responding to sudden market shifts.

Here is a short list of the key top team responsibilities that we have found to be relevant for most large organizations:

- Defining or modifying the organization's strategy

- Acquiring and deploying capital

- Building organizational capability (for example, by improving the operating model or the succession pipeline)

- Managing mission-critical initiatives (such as the acquisition and implementation of new production or service technologies)

- Monitoring the organization's performance

- Integrating major acquisitions

Small organizations also have a version of this list. Clearly, senior leadership must take on all of these items if they are to be satisfactorily dealt with by the organization.

Conceptualize the Team's Unique Contribution

When we say "conceptualize" we don't mean that you need to create a grand, abstract theory of team purpose. Instead, you need to identify and lift up the core themes in the team's collective responsibilities. A compelling purpose for a team is more than a short list of interdependent accountabilities, although even such a list is a great improvement over no clarity at all. But a true team purpose captures and encapsulates those items in a larger and more general idea. In that idea lies the answer to the question, What do you need this group of enterprise leaders to do that cannot be accomplished by any other set of people?

Conceptualizing your team's purpose in this way takes creativity and cognitive skill. Your conversations with the team members about their interdependencies creates the short list, but it is your own creative brain work that identifies larger themes in the list, connects them to the core challenges faced by the organization, and generates language to explain the themes and challenges to your team in a way that brings them to life.

Reg Smythe, the financial services CEO described earlier, began with a deep understanding of the challenges faced by the business, along with his short list of interdependent goals generated from multiple interactions and sessions with the team. With these, Smythe crafted a statement of purpose that captured why the members worked as a team and what they existed to accomplish. Figure 3-3 shows the concrete list from which Smythe generated the theme "seamless integration" as the core idea in his team's purpose.

Franz LeGuin studied his short list and ultimately identified "managing the matrix" as the core theme of his team's purpose. What he

FIGURE 3-3

Retail leadership team: From interdependent goals to a larger team purpose

Team interdependencies	Team purpose

• **Maintain a vision for profitable growth of the direct retail business.**
 	
  • Stay abreast of competitive, market, and consumer trends.
 	
  • Evaluate our current strategies and tactics and determine implications for future strategy.
 	
  • Identify new opportunities to create profitable growth (including "white space").
 	
  • Set goals for the organization, and ensure we achieve them.
 	
• **Provide leadership to ensure excellent execution by our organization.**
 	
  • Lead development of appropriate objectives, strategies, and tactics to support business goals.
 	
  • Ensure effective organization design, processes, and policy.
 	
  • Identify and develop high-performance managers.
 	
  • Proactively identify and remove barriers to progress.
 	
• **Create and maintain seamless integration of (a) the functions that constitute and deliver our customer value proposition and (b) our "face" to clients and prospects.**
 	
  • The *whole* of the team and the functions we manage must *exceed the sum of its parts*.
 	
  • Achieve true integration of what have been separate, coordinated functions.
 	
  • Maintain alignment across the business on key assumptions and strategies.
	• The challenge: Although our business still offers very attractive opportunities for profitable growth, the environment ahead is likely to be characterized by slower industry growth than that of the 1990s, intense competition, and consumers who will increasingly require proactive guidance from service providers to act on their financial goals. To succeed in this challenging environment, we will need to be strategically focused and nimble and to extract maximum leverage from our resources.
	
	• We will need to achieve *seamless integration* of the various centers of functional excellence that constitute our value proposition and value delivery chain in order to successfully pursue an integrated sales strategy.
	
	• This leadership team will be the focal point for integration, strategic focus, and effective execution.

meant—as the members understood it—was that the team shared responsibility for making those decisions for which it wasn't clear who owned what. By assuming collective responsibility for those matters, the team would reduce the likelihood that key decisions would slip through the cracks.

The Smythe and LeGuin examples illustrate a fundamental aspect of a leadership team's purpose: purpose evolves. It becomes clearer as team members discover what they can add if they take things on interdependently. The purpose needs to be revisited as leader and members alike learn to function as a leadership team and as the organization's challenges and must-win battles change over time. Slippage is natural in the course of a senior team's life. For that reason, the chief executive must personally take care to keep the team's main purpose at center stage, to reopen the conversation about team purposes when things change, and to continuously hone the purpose to make it ever sharper and clearer.

Use Your Authority

You are the team leader. Achieving clarity means being insistent and unapologetic about exercising your authority to specify your team's purpose.

Some teams actually work together to establish the organization's strategy. Many others focus on how to operationalize and execute a strategy that, as at AeroMexico, they had limited input in creating. AeroMexico's Barahona realized that no matter how good his team was, members couldn't be expected to create consensus and clarity on their own. He also knew that any clarity he might create by dictating his view of a purpose could be neutralized by the natural resistance of the various team members, with whom he had been a peer only months before.

But the new CEO also realized that the clock was running, the expectations of the board were high, and board members' patience was limited. So Barahona chose to achieve clarity about team purposes collaboratively with his team, putting members through a series of intense and at times exhausting discussions in which they decoded his new strategy. Starting with the overarching strategy, the team spent hours drilling down through the various levels of organizational strata until the members had defined the processes, tactics, and team responsibilities needed to make it come alive throughout the organization. Over time, the team developed a collective understanding of what the strategy meant and what the team had to do to drive it forward. It was a critical first step in creating the purpose and direction that members needed if they were to lead effectively as a team.

Such a process requires time, patience, and hours—sometimes days—of robust dialogue. You can accomplish clarity of purpose collaboratively, as it was here, or through the leader's independent reflections. Dave Knopfler, CEO of a company that was on a steep downward slide, took the latter approach. Because his company's major product was rapidly becoming a commodity, Knopfler decided to differentiate the firm from its competitors by providing integrated services and not just products. Providing consulting services to global clients would be a very different business from the regional, product-centered company his executives were accustomed to leading.

Knopfler went to his team with a non-negotiable directive. The company was going to offer integrated services to its large global customer base, and the team was the key to executing that organizationwide change of strategy. He told them that the purpose of the leadership team was twofold: to continue to monitor the performance of the company, and to design and execute the transition from a product-based to an integrated services company. He then asked his team to join him in identifying the particular accountabilities that the team would share as it pursued the directions he had set.

Not all the team members agreed with Knopfler's decision. One of his direct reports gave lip service to this concept but never contributed to its execution. After several discussions with this person that resulted in no observable change, Knopfler asked for his resignation.

A compelling purpose, a real team with real interdependence, the right people. The three essentials for building a leadership team all came into play as Knopfler acted to redirect his organization. Thinking through the new interdependencies created by the shift of strategy helped sharpen the team's purpose and brought into focus the special capabilities that his team members needed to have. Knopfler used his legitimate authority as CEO to get those three essentials in place and aimed in the same direction.

Conclusion: A Clear, Challenging, and Consequential Purpose

It took a lot of intense, iterative, and emotional work, but Arturo Barahona and his team eventually transformed the dust-covered, two-dimensional strategic plan that had stood forlornly on his bookshelves into a dynamic, living strategy for moving AeroMexico forward.

At an initial meeting with his 250 top global leaders one month after he took the helm, Barahona spoke for four hours outlining his overall vision and strategy, promising he would be back in six months to provide critical detail. Six months later, he made good on his promise. Only this time, it was his team members who spoke. Each provided a piece of the plan, each palpably aligned with all the others. "It said a lot about how my team took my vision into their hands," Barahona says. "That really got us going. People saw for the first time that we were really acting as a team."

At a presentation at a global management conference in Italy in 2001, Barahona proudly shared some of the results of his team's work, including a major increase in pilot and crew productivity even as the airline's costs had plummeted. Some of the victories the team savored seem small and tactical, such as renegotiating the airline's beverage contract and thereby saving $2 million. But those were early victories—moments of interdependence—that showed the team what else it might accomplish. Others were major wins, such as saving nearly $500 million in the purchase of new aircraft. The complex purchase negotiations managed by the newly energized team involved two aircraft manufacturers, the Mexican government, the U.S. ambassador and secretary of commerce, and major world banks. It simply could not have happened without Barahona's highly interdependent, purpose-driven leadership team.

Perhaps this team's most significant accomplishment occurred shortly after Barahona's presentation, when terrorists struck the World Trade Center. Suddenly the CEO and his team found their best-laid plans grounded—literally. As tragic and unexpected as these events were, AeroMexico's leadership team was aligned and poised to deal with crisis as a unit. In contrast to all other North American airlines, in only five days AeroMexico was again flying every route on its schedule except for the one that was entirely out of its control—New York City.

That AeroMexico was back in the air sooner than most of its competitors was no fluke. One had only to look back at an early team meeting to understand why. It was then, during an initial discussion of team purpose, that this leadership team decided to make security and safety a priority. The team members had never lost sight of that objective, and now it was paying off in ways they had never imagined: when disaster struck, the team was ready and collectively able to deal with it quickly.

Make no mistake: despite its successes, the flight Barahona and his team had taken was not a smooth one. Those initial lengthy discussions about direction and purpose were only the first leg. For more than two years those conversations about purpose continued, as Barahona, the team, and the airline grew and evolved. But without a clear, challenging direction and the commitment of the team to work together, the team's success never would have happened.

Articulating a Compelling Purpose for Your Team

As you prepare to articulate your team's purpose, keep these points in mind:

1. Your leadership team's purpose is already consequential; focus your attention on challenging the team and making its purpose clear and unambiguous. Ask yourself, If I were a member of this team, which would feel more challenging and vital—my individual responsibilities or our work as a team? If the answer is what we suspect, the challenge is to raise the level of challenge you pose to the team.

2. There is no one best way for a chief executive to arrive at a clear team purpose. You can do the conceptual work entirely on your own or with a trusted adviser. You can engage your team members in helping identify their interdependencies, and then create the short list of vital decisions on your own. You can test run an initial draft of your team's purpose and then revise it after hearing your team's reactions and ideas. Any or all of these processes can be helpful, depending on your own capabilities, preferences, and relationships with the team members. What is essential is to arrive at clarity; the path to it is yours to choose.

3. Expect the process to be emotionally demanding. All the leaders we worked with and studied struggled with the emotional aspects of setting direction for their leadership teams. Clarifying the team's purpose invariably uncovers discrepancies and conflicts about what members think their role is or should be, and using your authority to say, "This is what we will do" triggers anxiety for leaders and members alike. But when done persistently and well, it also energizes and inspires.

4

Get the Right People
on Your Team—
and the Wrong Ones Off

An executive suite is not a school yard. Just because someone wants to play on your team, has always been on the team, or was considered the heavy hitter of a past team does not mean that you are obligated to have him on your team. What's more, just because you have been chosen to lead an established team does not mean you must keep all the players when you take it over. No matter what anyone says or implies or believes, it is now your team. You must choose whom you need to be on it.

One thing that surprised us about senior teams is how often leaders who become chief executives take what they get and assume that leading their executive team means leading *this* team, of *these* people. Ask yourself whether you have allowed the history of the team, the structure of the organization, the importance of certain leadership roles—any or all of these—to drive your team's membership. Have you assumed that all your direct reports must be on your leadership team? If your team is too big to be anything but an information-exchange team, if some of the members are stellar individual performers but have toxic effects on collaboration, if the chief counsel has always been on the team but has nothing to contribute to its purpose—is that really something you should just live with?

No. It doesn't have to be that way. Once you know what you want your team to accomplish on behalf of the organization, it is time to address what may be the most emotionally challenging team leadership question of all: whom do I need on this team?

Although many organizational scholars have studied how the demographic mix of top team members affects organizational performance, we take a different approach.[1] Rather than take the mix of people as given, we explore what you should look for in members of your senior leadership team. Our research has identified certain team member characteristics that can enhance—or undermine—top team effectiveness, and our work with CEOs has identified the challenges many leaders face in using their authority to compose their teams.

The leaders we highlight throughout this book faced the challenge of shaping the composition of their team: Unilever's Diego Bevilacqua and AeroMexico's Arturo Barahona, as well as Applebee's Lloyd Hill (chapter 5) and Roche Canada's Pascal Mittermaier (this chapter). All are excellent, experienced leaders. All are assertive, confident, and successful. And yet every one of them struggled when it came time to address who should be on their team—and especially who should not.

Wanting to build member commitment, wanting to establish their worth as leaders, and wanting not to be seen as capricious or exclusionary, these leaders took their time in altering the composition of their teams. In many cases, they took too much time. Barahona, for example, lost many months in moving his organization's strategy forward as he struggled with two dysfunctional members. One was an airline veteran who was well loved by other senior leaders but ineffective; the other was a talented individual but a destructive team member. Barahona finally cut both from his leadership team, but only after months of anguish and lost momentum for his team.

Pascal Mittermaier, CEO of Roche Diagnostics Canada, tried at first to make do with a team he inherited. Mittermaier joined the Roche Canada organization at the tail end of six years of "dramatic growth." The company had gone from being a $50 million, 200-person organization to a $250 million, 400-person organization. Mittermaier arrived when growth was starting to slow and when SAP, the parent corporation, had begun more closely integrating Roche Canada—via a global SAP system, for example—and reducing its autonomy. Mittermaier explains: "I inherited a team that had pretty much been there for the previous six years. So they had been part of this phenomenal growth. It was all very externally focused, very market share driven. And you don't really ask yourself too many questions on what is the internal impact of all of this. So leadership team meetings were very tactical, very informative, and pretty siloed. Everybody came in and talked about their piece of the business. Really the only glue was the fact that I asked everyone to be there. Everyone was very cordial, but there was not a common goal. There was the attitude of, 'Things are okay as long as my area is okay.'"

But his functionally oriented, silo-minded leaders could not get past polite information exchange about their individual arenas to engage in the enterprise-level thinking required by the new challenges they faced. So, slowly, Mittermaier began recomposing the team to include only those who showed signs of an enterprise-leader perspective.

Hill of Applebee's at first believed that if he just worked hard enough with his current members he could infuse a collaborative culture into a divided team of cordial old hands and combative newcomers. It was only after some of those team members, frustrated and angry at their inability to work together, confronted their chief executive that he saw the problem. All the patience and coaching in the world were not going to save his less-than-merry band of followers unless he made the tough call to recompose his team.

Bevilacqua, as determined a leader as any we have encountered, was so intent on making strategic choices and making the merged entities successful that even when it was obviously futile, he kept trying to earn the respect of team members who clearly would never support the new organization and its new business strategy—nor their new leader. It was only after his chairman suggested that it was time to switch out some of his team members that Bevilacqua made several needed deletions from his team.

Although each of these leaders overcame the challenges he faced and eventually created a highly effective team, all of them bear scars from a process they will never forget. If you ask any of them what it was like, most likely you will get a shake of the head, a tired-soldier stare, and a muttered response. Hill calls it "painful." Bevilacqua says it was "unbelievably hard."

We cannot promise to eliminate the pain and difficulty of selecting the right members for your leadership team. But we can offer some guidance for making it easier, including which attributes to look for in potential team members, given your team purpose; how to help members understand their roles as individual leaders and members of a leadership team; how to identify and eliminate those obvious and not-so-obvious problem members—the team "derailers"; and when and how to make changes in your team membership.

Choosing the Best Players

Once you have created clarity about your strategy and operating model and have articulated the team's role in bringing it to life, you can thoroughly assess your current team members and determine whether or not you need to make any changes. It is at this time that you will stabilize the team's membership and create clear boundaries—in effect, saying, "This is us" for the foreseeable future. But it must be a thoughtfully crafted *us*. Composing a leadership team is not only a matter of selecting people by position or title or individual contributions to the organization. Your team members must also bring the essential competencies necessary to work as a real leadership team.

Most chief executives eventually reshape their senior leadership teams. If your team is to be effective, you must at minimum ensure that the members collectively understand and can represent the entire enterprise. But representing the enterprise does not translate into giving every division or function a seat at the table. As needed, those other senior managers and specialists who are not members can be invited to contribute to the team's work when the team can benefit from their expertise or knowledge.

We found that many leaders not only are hesitant to make changes in the team membership but also do not always make wise choices when they eventually change the team's composition. The challenge for a chief executive is to look deeper than the member's functional and operational expertise and focus on less obvious criteria as well, such as the person's ability to engage in robust but constructive debate with other team members and to think strategically about the enterprise as a whole.

We have heard leaders rationalize that they need the chief of technology for his systems knowledge, the marketing director for her knowledge of the customer, and so on. For a team engaged only in information exchange or for a team acting as consultant to you for key decisions, it's useful and productive to seek breadth of representation and expertise. Some leaders also make symbolic choices in membership. They may, for example, look for members who can broaden the demographic diversity of the leadership team, making sure that traditionally underrepresented groups have a highly visible role model at the leadership table.

Such choices are appropriate when they are part of a deliberate and thoughtful approach to the overall composition of a leadership team. Moreover, the presence of diverse viewpoints has been shown to significantly increase a team's creativity and decrease the likelihood that the team will congenially make plans or decisions that turn out to be fiascoes. However, having a single nontraditional member—a "token" from an underrepresented group—is not sufficient. It takes at least a pair to make a substantive difference in the quality of group performance. A diverse top team is poised to evolve into a forum for debate of strategic issues that is as vigorous as it is constructive.[2]

Our research indicated that in poor teams, members viewed the diversity of their teams as, on average, too high to be optimal. In fact, on demographic dimensions such as age, race, and gender, these teams actually were too homogeneous. This complaint in poor teams about diversity was most common in teams in which functions, regions, businesses, and the like all were represented in a top team that was an unbounded mass, but with the CEO also seeking to make a decision-making body of the team. Members themselves recognized that it was unlikely in the extreme that the chief executive could identify a clear purpose and a set of core tasks for such a wide group.

Too many leaders make the mistake of using a highly diverse mix of players as their core decision-making team without preparing either the team or the members to use their differences well. When all functions, regions, and operating units are represented on a leadership team, members understandably play the roles that they have been signaled to play: "I'm here because I represent my area. I should speak only as the SVP of sales."[3] When this happens, chief executives limit the ability of their team members to deal collaboratively with their interdependencies or to think together at the enterprise level. Moreover, they overlook and exclude the contributions of other individuals with broader perspectives, who could, if given a chance, add great value to the leadership team.

Seeking particular technical skills is another reason senior teams tend to grow steadily in size over time, until one day the conference room is filled with people who are pleased to be at the top table but who operate more like an unwieldy mob than a nimble, efficient team. Leaders, frustrated with the inability of their functional and operational "stars" to move the organization forward but afraid to let go of their technical expertise, continue to add members who, they hope, might be able to make things happen.

Look First for the Needed Skills and Experience

The first step in forming a well-composed senior leadership team is to ask what core skills and experience you need your team members to have if the team is to accomplish its work. Knowledge, experience, skills, representation of key perspectives, and functional or operational expertise are vital. Your first priority in choosing core members should be the expertise they bring to the table.

In our sample of senior leadership teams, leaders and members alike reported a reassuringly high level of knowledge and skill present in team members.[4] The essential capabilities of the members did not differentiate among the poor, mediocre, and outstanding teams, because there was little variation in task-related skills. The teams we studied were composed, by and large, of highly capable executives.

We have never seen a senior team that did not include the chief financial officer (at least initially). But we have seen effective leaders exclude CFOs who had rigidly narrow functional views and an inability to make joint decisions. Like any highly capable individual, a talented and experienced CFO who cannot work effectively as a team member can still contribute vital knowledge and experience to the organization—but not as a member of the senior team. Chief executives who take seriously the dynamics of their leadership teams invite these individuals to provide input to the senior team's deliberations when needed—as a guest appearance. But CEOs also make it clear that membership on the team requires certain teamwork capabilities beyond technical skills. Indeed, in at least one case in our sample, the CEO ultimately replaced the CFO with a better person for the job—the *whole* job, including the CFO's role as a member of the senior team.

If not a problem in acquiring basic technical abilities, then what were the most common kinds of difficulties that chief executives had in composing their leadership teams? In probing what differentiated outstanding teams from the poor and mediocre ones, we examined the hidden attributes of effective team members, searching for those that contribute to outstanding senior team performance.[5] We compared the competency profiles of outstanding teams to those of mediocre and poor teams for which we had complete assessments of all the team members. We found that although many attributes varied from team to team, there were a handful of competencies that members of high-performing decision-making teams consistently demonstrated.

Look for Signs of an Executive Leader Self-Image

Members of senior teams must conceive of their role as leading in ways that maximize the effectiveness of the organization as a whole. An often-overlooked characteristic that is critical for effective senior team members is a self-image as an executive leader. Self-image refers to an individual's dominant understanding of his or her main role in a social system.[6] If you ask a member of a senior leadership team what her role is, as often as not the initial response will be a functional or operational responsibility. She is, she will say, the head of human resources, or she runs a business unit, or she oversees marketing. Her enterprise leadership role is a bit of an afterthought, if mentioned at all.

Most managers, as they move up the ranks of organizational leadership, find that their self-image lags behind their increased breadth of responsibility. When an individual enters the management ranks she still sees herself as an employee; when she becomes a middle manager, she still acts like a first-line manager for a while.[7] And when she becomes a member of the senior team, she still thinks of herself primarily in terms of her operational or functional leadership roles.

To transition one's self-image from line or function leader to member of an enterprise leadership team takes time, coaching, and patience. Some experienced senior team members may already demonstrate an executive leader self-image, but you may need to encourage newer senior executives to see themselves as leaders of an enterprise. The transition of self-image involves not only adjusting one's self-perceptions but also modifying behavior that has been practiced and reinforced for so long that it has become habitual.

Some executives respond well to feedback and coaching about their new role as a member of a team leading an enterprise. Others have great trouble viewing themselves as anything other than representatives of their areas of responsibility. It may be best to move such individuals off the senior team and instead invite them to contribute as individuals when the team needs their specific expertise. The judgment call for a chief executive is how much time to spend coaching an individual before deciding that the transition is taking too long.

Consider the case of Philippe Reymond, who struggled with the transition from a functional manager to an executive leader self-image but, with coaching, succeeded in making it. Reymond was CFO of a technology company that had recently been spun off. He had a brilliant financial mind and had played a major role in taking the new organization public. But with that victory behind him, he found himself at loose ends as a member of the new senior leadership team. When he discussed his frustrations with his long-time manager and mentor, the mentor acknowledged that Reymond needed to rethink how he viewed his role. But his advice about how Reymond should change ("You need to be more of a leader") was vague at best.

When we began working with Reymond, he was confused. "I'm not sure what he wants me to do," he said. "I work hard making sure that my direct reports are on top of critical issues, making sure we meet all our financial requirements and filing deadlines. I spend a lot of time working with them and providing financial expertise to our senior leadership. And I think we're seen as doing an excellent job."

It was clear that Reymond's problem was not with his financial skills and expertise nor with his commitment to the new organization and its leadership. Rather, the problem was that he was still holding on to his old self-image. He saw himself as a functional leader whose role was to make sure that his unit was doing a first-rate job and that the top leadership of the organization received sound financial advice. So he spent most of his time focusing on *his* team, making sure his reports were up to speed on the latest financial requirements and that the proper reports were filed and deadlines met. When he was not working with his finance team, Reymond was often cloistered in his office making sure that he personally was on top of these same issues so that he could provide the rest of the leadership team with the best advice possible.

But the CEO and Reymond's peers wanted more than a finance expert, and they told him so. They wanted Reymond to be a full-blown member of the team, someone who could provide financial expertise but also a colleague who would engage with them in discussing broader business issues. It was only after he understood this, and after he got behavioral coaching about how he might enact his new role, that Reymond began to change his self-image. This change, in turn, shifted both how others viewed him and how he behaved on the leadership team.

Look for Signs of Conceptual Thinking

Senior leadership teams benefit from a high level of conceptual thinking by their members. *Conceptual thinking* involves the ability to synthesize complex information from divergent sources and extract their implications for the enterprise. At its most sophisticated, it is the ability to reinvent an organization, incorporating sophisticated knowledge of the organization and its environment into a new way of succeeding. Competency research on senior leaders suggests that few individuals have the ability to reconceptualize an entire organization on their own. However, an effective team, by elaborating and incorporating one another's ideas, often can discern exciting new ways of understanding what their organizations are and what they might become.

To identify team members who are capable of this level of thinking, you should look for people who have demonstrated their ability to speak about the whole enterprise and its context, beyond their own area of expertise. Be sure to choose a relaxed, reflective time to test for this competency, because it shows itself when a leader has the time and latitude to reflect, and not when she is fighting fires.

As you reflect on the leadership teams you have known, you may wonder why you have not seen more of the fruits of conceptual thinking. The reason is that teams rarely engage in the kinds of discussions that would allow conceptual thinking to emerge. Many senior teams take a simple goal-oriented view of a team meeting, for example, and try to cover the largest number of items in the least amount of time. These sprints allow no more than a cursory discussion of an issue before the team is on to the next item. Other teams spend a great deal of time in meandering discussions about historical, tangential, or trivial matters rather than those that are vital to the organization's future. Both of these uses of team time rob the organization of the collective wisdom that exists in a well-composed and well-structured team.

Consider Hong Rui, brought in as chief executive officer to save a failing multidivision organization. Once Hong and his team had success-fully stabilized the organization and reversed its declining fortunes, he was ready to move to his next agenda item: growing the business. At that point we were asked to conduct a competency assessment of all mem-bers of his senior leadership team.

We did not find anyone in this team demonstrating high-level con-ceptual thinking. That got the CEO's attention. Hong challenged our findings, pointing to Bei Zhe, a division president handpicked by Hong. The two executives had worked together in the past and indeed had in-vented a whole new business in another organization—something that requires a very high level of conceptual thinking. We believed Hong's claim. But we countered by pointing out that to do conceptual thinking, a person or team needs the space to think. Bei had been running nonstop since joining the company, first to stop the bleeding and then to come to understand the business well enough to contemplate strategic change. Moreover, Hong ran his meetings as though the team were still in turn-around mode, with agendas so operational and so crammed with items that getting through two-thirds of the list was considered a good meeting.

Upon reflection, Hong affirmed our observation. He agreed that he had not been hearing the type of groundbreaking thinking he had come to rely on from Bei. So he decided to relaunch his executive leadership team, working with the members to identify a short list of team account-abilities. Hong began setting his own agenda rather than leaving it in the hands of his administrative assistant. The four to six items that he puts on a meeting agenda are tightly tied to the team's purpose. He and team members report that they are now dealing with the important issues and are having the kinds of discussions they did not think possible. As one member told us, "We are now a team that can work with hard ideas, make complex decisions, and execute them."

Even the best teams, however, do not brim over with highly creative conceptual minds. This talent is rare. In reality, the most effective teams may have only one or two members who are first-rank conceptual thinkers. It can be inspiring to watch these individuals work. With little apparent effort, they synthesize disparate information, arranging pieces of an organizational puzzle into a coherent and interesting mosaic. They listen carefully to the various concepts, perceptions, and arguments that their peers toss about and then succinctly offer a synthesis or solution that is far more powerful than the sum of the individual suggestions.

Conceptual thinking is critical to the success of almost every senior leadership team. To achieve it requires time and an appropriate agenda, as we've noted. But it also requires at least one or two members who have the rare—and extraordinarily valuable—ability to work at high levels of conceptual sophistication. The best chief executives make special efforts to include on their teams senior leaders who have that capability.

Look for Signs of Empathy and Integrity

Members of senior teams charged with making decisions for the entire enterprise must be able to engage in robust discussions that explore divergent ways to address a problem or opportunity. Indeed, the ability to have these kinds of discussions is a sure sign of leadership team effectiveness.

Teams that anchor either end of this spectrum are headed for trouble. On one side are the teams whose members nod their heads in unison to the ideas and directives put forward by the leader. Silent compliance is a terrible waste of brainpower and money, especially the expense incurred by global leadership teams meeting face-to-face several times a year. What's more, such public compliance with a leader's directives almost always is *mere* public compliance and not genuine commitment. If members view their leader as combustible they understandably may collude to avoid a direct confrontation. Or they may be unwilling to open their own areas to scrutiny and influence by other members of the team because they have yet to see evidence in their interactions that the other leaders can be trusted to address their concerns. Ultimately, these publicly agreeable teams balk when it comes time to execute the leader's directives. That choice is understandable if they have never laid their concerns on the table and heard them addressed.

At the other end of the spectrum are the teams that become so argumentative that they cannot make decisions that stick. Observing them, one often gets the feeling of being on an aircraft with them, just when all the passengers can see the runway ahead and feel the landing gear coming down. Suddenly the engines rev up and the plane takes off in a new direction as someone reopens the discussion, one more time. And this time, it's noisier.

Our research has identified two competencies that consistently enable teams to engage in real and robust discussions of strategic issues that result in shared understanding and a collective decision. These two competencies are empathy and integrity. Here is how to look for signs of these competencies in your potential team members.

Empathy

This leadership competency is demonstrated in three ways:

- The ability to understand the content of what a person has just said

- The ability to understand the meaning it holds for the speaker

- The ability to reflect back the feelings the speaker has attached to the content

These abilities show themselves in the way the individual deals with the spoken words of other team members. Individuals with great empathy can paraphrase their colleagues' ideas; they identify the underlying organization-relevant concern that the speaker has communicated, and they address that concern directly in their responses. Of these three abilities, open reflection on a colleague's feelings about a concern is especially rare in senior leadership teams.[8] Senior team members seldom say, "I hear that you're frustrated about that, Marcus." However, we have found that teams can be successful when they consistently demonstrate even the first two ways of showing empathy.

Overall, we find that members of outstanding teams are far more empathic than their counterparts on mediocre and poor teams. On outstanding teams, nearly three-fourths of the members were identified as being able to consistently understand the content and meaning of others' expressed concerns. On mediocre and poor teams, however, fewer than half demonstrated such empathy.

Why does empathy matter so much as a competency for leadership team members? Here is an example of its absence in a team interaction in which the consequences for team agreement are readily observable. This leadership team (in the financial services industry) was engaged in a tough and emotional discussion of drastically reducing organizational costs. The leader, Vera Castanelli, had asked that all team members respond to the current economic downturn by identifying, among other things, opportunities to cut staff.

The team was in the middle of this painful conversation when David Meyers, leader of a high-revenue division, began speaking: "Talking about the cutback in staff—" That was as far as he got. Far from exercising the ability to understand the content of what her colleague was saying, Frances Lanstrom leaped in angrily. "David, quite frankly, I don't see why you're worried about *your* job. You're in a mission-critical role." Neither Meyers nor CEO Castanelli responded, and the debate continued, with little progress toward any kind of agreement.

A few minutes later at a break in the conversation, one of us intervened, saying, "David, I think you never finished your sentence back there a few minutes ago." Meyers leaned in and turned to look the length of the table to pin Lanstrom with full eye contact. "Thank you. I am not worried about my job. I was about to say that I believe we are doing the right thing. Cutting staff right now is the right decision. But this one is especially hard for me, because I will have to let go someone who started the same day that I started here, eighteen years ago. And that is *hard.*"

This example occurred in the context of a highly charged topic. Similar patterns of behavior arise in senior teams in even the most mundane circumstances, and they prevent genuine understanding of other people's perspectives. Team members fail to seek clarity in what people's words mean, they move too quickly to accept loose terms without defining them, and they fail to calibrate their understanding. They create conditions that make understanding, let alone agreement, impossible.

Empathy is not about being nice for the sake of being nice. It's not about being nice at all. In fact, the outstanding teams in which empathy is a common competency have vocal disagreements and lively conflict—like the thoroughbreds they are.

The problem is that without empathy, members cannot do the work of leadership teams. It is essential that such teams harvest the collective knowledge and skill in the room to make wise decisions on behalf of the enterprise—decisions that take into account all the tough trade-offs among alternatives. Without full information about those trade-offs, they cannot make good choices. Without empathy in the team, members are not likely to feel that others have understood their own legitimate concerns and have taken them into account in the decision process. So they raise and reraise objections, a dynamic commonly seen in teams that have trouble landing the plane. Ultimately, a member who feels not heard or understood may withdraw from engaging with other members in the real work of the team.

Empathy also makes it possible for the team to accomplish real work—and make real decisions—even when some members cannot be present, and that contributes greatly to a senior team's efficiency. When members are empathic with one another's concerns, they trust one another to represent their concerns when they are absent. Decisions made by this kind of team will stand even when not all members have been present for all the discussions.

What signs can help you identify potential members who have the empathy needed for a senior team's effectiveness? Look for members who not only actively listen to their peers but also speak directly to the concerns they raise. Listen for signs that they reflect what they have heard when others speak. We have seen that many such individuals use common turns of phrase such as, "What I heard you say is . . ." or "Do I have your point right?" The choice of phrase alone is not diagnostic of empathy. What is critical is a team member's tendency to listen to corrections or to affirm an expressed concern before continuing to express his views. Look also for members who can hear criticism of their perspectives without automatically dismissing it and who can tolerate even outright rejection of their ideas.

Select members for your leadership team who are capable of empathy, and then reinforce it every time you see it. You need at least moderate levels of empathy to have any hope of robust discussion, wise advice, real coordination—and actual decisions—from your team.

The costs of having a member who is incapable of empathy are evident in the behavior of Paul Cooke, a leadership team member at a major health care provider. Cooke, who ran the top-performing hospital in the organization, dominated team meetings with his personal demands. Ironically, his stellar performance as an individual leader was a large part of the problem. He knew he was a star, and he made sure everyone else on the team knew it, too. During discussions of capital expenditures and other resources, he often took over the discussion to the point of turning it into a monologue. "With Paul it's always, 'I can only see it this way' and 'I can't sign up for that,'" observed CEO Bill Taunton. "It seems like three-quarters of every meeting is about his issues. He never has any clue about the concerns of others on the team."

Cooke's self-absorbed behavior showed an inability to self-manage the destructive impact of his lack of empathy. His relationships with other team members deteriorated to the point that it was difficult for them to work as a team at all. Because Cooke was unwilling, or perhaps unable, to change his behavior, Taunton eventually removed him from the team. Although Cooke ultimately left the company, Taunton believes the move was necessary. "Paul was a smart guy, and a great performer, but in the end I felt he was holding me and the rest of the team hostage. A guy like that can destroy an executive team."

Integrity

When we refer to integrity, we are not referring to its popular definition—things such as not stealing from the company or being generally honest. Rather, integrity was manifested in the senior leadership teams we studied by these behaviors:

- Putting enterprise-affecting issues on the table for discussion by the group even when resolution of the issues could have negative implications for one's own area of responsibility

- Keeping discussions among senior executives confidential, not sharing them with one's group or gossiping to others about who argued for which position in senior team meetings

- Actually implementing decisions that have been agreed to by the team

- Holding the team accountable for making choices that are consistent with publicly espoused team and organizational values

Members who have integrity do not agree to something in the heat of a group interaction about which they have unexpressed reservations. They do not enact their resentment of team decisions by failing to follow through to implement them. They do not reach the real agreements in hallway conversations with a select colleague or two. They do not return to their home turf after a tough decision and communicate it by saying, "I didn't want it that way—it was all Mike's doing." They do not revert under stress to acting independently when they agreed in the team to share accountability for something the team has done. Members with integrity manage themselves honorably and make good on their promises to the team.

When a CEO has composed a team of members who have that kind of integrity, even the most difficult decisions can be handled competently, as we observed in a leadership team that had to decide whether or not to close an unproductive manufacturing plant. Several members argued in favor of closing the factory immediately because it would save millions in costs and would substantially help the company's overall performance. This hard-line view was gaining steam when Jeff Oakes, a team member, spoke up: "One thing we always say at this company is that we show respect for people. How is closing the factory this way consistent with that core company value?"

It was a risky position to take. On some leadership teams such candor could be tantamount to political suicide. But Oakes took the risk of reminding the team of its own stated values. After lengthy debate, the team agreed that shutting down the plant right away could have serious repercussions with employees, the union, customers, and the community. They decided instead on a plan to shut the plant within one year. That would give them time to meet the needs of their customers through other plants while helping employees locate new employment and assisting the community to adjust to the lost of a major employer. At no time did members of the organization or community hear mixed messages coming from the executive suite. The team implemented its choice with no sign that many of the members had vehemently expressed an entirely different point of view.

To repeat, acting with empathy and integrity is not about "playing nice." Quite the contrary: you should expect a well-composed team, like the one just discussed, to be a place for serious conflict and debate. What you are looking for in potential team members is not deference to each other or politeness or smooth and harmonious relations—hardly a likely characterization of a room full of thoroughbreds in any case. What you are looking for in team members is the ability to put hard questions and strong disagreements on the table and work them through to a conclusion that benefits the enterprise and its stakeholders.

Onboarding as a Tool for Forming Senior Leadership Teams

Onboarding is a form of individual coaching that helps a senior executive prepare for a role as part of a leadership team. (In chapter 7 we address coaching the team.) Yes, when you're bringing new members to the team, you should clarify the individual's functional role within the organization—but you also should define her role and your expectations of her as a member of the leadership team. Be especially clear that you seek her expertise about the whole enterprise and not only about issues that lie within a particular function. As enterprise-level leaders, members contribute by seeing the interconnections among parts and managing the white spaces between defined accountabilities. Only by being attentive to those interconnections can the new member come fully to terms with both her enterprise role and her team role.

Here are some questions you might want to address with new members of your leadership team.

1. What are they expected to contribute to the team? You have established a set of team accountabilities for the leadership team through discussions and initial agreements and through revisions to those agreements as circumstances have changed. New members have not had the benefit of those discussions, so they need to be oriented to what you expect of your team now.

2. How are members expected to behave—both in and out of meetings? You may have gone from some initial rules of

engagement to developing team norms that are now so deeply held that they are no longer discussed. Everyone on your team understands what goes and what does not in this team. Your newest members need to know that, too.

3. What characteristics of this individual's behavior risk hurting the team? What behavior shows the greatest promise for facilitating the team's work? Leaders learn some habits in the course of their careers that are effective in some circumstances and destructive in others. Draw on what you know about this leader and what you know about your team to help the person bring the best she has to offer to the work of your senior leadership team.

For more information on this topic, see "Onboarding Leadership Team Members."

Onboarding Leadership Team Members

Think back to the last time you welcomed a new executive to your organization and to your senior leadership team. How did you talk to him about your expectations? Next time, consider having three conversations.

1. Expectations for the individual role.

In this conversation, you identify for the new executive your expectations for her individual contributions to managing her function, operational unit, or region.

2. Expectations for the enterprise role.

In this conversation, you identify for the new executive your expectations for her contributions to the leadership of the enterprise as a whole. You explore strategies she can use to develop constructive relationships with other functions, units, and regions.

3. Expectations for the senior leadership team role.

In this conversation, you identify for the new team member your expectations for her contributions to the senior team's accountabilities, and you help her understand the team's behavioral norms or rules of engagement.

Eliminate Dangerous Derailers

Most senior executives, with coaching and support, can adopt an executive leadership self-image and develop competencies such as empathy and integrity. But there is one kind of team member who poses a serious risk to the success of any team: the derailer. The most obvious derailers are members who refuse to accept the chief executive's leadership. They may not agree with the enterprise's strategy, its operating model, or the senior team's main purposes. They may not commit to the team norms. For whatever reason, they refuse to play the game you have asked your team to play.

Most chief executives are willing to spend a lot of time and effort trying to convince such members to commit to the team and move forward. Certainly some of that patience is necessary, especially if the derailer has expertise or experience that is vital to the enterprise. Yet no matter how talented the individual, eventually you must remove a chronically mutinous person from the team.

How much time should you give a balking member to make up his mind? Looking back, many of the leaders we interviewed about this issue took six months or more to remove team derailers, and all of them regretted not moving faster. Some noted that when they acted, it not only eliminated a powerfully disruptive force but also reinforced among the remaining members the importance of adhering to the team's agreed-upon purpose and norms.

Such was the case for Fritz Fein, president of a division in a global manufacturing company. Fein's company, at the time we studied it, was embroiled in difficult and protracted negotiations with labor unions. Learning from a history of upheaval and tragedy in relations with the unions—including riots, one resulting in the death of a man who had crossed the picket lines—Fein's team agreed unanimously that it would allow only specifically designated individuals to be in contact with the union leadership. Despite this agreement, Bill Selva, head of human resources, decided to have an off-the-record Sunday morning breakfast with the union president. The following Monday morning, when Selva arrived for the leadership team meeting, the organization was abuzz with rumors that Selva had met with the union president and that the union had "broken" the company's leadership team. Selva, unaware that the meeting was common knowledge, headed for his chair among the team members. As he began to sit down, Fein spoke: "You have something else to do this morning. Go do it." Not a person spoke or moved as Selva left the room.

Fein had kicked Selva off the team in front of the other members. "This was a betrayal—of me, of the team, of everything we had agreed to," Fein told us. "He had ignored it all. He was no longer a member of the team." It was a tough move, but the message was clear. As Fein later put it, "Honest mistakes will not get you off the team. Foul play and a lack of commitment will."

How a Derailer Can Take Down a Team

The most dangerous type of derailer is someone who publicly appears to buy in to the program but who actually is quietly working in the background to subvert it. One derailer was Georg Nigilievsky, head of operations for a regional tire company. For years Nigilievsky had labored as the number two leader, assuming that when the CEO retired he would be summoned to take over. But the call never came. The board saw Nigilievsky as coercive, paternalistic, and rigid—unable to take the organization where it needed to go. They wanted someone with a new perspective, a leader who could develop a real team and think new thoughts. So they gave the leading role to Jane Dupres, a rising star at a competing firm.

But the board made a critical mistake: because Dupres was an outsider, new to the company, they urged her to keep Nigilievsky as second in command. Nigilievsky, they reasoned, not only knew the company but also was respected throughout the industry for his knowledge of tire production. Nigilievsky graciously, even humbly, agreed to stay on. After all, he told the Board, he wanted to see the company succeed; after all, he told Dupres, he wanted her to succeed. He recognized the need for new blood, he told her, and he respected the talent she brought to the company.

In truth, Nigilievsky detested the new CEO. She was young; he was old. She was from the North; he was from the South. She was, dare he say it, a woman. He was a man. And manufacturing was really a man's world. So Nigilievsky made a plan: plant seeds of discontent wherever he could, sit back, and wait for trouble to take Dupres down.

For the next two years, with Nigilievsky quietly working against her behind the scenes, Dupres struggled to move her team and the organization forward. To hear Nigilievsky tell it, she was in over her head. And tell it he did—behind her back to anyone who would listen: his direct reports, other senior team members, even sympathetic board members. For all his public talk about mentoring her, he did everything in his power to exclude her from operational issues under his control.

By the time we studied Dupres and her top team, the situation had become ugly. Nigilievsky's campaign of disinformation had sown doubt among the board and some of the team members. He had effectively sabotaged Dupres, all but destroying her credibility and self-confidence. And he had taken the top team hostage with his political maneuvers.

There was no doubt that Nigilievsky knew the organization and operations intimately. There also was no doubt that he was doing everything he could to destroy Dupres. We recommended that Nigilievsky be removed, not only from the team but also from the organization. He was. But the damage had been done. Dupres, in essence, had to start from scratch, not only to rebuild the team but also to rebuild her reputation as a leader. The last time we spoke, she confided that although she'd been offered the top position with a larger competitor, she'd turned it down and was thinking about changing careers. She was tired, she said, and ready for a change. The struggle of the past few years had taken its toll.

Looking back, no one came out a winner—not Dupres, not Nigilievsky, not the organization. That is the trouble with derailers: they tend to bring everyone down with them. Worse, they tend to be closed to corrective feedback and relatively immune to coaching. When confronted, derailers explain how well they understand themselves and why they do the things they do. But the critical information is in their behavior: they tend not to suppress their destructive actions even after being confronted, and any changes they do make are not sustained over time.

Identifying Derailers

Identifying derailers is sometimes difficult. Although some can be sneaky and manipulative, most derailers have common behavioral patterns that, if you watch for them, are readily recognizable. To tease out the common themes in derailers' behaviors, we turned to our group of expert observers (who had deep knowledge of the teams in our research sample) as well to our competency assessments and interviews of team members. Our group of expert observers nominated fourteen team members who had persistently and continuously prevented the senior teams of which they were members from improving over time. Then we examined the interview content and competency assessments of these individuals to identify their characteristics and the behaviors that they consistently displayed more (or less) frequently than other team members. Here is what we found.

First, derailers are not unskilled technically. Indeed, it is their technical talents that make it difficult to justify removing them from a leadership team. Second, they are not merely argumentative, opinionated, and loud. Such individuals may indeed be irritating. But if they also are loud in praise of other people's ideas, and if their argumentativeness elicits smart thinking from other members, and if they agree as vehemently as they disagree, then they are not derailers.

Derailers almost always lack critical people skills and competencies. They often are low in both empathy (they tend to be blind to the concerns and needs of the rest of the team) and integrity (there often is a great discrepancy between what they say in public and what they do in private). Derailers also tend to have two specific characteristics, relatively rare among senior managers, that cause problems in leadership team dynamics.

1. *A victim mentality.* If you ask a derailer about his career, you get a tale of times when he felt badly treated, his work was unfairly assessed, his contribution was not recognized, he was overlooked for a promotion that rightfully belonged to him. Years later, the bitterness is still fresh, and the individual expresses little or no recognition that he has in any way contributed to these patterns. And he has not taken any useful or constructive learning from those disappointments.

2. *A tendency to make blanket negative assessments of other people.* Derailers' descriptions of others are filled with sweeping judgmental statements: "He's a moron." "She's a rotten manager." A derailer's conversations are full of disparaging adjectives applied to other people, other programs, other ideas. A derailer rarely offers compliments or speaks in praise of others.[9]

Although there is no simple test that will root out every derailer, there are some symptoms to watch. Beware of any team member who does the following:

*   Frequently complains about and criticizes others in public

*   Brings out the worst in other members

*   Attacks people instead of criticizing the issues

- Talks in the hall but not in the room

- Constantly disagrees with everyone and everything

- Displays chronic discrepancies between public words and private actions

- Claims to understand her behavior but seems unable to change

A derailer kills momentum in the team by cutting down ideas before they can have a fair hearing. A derailer's real views of what should be done do not come out in the team meeting but in private conversations and conferences outside the leader's scrutiny. A derailer does not tell what he thinks to a powerful individual's face, but is more than willing to criticize behind one's back. And he can be merciless to those who are less powerful.

Dealing with Derailers

When a derailer is in the room, other team members may engage in their worst rather than their best leadership team behavior. They revert to siloed thinking, keeping critical issues in their domain off the table lest others get to assert their views. They agree publicly with what is being said in the team but then act according to their own judgment. And why shouldn't they? If you have left untrustworthy and destructive people on the team, their best shot at taking care of their own responsibilities and challenges is not to expose them in front of the team.

Confront such dysfunctional behavior early. Confront it as soon as you see it, especially if the team or the member is new, or the member is well respected or an expert in a specific function. Letting it slide teaches the derailer and the other team members that such behavior is tolerable. Do not let such behavior fester until it has significantly damaged the team; it is much easier to prevent damage than to undo it.

The key is to move quickly and address derailing behavior forthrightly. One of the best leaders we have observed do so is Lynn McCaffrey, CEO of a major consumer goods company. In a prior role in an underperforming division of the company, McCaffrey was known for laying it on the line with her teams. Within the first three or four weeks in a role, she would pull her team together and describe its purpose and her goals. Then she addressed each member, explaining the competencies she'd seen that made the person a good contributor and any behaviors that would lead to dismissal from the team.

Finally, she asked team members whether they were committed to her agenda and committed to changing those behaviors that needed changing. If so, she told them, she would work with them and help them change—and that is what she did. But if team members showed no sign of change, even within as short a period as two weeks, they were gone. McCaffrey's approach was both fair and effective. In essence, she put the decision to change in members' hands. The choice was theirs.

A word of warning, however: do not use the "derailer" label as an excuse for getting rid of team members with whom you simply disagree, who take the risk of disagreeing with you, who are argumentative, or who are difficult to manage. Indeed, the choice by U.S. president Abraham Lincoln to include in his closest cabinet of advisers his chief political rivals—men who at times vocally and passionately disagreed with his point of view—is core to what historian Doris Kearns Goodwin describes as his "political genius."[10] According to Goodwin, Lincoln sought the principled disagreements among these highly capable individuals for the perspective, intelligence, and depth they brought to bear on the complex problems of the Civil War, which he faced during his presidency.

A final word about behavioral problems in your leadership team: ineffective behaviors in your team are most often a symptom of poor team design. The primary causes are a lack of clarity or consensus about the team purpose, poor or unclear norms of conduct, and badly designed reward systems that pit members against one another for valued outcomes. Sometimes a member acts up because of the frustration of trying to work in a poorly designed team. So before you assume the worst of the individuals and label them derailers, look first to the team purpose you have articulated and to the structure you have created.

Composing Your Team

Unless you are choosing a new team from scratch, team selection is not a linear process. Most new team leaders inherit an initial team and often get to know the members first. Before leaders make changes to the membership, they invest time in coaching talented members who need to develop their self-image or to display more empathy and other teamwork competencies. The wisest of those leaders also pay close attention to matters of timing: they do not give up easily, but neither do they linger too long before they begin to reshape the team and create clear boundaries.

Getting the composition of the core team right makes it easier and more straightforward to do the ongoing work of composing subteams for particular purposes. For example, Bob Lee of Millennium Chemicals, whose relaunch was described in chapter 3, explained his thinking about the formation of the subteam charged with identifying potential acquisition targets. This subteam was not limited to members of the Operational Team (the smaller, six-person team). The person responsible for business development was asked to lead the subteam. He, in turn, invited the chief financial officer to be on the team. The other four members of the core acquisition team were from the larger Management Committee. This core team collectively oversaw the teams of people involved in the various stages of acquisition: target identification, negotiation, due diligence, and integration. In effect, the core team stayed together as a decision-making body and did the work of forming and coordinating these "sand dune" teams as the effort progressed.

In many situations, a leader is constrained in the choice of team members. For example, in countries such as China, the CEO may not be free to select all the members of the leadership team. Organizations in China are in transition, moving from state-owned and state-run companies to publicly owned entities. During the transition, the Chinese government appoints government officials to be part of leadership teams. This action ensures that the government's interests are represented at the table.

It may not be feasible to expect an enterprisewide perspective from individuals whose sole function in the team is to represent one constituency, although certainly they have no reason to want the enterprise to fail. Their presence, however, often constrains the range of strategic initiatives that the senior team considers, taking off the table any options that are thought to undermine the interests that these members represent. However, even though having obligatory members expands the size of the senior team and broadens the constituencies the team must address, it is unlikely to be disastrous for the team unless the individual is both very powerful and a team derailer.

As with many leadership challenges, there never is an ideal time to make changes on a senior team. There is no off-season hiatus during which the leader can take the time to sit back and, with no distractions, ponder potential moves. Leaders must make these critical decisions on the run, in the heat of the moment. Composing an executive team is an iterative process, one you will no doubt revisit as members depart and as organizational strategies and team purposes evolve.

Ultimately, selecting the best players for your team takes deliberation and courage: a keen understanding of people and the will to act quickly. The leaders that you have heard from in this chapter are right: it is difficult, at times painful, work. But it is necessary if you want to build a successful team.

Here are some points to remember as you go through the process:

- This is your team. It is your call whether someone is on your team. You ignore that responsibility at your own risk and that of your team. Remember: next to defining the team's purpose, this may be the most important action you take as team leader. Consider carefully whether you really want to take on those rare situations, such as the one Dupres faced, where you cannot control the team membership at all.

- Your task is to select a carefully assessed group of highly competent leaders to help you run the organization. Select the best people you can find for the team purpose you have crafted. Function, title, and past experience or expertise are not adequate tickets for admission. Not all of your direct reports may be appropriate as team members, whereas others who do not report to you may make vital contributions. Seek people who can think like general managers and who display empathy and integrity in their interactions.

- Eliminate the derailers. Taking them off the team does not have to eliminate their contribution to the team or to the organization. Find another way for valued individuals to provide what they know to the team—but do not keep derailers in the mix.

- Plan for the future. Organizations change, and people depart. Make sure you are developing potential team members who can, when the call comes, quickly take their places on the team. Look for potential members who exhibit—or who can develop— the self-image and competencies that we have detailed. It is far better to begin the development process now rather than when organization members suddenly find themselves in the cauldron of the day-to-day work of a senior team.

Selecting the best players is only one step in creating a great senior leadership team. Now you must turn those well-selected thoroughbreds into a functioning unit. You have the people and the purpose—and now you are in a position to breathe life into this entity and give it the structure and support it needs to really work. In part II we turn to the enablers of great senior teams and the processes by which you can get them in place for your team.

PART II

THE ENABLERS

*C*hapters 5, 6, and 7 explore the three conditions that facilitate the work of senior leadership teams: a solid structure (chapter 5), a supportive organizational context (chapter 6), and competent team coaching (chapter 7). As you will see, all three enabling conditions can greatly aid the work of senior leadership teams, and serious flaws in any of the three can spawn significant problems that consume both your own and team members' time and energy. The enabling conditions make it possible for a leadership team to take full advantage of the solid foundation that is created by the presence of the three essential conditions discussed in previous chapters.

Although none of the three enabling conditions is inherently more important than the others, there is a preferred order for implementing them. First is creating a solid team structure, because without that the team will not get the full benefit of the organizational and coaching support at its disposal. Second, you need to create a supportive organizational context. Third is providing competent coaching, because our research has shown that coaching is far more helpful to teams that are otherwise well designed and supported than it is for teams whose structure or context is significantly flawed.

5

Give Your Leadership Team the
Structure It Needs to Work

As a kid playing high school football in Texas, Lloyd Hill learned early the importance of good teamwork. "I came to understand the power of teams," he says, "and the fun they are." So when Hill took the reins of Applebee's, a rapidly growing Kansas City–based restaurant chain, he set out to recapture that power and fun "the way we played football in Texas."

At the time Hill became CEO, Applebee's, which had started as a small Midwestern chain of casual dining restaurants, had been growing rapidly and expanding geographically. But Hill, who has since become chairman of the board, knew that if it was to continue such growth, given the intense competition, he and his team would first have to take their leadership to the next level. "Externally, we were moving ahead, making our numbers. But internally, we were struggling," says Hill. He was concerned about the negative impact such internal dynamics might have on the company's franchisees—smart businesspeople who expected strong support from the executive team.

He assembled what he thought would be a world-class executive team. It was composed of talented, experienced, and successful individuals— each a strong player in a particular arena. That individuality, however,

111

was exactly what worked against the team members when they tried to work together. Part of the problem, team members say, was a culture clash. Although Hill wanted to create a collaborative, supportive, people-based culture, there remained an unstructured, entrepreneurial atmosphere from Applebee's start-up period of only a few years earlier. Team members themselves had different ideas of what the right culture should be. For some, especially those who had "grown up" with Applebee's, the ideal culture was one, as one executive put it, "of Midwesterners trying to do the right thing." Others, especially those who had worked for larger, more traditional, long-established companies, were more at home in a culture that fostered a structured, formal, and siloed approach.

The close-knit team that Hill had envisioned, one in which everyone listened and collaborated to achieve common goals, failed to materialize. Turf battles broke out, and factions formed. "We were definitely dysfunctional," recalls the CFO at the time. "We were experiencing the white-hot heat of a team that wasn't working. There wasn't trust. There wasn't the sense that other members were looking out for your best interests. We weren't valuing each other's concerns because we had built up walls and weren't even listening to each other anymore."

Initially, the team avoided facing its problems, although every member knew that the team was not working. Hill continued to hold on to his dream of a people-centered culture. Publicly, team members agreed with the concept, but privately, many were having their doubts. Finally the CFO confronted Hill. "Lloyd," he said, "we're headed for a heap of trouble."

It was then that Hill acknowledged the urgency of the problem and moved to address it. He began by conducting a two-day retreat, asking the team to examine its dynamics, including members' own behaviors as well as other obstacles that were impeding their ability to lead as a team. Together, they began developing team norms and an action plan for improving their effectiveness.

The team identified several key themes that were keeping it from accomplishing much together. These included an inability to develop joint strategies and initiatives that would drive the business forward, as well as troubles in implementing the decisions that the team did make. The lack of focus on team initiatives, in turn, led to confusion, frustration with wasted time, a lack of accountability to one another, and ultimately, a poor result.

After more discussion, members distilled their findings into three key issues:

1. The dysfunctionality of team norms ("bad habits") presented a significant obstacle to improving the operating performance of Applebee's.

2. Differences of opinion in how the team should be organized into roles and accountabilities acted as a disruptive force on the team's work.

3. The performance management system did not drive business performance because of poor alignment between what the team was attempting to measure and Applebee's most critical strategic priorities.

These three issues were hammered out through lengthy, and at times stressful, collective analysis. Yet for all the difficulty, participants now agree that it was time well spent. Applebee's chief people officer described it as a defining moment in the team's development into an effective leadership team. "We knew what was broken," he says. "We were not working as a team. We didn't have ground rules. We weren't treating each other with respect. We didn't have a common score card."

The problems faced by Hill's team are similar to those of many top teams we've worked with: members of the Applebee's top team didn't have a clear sense of what to work on together as part of the leadership team or how to interact effectively when they did. Although team members were excellent individual performers and good leaders in their areas of responsibility, they had no experience collaborating as a leadership team. They were clear about the team's purpose, but they did not have a common understanding of the work they had to do to make it happen. They did not understand the tasks that the team needed to accomplish. What's more, they did not know how to conduct themselves in a way that fostered teamwork. The team's norms, or rules of conduct, were not helping.

These elements—team tasks and norms of conduct, along with team size—make up the fourth important attribute of an effective top team: its structure. According to our research, a solid team structure significantly enhances the ability of members to work together to achieve their purpose. The better the structure, the more effective and productive the team.

Indeed, our research showed that the quality of the team's structure, more than any other of the six conditions, determines which teams are outstanding and which are not. Let's look at the elements of structure in more detail.

- *Team tasks.* Great senior leadership teams performed genuinely meaningful tasks. By *task* we mean a concrete piece of work— such as a decision about moving into a new geography, a succession plan, or an analysis of whether to move the corporate headquarters—that a team performs together. Tasks can be complex, intellectually demanding, and meaningful, such as deciding whether to acquire another company or allocating resources for leadership development in the organization. Or like many agenda items on a leadership team's list, tasks can be simple, undemanding, and trivial, as you'll see. We compared the tasks of outstanding leadership teams to those that were poor or mediocre and found a clear and strong tendency for struggling teams to be cursed with overly simple and trivial team tasks.

- *Team norms.* The presence of clear norms of conduct—shared expectations about member behavior—had the largest impact of any subfeature of the six conditions on whether a leadership team was effective.

- *Team size.* For teams that must make collective decisions (as contrasted, for example, with information-sharing teams), the smaller the better.

Figure 5-1 shows the effects of these three structural features on senior team performance. In the outstanding teams, all three aspects of structure were better. The biggest difference between outstanding and mediocre or poor teams, as we noted earlier, was the presence of clear norms of conduct. On outstanding teams, members know precisely what is and what is not acceptable behavior in the team, and it helps them not only to serve their constituencies well but also to grow increasingly capable as teams and as individual leaders over time.

As we've discussed, creating a clear and challenging purpose requires demanding cognitive work by the chief executive, often performed after consultation with senior team members. And we've explained that getting the team composition right can involve difficult choices and conversa-

FIGURE 5-1

Effective senior leadership teams have sound structures

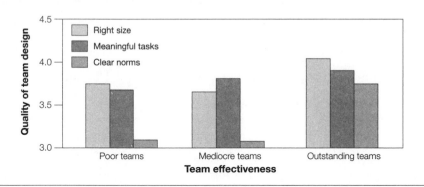

tions. At this point, you have a bounded entity that has some understanding of why these members are on the team and what the team exists to accomplish. Now it's time to get down to work, yes?

Yes—and no. The early life of a leadership team offers a crucial opportunity to get it well structured and on a positive trajectory. In a sense, the team that's now emerging needs you to breathe life into it and give it the core structures it needs to grow in capability.

As at Applebee's, we have seen many leaders reach this point and then neglect key structural elements, falling into the trap of putting up the same old agenda and allowing the same old habits to determine what occurs in the interactions of the team. When that happens, a team becomes lost in day-to-day minutiae of habitual work, and members fail to collaborate well—both inside and outside team meetings.

To be sure, it's easy to overlook the issues we discuss in this chapter. If you are a busy executive with many pressing matters on your mind and your agenda, then creating a solid structure for your team may not feel like an urgent leadership task; the executives are, after all, smart, experienced, grown up, and presumably knowledgeable about what it means to be a member of a leadership team. But they need structure. Well-chosen team members are capable of handling their individual responsibilities, but most have very little experience in working as a member of a truly interdependent leadership team. If you let them focus on trivial tasks in team meetings, you add the frustration of seeing that the real work is happening outside with not all the members present, and what happens inside the team ranges from inefficient to inappropriate. Given such dynamics, it is not surprising that senior teams often end up in the same place that the early Applebee's team found itself: experiencing the "white-hot heat of a team that is not working."

Building a Solid Structure for Good Work

Bring together a small group of people—the smallest you can for the work to be done—give them the tasks they need to do to achieve the team's purpose, and establish the basic norms that govern how they will work together. That is the essence of a solid team structure. As important as it is, once it is in place it becomes all but invisible.

What you observe on a well-structured team is simply good work and great team habits inside and outside team meetings. There are times when they come together to share information, brief their leader, and coordinate with one another. But they also tackle major issues and make important decisions as a team. They act with autonomy and authority, not waiting for instruction: members are expected to take the initiative and use their knowledge and judgment as a team. They participate in discussions outside their area of expertise. They do not defer to the team content expert—for example, the CFO on financial issues. Nor do they become defensive of their own turf.

Well-structured teams are future oriented rather than focused on the past. Certainly they review past actions and performance. But they spend most of their time attending to the issues, strategic or tactical, that are critical to the future of the enterprise. Much of their work takes place outside the venue of formal meetings. Meetings are important. But if you observe an effective team you will see that much of the heavy lifting is done between periodic meetings. Finally, well-structured teams continually assess their own effectiveness. Members seek data, feedback from others, and signs of progress that tell them how well they are doing.

How do you establish these patterns in your team? You must attend to the three core elements of structure:

- *Bring together your small but significant group of individuals.*
  The best senior leadership teams, as we have noted, are small, typically made up of no more than eight members.[1] But each

member brings something unique to the team. The members are carefully selected not because of their title or status but because of the value they add in realizing the team's purpose.

- *Give them well-defined team tasks.* Invite your team to tackle work that is core to the purpose. Members need a short list of well-defined tasks that are mission critical and engage them in generating meaningful assessments of the quality of their work on those tasks.

- *Get constructive norms in place from the beginning.* Establish for your team a clearly defined set of norms of conduct that are critical for working together. Ask members to hold one another accountable for maintaining these rules, and model and enforce them yourself. Understand that those who cannot abide by them you will ultimately have to remove from the team.

Beyond Boundaries:
The Importance of Being Small

As we've discussed, having clear boundaries—knowing who is on the team and who isn't—is a necessary condition for a real senior team, and the most clearly bounded teams tend also to be small ones. But team size affects more than boundaries. The bigger the team, the harder it is to establish and enforce the rules of engagement. The bigger the team, the harder it is to create genuine team tasks. The bigger the team, the harder it is to accommodate all the voices for the robust discussions that great senior leadership teams must engage in and the subsequent tough decisions they must make. Indeed, the large, underbounded teams we have studied do little beyond sharing information.

Figure 5-2 illustrates how process problems grow as you appoint each additional member to a leadership team. The larger the team, the greater the number of links and relationships that must be managed. The greater the number of links, the greater the number of relationship issues and coordination problems you will likely experience. Trouble in teams is not a linear function.[2]

Large teams, if given a clear direction and shared norms, can serve important alignment purposes for the organization. At IBM, then-CEO

FIGURE 5-2

Group size and the number of links among members

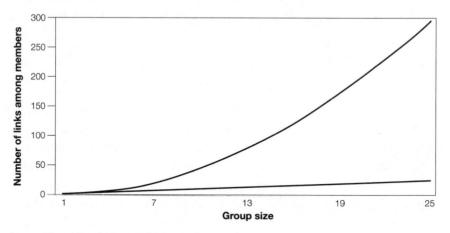

Source: Adapted from Hackman (2002). Used with permission.

Gerstner created a group of three hundred leaders, charging them with being change agents for the transition to the new strategy. Members of this Senior Leadership Group (SLG) were nominated by other leaders in the organization as exemplars of leadership consistent with the change, and Gerstner himself and his executive team appointed select nominees to the SLG.[3] Membership changed each year based on contribution to the change effort. Members met face-to-face annually to create connection and alignment within the group and to focus organizational attention on leadership and change.

This widely dispersed group of leaders had clear norms about how they operated, including showing active support for the change effort, responding to one another's calls within twenty-four hours, and speaking well of one another outside their face-to-face interactions. But the team was too large and fluid to make decisions on behalf of the organization; it was designed and led as an alignment team only.

For decision-making teams, by contrast, smaller teams are essential. Although many executives complain about the size of their leadership teams—"We're too big to accomplish anything significant together!" said one member of a team we studied—it is rare for anyone to want to be taken off the team, no matter how dysfunctional it is. So the question for CEOs is this: "How do I reduce the size of my senior leadership team without alienating and losing the very people I need to run the company?" It is doable, as you have seen, but it takes considerable leadership skill to make it happen without distress and alienation among former team members. We outline here some steps you can take when addressing the issue of team size.

First, take the work you do in clarifying the team's purpose as an opportunity to relaunch your leadership team. Many CEOs that we have studied appreciate this concept because it allows them to remove some people from an overlarge team. Doing so can signal that the change occurred not because the person wasn't a valuable leader but rather because the purpose of the team had changed. A relaunch—bringing together a new core team, articulating a new purpose, reestablishing norms—allows a graceful exit for those no longer on the team.

It also can be helpful to launch other leadership teams having different purposes. For example, many CEOs also form a team of key line and functional leaders to align resources, and yet another team composed of those who coordinate the execution of major initiatives such as product launches and brand repositioning. Typically, members who are not included in the smaller core decision-making team find a seat at the alignment or operational table. These latter types of teams generally meet face-to-face less frequently than the core group. Although members of the core decision-making team usually serve on the alignment or operational team, the purposes of these types of teams are distinct, and they are positioned as interlocking horizontal teams rather than hierarchically, with everything that kind of structure implies.

Many CEOs who have successfully implemented the steps sketched here have been able to retain all their key senior leaders. In other cases, there have been departures. When you reform the set of leadership teams, not everyone is protected from potential loss of face. For example, Walter May, a new CEO who implemented this multiple-team plan, lost a highly talented senior vice president, much to his dismay. Upon reflection, however, May wondered whether this SVP would have gone anyway, for reasons having less to do with his status on the top team than with general dissatisfaction with his work. If it hadn't happened now, May reflected, it would have happened in the near future. May ultimately concluded that changing the core team was the event that triggered the SVP's swift departure—but he had no regrets about relaunching his team.

Snowblowers Versus Sales Strategy: Why Old Team Habits Die Hard

Size is not the only aspect of poor team structure that can create trouble. Just ask Pascal Mittermaier (introduced in chapter 4), head of Roche Diagnostics in Canada. He can attest to the importance of well-designed team tasks and clear norms of conduct.

When the young executive took over the business, he found the leadership team he inherited primarily focused on the minutiae of operating a small company. The problem was that the Canadian subsidiary no longer was small, having grown in a few years from $50 million to $250 million in sales. The early team interactions, Mittermaier recalls, were tactical and siloed. This pattern of behavior and attitudes often appears when the team has never been charged with significant tasks as a team; the accountabilities with real punch remain at the individual level.

The few tasks that Mittermaier's senior leaders performed as a team had little meaning. There were few discussions of critical issues such as shifting the company's sales strategy to better meet customer demands and competitor challenges. Instead, the talk focused on minor issues such as where the team members would stand at the kickoff reception at the national sales meeting or what kind of snowblowers it should purchase. "The facilities guy came in and said, 'Alright, we've got four snowblowers that need replacing. And here are the five options.' And all of a sudden we all became experts on snowblowers. 'No, don't get that kind, it blows the snow the wrong way!'"

It was the issue of office security that finally made Mittermaier realize the triviality of what the team was tackling. "After the theft of some computers, we decided to improve security. And for two or three meetings we discussed such issues as the size of the security badge, whether it should be swiped or held, which way the doors should open. Finally I said, 'Look, you need to come here and present us a couple of options. If you recommend we go for the one that costs $50,000 more, and we approve it, then five minutes later go implement it!'"

Looking back, Mittermaier now understands that the snowblower and security card incidents were merely symptoms of a larger problem: a lack of understanding of what the team's tasks really should be, and, in its place, a natural tendency to cling to old, outmoded habits. Like so many teams, members continued to go through the "historical motions" of how they thought they should work together—motions that over time, tradition, and repetition had become seemingly essential parts of the team's identity.

Mittermaier's team spent far too much time and energy on narrow, tactical issues that would better have been handled at a lower level of the organization or by one of the team members individually. Team members also returned repeatedly to familiar but often tired approaches to addressing issues, and that inhibited any conceptual or creative thinking that otherwise might have arisen from their interactions.

Creating a High-Quality Team Structure

You often can begin changing the pattern, as Mittermaier did, by refocusing the team on work that is aligned with its purpose and then continuing to keep the team on those tasks. You can best refocus the team's work in the context of the face-to-face team meeting, because in that setting all members can be involved in the discussion. However, the best top teams aren't exclusively meeting oriented. Expect that your team, at its best, will work informally, individual-to-individual or in subgroups outside a formal team setting.

Team meetings themselves require careful planning, because they can easily slip onto a spectrum of inappropriate tasks, as discussed in "Executive Teams Doing the Wrong Work." At one extreme are those that generate the white-hot heat of discord, described earlier: meetings filled with passive-aggressive antics and territorial battles, where the weapon of choice is the executive power play.

At the other extreme are never-ending loops of mind-numbing, must-attend meetings, at which members are beaten into boredom with an equally effective force: the dreaded slide presentation. (As a frustrated member of one team said after traveling thousands of miles for what was little more than a PowerPoint version of a corporate film festival, "I came halfway around the world for that?!")

Executive Teams Doing the Wrong Work

Although the structure and content of meetings are important elements of almost every senior team, they often are overlooked in the quest to improve the team's performance. Run well, meetings can be powerful and energizing; poorly managed, they can be demoralizing and demotivating. Here are some common types of dysfunctional senior team meetings to avoid.

The Show and Tell: In this forum, some or all of the team members are asked to present briefings on their areas of responsibility. During these briefings—usually accompanied by colorful handouts and thick slide decks—the other team members and even the CEO (a) silently work on their own presentations or responses, (b) focus on some of their real work that must be handled following the meeting, or (c) make an honest attempt to multitask, listening to the speaker while answering e-mails or composing memos.

The Retrospective: The focus here is on the past—the past week, the past month, the past quarter. The upside: the focus is on performance and not only information download. The downside: it is much too reactive. Instead of proactively strategizing about the future, the team engages in soul-searching, finger-pointing, and second-guessing about the past, followed by reactive decision making about the short-term future.

Although these descriptions may seem extreme, they are not rare. Even otherwise solidly performing senior teams often select tasks and engage in behaviors that distract them from constructive work and subtly take the edge off the team's performance. Items wind up on the team's agenda through thoughtless or habitual processes, such as having the CEO's executive assistant ask everyone what they'd like to discuss and then including every item in the list. Such practices are the single greatest threat to getting a good task structure in place.

Roche's Mittermaier and Applebee's Hill both worked with their teams to define an appropriate set of tasks, along with a set of norms to keep them constructively focused. In both cases, it took open, frank—and at times stressful—discussion as well as considerable coaching to get

The Monologue: In these sessions, also known as The Harangue, the leader speaks and the members listen. There is little room for discussion or input. Decisions, most of which already have been made, are the sole responsibility of the leader. Monologue meetings can be appropriately informational, or inappropriately directive, and even coercive. It is a forum in which marching orders are given or received.

The Dialogue: Somewhat more democratic than The Monologue, The Dialogue often accomplishes even less. Such sessions usually reflect the best of intentions: agendas are created, priorities are set, and issues are discussed. But then the problems start. Members engage as representatives of their areas of responsibility and not as representatives of the enterprise. When not speaking, they are preparing what they want to say next rather than truly listening. Most frustrating of all, despite lengthy discussion, there is no consensus and no group decision making.

The Anarchist's Ball: What's worse than misguided team norms and tasks? Having none at all. Welcome to The Anarchist's Ball. At their best these meetings turn into executive blabfests, where everyone competes for a speaking part, no one listens, and little of importance happens. At their worst they can become nasty skirmishes, executive free-for-alls in which members covertly or overtly attack one another and sometimes even go after the leader.

it done. It also took a lot of practice for the new tasks and behaviors to become second nature.

Both leaders began by pulling the team together, identifying positive behaviors and confronting behavior that got in the way of the team's work, and then clearly defining critical team tasks and the most-needed behavioral norms. That initial forum, says Hill, "was the starting point for major change—the confluence of people, organization, and strategy. We had to reteam this thing. We all had to know how to work together." Mittermaier acknowledges that his teamwork restructuring effort was arduous. But it also was a defining moment for the team. "We're talking years of hard work," he says. "But for the first time, we really thought about what it means to be leaders."

Defining and Staying On Task

Mittermaier makes an excellent point. A senior team's tasks should be far more than a list of duties that can quickly be addressed and then checked off. Instead, the tasks should be defined in the context of the team's purpose and in the context of what it means to be an enterprise leader.

At the same time, however, the team's duties need to be tethered to the day-to-day operational realities if that is what the team needs to be doing. The work of a truly effective executive team should be focused on key strategic and tactical issues that affect the enterprise. Certainly the team must occasionally dip into the mundane. But for the most part it should focus on broader, more significant organizational issues that directly advance the team's purpose. Figure 5-3 shows various kinds of tasks that a leader can pitch to different types of teams—information-

FIGURE 5-3

Examples of senior leadership team tasks

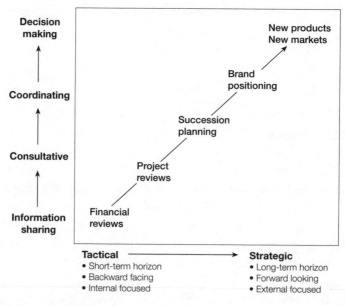

Source: Hay Group. Used with permission.

sharing, consultative, coordinating, and decision-making teams—with tasks arrayed from the tactical to the strategic.

Here are some actions chief executives can take to make sure that the senior team stays focused on the most essential tasks.

Create and Follow an Agenda

No matter how brilliant and knowledgeable the team members, no manner how well mannered they may be, every team meeting needs an agenda. Good team agendas are more than administrative checklists. They are important tools for keeping the team on task. Therefore, they are the responsibility of the team and its leader, and not the leader's executive assistant. Craft a focused agenda with your team. Do not, as many CEOs do, rely on phone calls to the team members from your assistant asking, "What do you want to talk about?" Make the list yourself, or have a trusted adviser on the team do it, and circulate it in advance for revision. Whatever method you choose, take it seriously as a statement of your team's tasks.

Here are some guidelines:

- Make sure every item is meaningful—has real impact on the organization—and is connected to team purposes. On the Roche Canada team, for example, no item goes on the agenda that doesn't meet three criteria: it's strategic, it's mission critical, and only the top team can do it.

- Keep the agenda short. Because all the items will be meaningful and important, you need enough time to discuss each one thoroughly, and that cannot be done if there are a dozen items to be processed in a single meeting. Bevilacqua's team, for example, often limits its agenda to three or four items, all focused on its must-win battles.

- Define the outcomes you want from your team for each item. Do you want everyone at the table to be better informed? Do you want the members to discuss an important issue for future reflection? Do you want them to make a team decision? Know when you begin a top team meeting what you want to have accomplished when it ends.

- Define the measures that will tell you and the members whether the team was successful. How will you assess the consequences of your decisions? How will you know whether the team is making significant progress on its shared tasks? What information should the team be sure to get about the consequences of its work, and from whom?

Start with the Most Important Issues

Often, in hopes of clearing the decks for more important, strategic matters, executive team meetings begin with tactical issues such as reviews and updates. Unfortunately, that practice runs a big risk of diverting the team from its real work. Someone throws down a challenge or asks a question about a small item. Someone else responds, defends, or argues, and then everyone weighs in. And forty minutes into the day-long meeting the agenda is already forgotten, along with the important issues that should have been discussed.

Teams, like individuals, have difficulty moving from tactical work to the greater conceptual effort involved in strategic tasks. By contrast, the transition from the strategic to the tactical is much easier. Therefore, start by directing your team's attention and energy to the most significant issues on the agenda. Give the team time for the robust discussion these issues deserve, and tell them that you are doing so because that is what you want of your leadership team. If you need the team also to tackle a few routine or tactical matters, do it at the end of the meeting. If you have managed the agenda well, there should be no mention of snowblowers, security cards, or whether to serve chicken or beef at the next gala dinner.

Face the Future

Based on their tradition of meeting to share information, many executive leadership teams continue to spend much of their time living in the past—examining, analyzing, and second-guessing recent decisions and results. They work much like the top team of a major pizza chain that we studied, which spent the better part of every Monday morning reviewing the sales numbers for the past week. Each member brought a large notebook filled with details and numbers, and the discussion frequently centered on what kind of pizza did best in which market and why. Unfortunately, that left little time to focus on the weeks or months ahead and what could be done to improve performance. As Dave Levy, one frustrated team member, noted, "We had the whole company looking backwards instead of figuring out what we needed to do tomorrow. We didn't talk about any initiatives coming up. Week to week was important because we had to drive sales, but we also had to think about the future—what our business was all about—and provide a strategic framework for moving forward."

Levy makes an excellent point. Start by focusing on upcoming issues. Relegate reviews of past performance to the end of the meeting unless their discussion is critical to future actions. If reviews are purely informational, put the relevant data in an easily readable summary.

Prepare and Participate

Alert your team members to the fact that they must be prepared for the team meeting and are expected not only to attend but also to participate in collective discussions. Briefing papers should be distributed well before the meeting, and members should know that they are expected to read them beforehand. Reading while sitting around a table is not a meaningful team task. Neither is getting everyone up to speed with slide presentations of "what's happening in my area." That is individual work, better done in advance. Make sure your team members understand that you expect them to actively listen to their peers and to be prepared to discuss issues beyond their individual areas.

Over time, expect that many of the initial discussions of important issues will take place among team members outside the formal team meetings. At Roche and other organizations we studied, the most effective team members have learned the art of pre-work. They know how to prepare and align their fellow members so that they create necessary agreement before the meeting. We are not describing secret deals in smoke-filled rooms or sneaking behind other members' backs, but straightforward discussions and negotiations that effectively move the team forward so that meeting time is well spent.

Challenge Questionable Tasks

No matter how good your intentions, trivia and inappropriate tasks sometimes sneak into the senior team's interactions. After the infamous snowblower incident, members of Mittermaier's team became aware of their core team tasks. Late in the day, at the end of a long meeting, the CFO raised the issue of archiving records, asking the team for agreement on a proposal to purchase a couple of thousand storage boxes. "It was the snow-blower incident all over again," Mittermaier recalls. But this time, the response was different: "The team just looked at him and said 'No, you make the call. That's not for us to talk about.'" Although the CFO was clearly disappointed, Mittermaier was delighted. From that point forward, the team was much more discerning about which issues it chose to address.

Delegate

Much of what many top teams deal with could and should be delegated, either to individual members or to others outside the team. That is the approach the Roche team took to free itself from unnecessary tasks that were weighing down its agenda. "We realized that we needed a deeper level of empowerment—a stronger second wave of decision makers," Mittermaier recalls. "So we created a new director level between our managers and the leadership team, and, as a group, we defined what they should be doing, and that helped define what our team should not be doing." It is well worth your time to ask your team to identify the issues that might reasonably be delegated to other leaders and teams.

Keep the Large Tasks Large

One of the most common reasons leadership teams wind up focusing on small issues is that leaders and members alike tend to disaggregate the big tasks.[4] Rather than take on the largest tasks as a group, some chief executives and their team members break those tasks into small pieces and dole them out to team members. The understanding is that the individual pieces subsequently will be sewn back together. It can feel as if disaggregation will make the work more manageable. But it sidesteps what should be the real work of the team: making the big decisions interdependently. Avoid this kind of piecework. Keep the core team small and the large tasks large.

Norms: Establishing the Rules of Engagement

As Pascal Mittermaier discovered when his CFO rose to discuss the two thousand storage boxes, no matter how well you have defined its tasks, the team also needs a set of operating norms that specify what team members must always do and what they should never do in their interactions. As small an issue as it may have appeared, only after team members called their fellow executive on his inappropriate behavior did the team confidently tackle only those matters that truly belonged to the senior team.

Developing a set of shared expectations about behavior makes it possible for a leadership team to tackle large tasks effectively. All the outstanding teams we studied have a set of norms tailored to their unique challenges. Like the list of team tasks, team norms should be clear, few in number, and specific. Although a handful of norms are valuable "must-dos" for any senior team (see figure 5-4), an effective team creates norms that address issues that are specific to it and its circumstances.

Team norms will form whether or not you take steps to put them in place. The norms that arise naturally, however, often are not helpful to leadership team effectiveness. As often happens in the absence of explicit team agreements, each member assumes his own code of conduct. This implicit process often starts a descent into lowest-common-denominator behavior, a downward spiral of decreasing effectiveness. For example, if one member misses a meeting and is not confronted, then the norm becomes, "Missing one meeting is OK." It applies until a member inevitably decides to test those boundaries and misses two—and also is not confronted. Now the norm is, "Missing two meetings is OK." And so it goes, with members testing the boundaries to see how far they can go without spending political capital, and often that is very far indeed.

This process is understandable. When a member chooses to miss a leadership team meeting and spend that time on other work, for example,

FIGURE 5-4

Four universally useful senior leadership team norms

- **Commitment:** Treat the role of team member as seriously as your individual leadership role.
- **Transparency:** If it affects more than one of us, put it on the team table.
- **Participation:** Each member's voice is welcomed on issues affecting the enterprise.
- **Integrity:** What you say and do when you are with the team is what you say and do when you're outside the team.

he is expressing what he believes are the right priorities. When the leader fails to correct that belief, she affirms those priorities—and confirms to the members that the work of the team is less significant than individual responsibilities. If the team is already plagued with a trivia-filled agenda, their choices make perfect sense for executives who want to do what seems right for the organization.

Yet for all the difficulty and fragmentation caused by bad norms, leaders are often hesitant to create formal expectations for members' behavior. These are, after all, experienced leaders. They should not have to be told how to behave, and they likely do not want to be told. And sitting them down and hashing out a set of dos and don'ts can be a disquieting experience. But just as a leader who will not address the team structure is the main reason that the team winds up with unhealthy norms, a leader who helps the group take them on is the essential solution.

We have seen many leadership team members—and leaders—behave in ways that quickly kill effective collaboration: individuals who do not respond to e-mails from other team members or who spend much time in every meeting noisily going through a large stack of mail. In one egregious case, a CEO called a special meeting to hear reports from twelve committees on a critical new branding initiative—and then failed to turn up for his own meeting, leaving a roomful of executives angry and frustrated, especially as this was not the first time such an event had taken place.

Most of the bad behavior we have seen is less outrageous than that, but still it can be debilitating to the team: members who talk over each other, those who detach from the conversation and check their e-mail when the subject is not of personal interest, and those who criticize other members and team decisions after they have left the table. Unchallenged, these inappropriate behaviors eventually derail the team and its efforts. Effective norms must rule out the kinds of actions that prevent a team from conducting a vigorous discussion of the issues. To be effective, norms must be more than eloquently stated team values. They must be specific behavioral rules to which the team agrees. Ultimately, it may even become necessary to enforce the norms by removing a member who persistently violates them.

That was the nature of the norms developed by the Applebee's team. Hill describes the offsite meeting at which he began establishing team norms as "the two most painful days of my life." After lengthy, at times awkward,

Applebee's Team Norms

Build trust. Honesty and integrity, being loyal to and defending others—even when they aren't present—honoring commitments, no matter how small, keeping no secrets, respecting others, welcoming others' interest and questions about your area (no protecting of one's turf), collaborating, giving feedback, and developing others.

Be decisive. Taking measured risks, being innovative, admitting mistakes (recovering quickly and sharing your learnings), being courageous, and taking a stand on issues.

Be accountable. See it. Own it. Fix it.

Hold great meetings. Meetings should be well planned (with an agenda), start and end on time, and involve all attendees. Only one person should speak at a time. No sidebar conversations. Next steps and accountabilities should be summarized at the meeting's close.

Deliver results. Members should deliver on commitments by demonstrating "iron will determination to make it happen."

Demonstrate balance. Members should demonstrate and support work/life balance.

Have fun. Life is short.

discussions, team members finally achieved a rare consensus: they acknowledged they had no ground rules. One by one, they came to the realization that the team would be successful only if every member committed to changing his or her own behavior. "It hit us like a ton of bricks," says one of the team members. "We looked each other in the eye and said, 'You know, we are the problem. It starts here.'"

With that starting point, members proceeded with the sometimes painful process of hammering out a set of norms, as shown in "Applebee's Team Norms." They address the inappropriate antics that had often derailed the team in the past—basic things like showing up on time for meetings and not interrupting other members.

The Unilever Foodsolutions team came up with a similar set of norms (see "Foodsolutions' Executive Norms") that members believed were critical for its success. As for Applebee's, it was an intense, at times painful, discussion. But looking back, members viewed the outcome as an important turning point for the team.

To an outsider, such lists look simplistic. Indeed, the content, void of context, may seem like pabulum. For the team, however, the discussion that leads to the list has great power. For an outsider, the soft-sounding norm "treating everyone equally" may pack little punch. But knowing that the norm was the result of the members bravely confronting the CEO about his tolerance of the CFO's frequent absences from team meetings gave it deeper meaning to the team. Its presence on their list of norms gave permission to the whole team to call others—including the leader—on their behavior when it went against what they aspired to and had agreed to live by.

Creating, Modeling, and Enforcing Norms: The Role of the Leader

The chief executive is key in establishing team norms of conduct: whatever behavior the leader tolerates becomes part of the rules. As with the core purpose and membership of your team, you ultimately are responsible for establishing the norms and for making sure that members follow them.

Establishing the rules is an iterative process. Often, a team needs to begin with basic behavioral guidelines, such as, "Don't interrupt; everybody participates in the discussion; put your cell phones away." These initial norms can guide team behavior even in the early stages, as your team membership and purposes are evolving. But once a chief executive has settled on who stays in the team and who goes, it is time to engage members in conversations about what is expected of them, both inside and outside meetings.

One simple but important norm, for example, is that team members consult with one another on shared accountabilities—not only in front of you but also in the course of their daily work. If a division is hiring a person to fill an important position in the succession pipeline, the division leader should ask for input from the leader of human resources at the start of the process, and not at the end. Additionally, subteams should

Foodsolutions' Executive Norms

Clarity of roles and responsibilities. We believe in clarity of roles and responsibilities.

Transparency. We believe in sharing our ideas and knowledge. Hidden agendas are not tolerated.

Active listening. In our meetings each member will genuinely listen, acknowledge the contributions of others and play a positive role in developing team decisions.

Common language. We will adopt "common language" for presentations, explanations, and measurements.

Participation. To be present in our meeting and be well prepared is a priority for all of us.

The leader leads. The leader will decide when a decision will be made by 100 percent agreement, by majority, or by his decision.

A decision is a decision. Once a decision has been taken, each member will support it as the team's decision. We will not continually reopen decisions made. Passive disagreement is not an option.

Ambassadors. One voice will come out of our meetings. Each of us will speak for the whole team.

We are customers. We will care for each other the same way we care for our customers. An "empty chair" will always be left in our meeting as a metaphor for the symbolic customer in the room.

Reaching in and out. We will ask for and offer each other help.

---

work on critical assignments together. If you run a global organization, expect team members to use video and telephone conferencing or whatever it takes for them to collaborate.

Another example: some teams benefit from an explicit norm of defining key terms. The leader of one senior team we observed asserted that the organization needed to go into "cost containment mode" for the last two quarters of the fiscal year so that it could meet its financial objectives. Team members nodded, and the discussion moved on. One of us was present and said to the group, "I heard the words *cost containment,* but I don't know what you mean by that." The leader scowled at the inter-ruption. But one member responded, "It means we stop all hiring." Another said, "No, it doesn't mean that at all. It means we fill those positions that we started the process for, but nothing beyond that." A third person said that hiring was not the issue but that unapproved travel was. It was a sharp lesson for this team as the members contemplated what would have hap-pened had they continued their discussion without defining the term.

Good norms always are the result of careful assessments of what is getting in the way and what helps the team, and are established and refined through conscious decisions and hard collaborative work. It is essential that you model any norm that you advocate. Unfortunately, leaders often underestimate the impact they have when they break the team norms. The leader of one large organization we studied, for example, was the first to proclaim that the team meetings should be a venue for transparency and honesty. But members noted privately that he also was the first to be offended should the discussion be in any way critical of his actions.

Good team leaders not only model appropriate behavior but also ac-tively foster it. Unilever's Bevilacqua, for example, reviewed the team's agreed-to rules of engagement at the beginning of team meetings and was not shy about reprimanding members who violated the norms. Although members' input is critical in defining team norms, it is you who must ini-tially coach and correct members when they get off track. That is likely to feel awkward, but ultimately your public affirmation of your expectations will make the norms a self-sustaining part of the team structure. And the best team leaders also use the enforcement of team norms as an opportu-nity for team learning.

Consider Gina Palermo, who led one of a global technology com-pany's biggest businesses. Palermo's team had struggled for a long time with the aspiration of putting the team ahead of the concerns of the indi-vidual members. Repeatedly she told them, "Guys, we've been siloed too long. Now you are a member of this team. You have to put our collective performance ahead of your own business units." For a while, the team seemed to be embracing the notion. Then one day it all seemed to un-ravel. Shortly after team members had agreed to reduce the pool for merit increases by a small percentage in order to cut a critical $30 million from the budget, Palermo discovered that someone had reneged, leaving a $10 million shortfall.

Although furious, Palermo waited until the end of the next meeting to address the issue. Then, in a calm but serious tone she asked the members to tell her what had happened. "The last time we met, I said we had to put the group ahead of our individual interests. We all agreed to do this, but in the end, we were $10 million short. Can somebody explain to me what happened?"

One by one, members admitted they had gone back on the agreement in order to protect their own people. Rather than further castigate the culprits, Palermo, palpably angry, nevertheless calmly reinforced the importance of putting the team first. She told the members that although she understood their individual concerns, they had to "raise such issues with the group rather than go behind the backs" of the other members. Then she held them to account for how they were going to make up the deficit they had created.

Palermo's example underlines a crucial point about team norms: they get established in a meeting, but their purpose is to guide the behavior of team members in all their work as a team, including and especially the work they do outside meetings, in the absence of other members. The norms you establish for your team reinforce the interdependent team tasks you have assigned them. Strong team norms pay off especially after a decision is made in a meeting and then must be implemented. When your team members have come to agreement—however contentious the discussion was behind closed doors—you have the right to expect that outside that room the team will present the decision as a team decision, from a united front. Remind them that dissenters must not go back to their own organizations and blame others for the decisions they helped make.

Only if you call out an offender will the norm in question be seen as a real norm by the other team members. Consider the example of Lev Landan, divisional president of a large corporation. Landan had established with his team a norm of integrity: what you say and do when you are with the team is what you say and do when you are not. Landan brought his team together to identify divisionwide accountabilities for which the team would be responsible, one of which was managing the succession pipeline.

At the meeting, members agreed that division HR would have a hand in the assessment and hiring of anyone hired to fill leadership jobs identified in the succession plan. But it turned out that one team member, regional business head Avi Mier, subsequently complied only with the letter, and not the spirit, of the agreement. When Mier had a position to fill in his business, he habitually called divisional human resources only a couple of days before a candidate was scheduled for a final interview. Mier's business was headquartered a plane ride away, and at least twice human resources manager Jaan Page could not get there in time to play a role in the hiring. When Page confronted Mier after the first incident, he apologized and said it wouldn't happen again. When it happened a second time Page brought it to Landan. After talking to both team members, Landan made it clear that this game playing was unacceptable and he would not tolerate it. He expected both of them to work it out. It did not happen again.

Over the long term, members of the best senior leadership teams increasingly take responsibility for the refinement and enforcement of team norms, gradually reducing your responsibility for keeping team behavior on track. Jen Warren, a division president we studied, made that sort of transfer of enforcement by initially playing the heavy. Tired of hearing team members blame missed deadlines on the fact that corporate had not sent them requested data, she finally unloaded: "From now on, it is no longer acceptable to blame it on corporate when you blow a deadline. You are senior managers. I expect you to work it out and get the work done on time." For this team, in its circumstances, that unique norm was essential to its effective functioning. Several months after that incident, Warren happened to overhear her newest team member on his way to his first team meeting asking a veteran for tips. The telling response: "Whatever you do, if your work is not completed on time, don't blame it on corporate!"

Refining Structure

The core elements of a solid team structure—keep it small, give the team meaningful team tasks, establish the norms of conduct—are the acts that breathe life into a team and make it work. We summarize here the core steps in establishing a good structure for your team.

1. *Look for signs that the team is too large.* Troubles in teams escalate fast as team size increases. Consider using a team

relaunch to make the team as small as it can be to accomplish the work you want it to perform.

2. *Get meaningful tasks on the agenda, and tactical trivia off.* The work that senior leadership teams do together should be more important to the enterprise than that of any individual team member. Choosing those tasks takes care and deliberation, and you cannot do it by calling around to see what members would like to put on the agenda. Make sure you give the team only tasks that require collaboration and that bear directly on the effective leadership of the enterprise.

3. *Establish and enforce healthy norms, and engage your team in refining them.* Agree on some basic norms for constructive meeting behavior, enforce them when you see members violate them, and model them yourself. Once your team is well established, engage the team in identifying those critical few rules that experience suggests are the most critical "must always do" and "must never do" guidelines.

4. *Revisit your team's structure with your team.* Crafting a solid team structure is never completely finished. We have discussed here the various aspects of team structure—deciding who's on the team, identifying the tasks you will ask the members to do, establishing the rules of engagement—as if they were steps in a linear process. That was necessary because the pages of a book come one after another, in linear fashion. But creating and refining a team structure is an iterative process. Each aspect of the team structure that you put in place will have to be revisited in response to other structural changes you make. The best senior leadership teams frequently refine their norms and reassess their shared tasks as their environments change and as the teams themselves mature.

We turn next to actions you can take to strengthen the organizational context of your leadership team: getting in place support and resources that smooth and facilitate teamwork. But for now, let's return to the place where we began this chapter. Do you recall that Applebee's team? The one that, early in its life, was not really a team? Once team norms had been established, it became clear to Hill that some members were not going to behave in accord with them. He eventually concluded that they were not suited for their roles on the team.

Ultimately Hill reorganized and relaunched his senior leadership team, reducing its size from five to four and replacing one of the members. Even now, long after it happened, Hill feels uncomfortable discussing it. Yet he takes full responsibility for the decisions. Looking back, he says he knew long before the intervention that the team was not working but avoided making the tough decisions needed to fix it. "My gut told me I had the wrong people on the wrong team," he says. "I struggled. In my view, I failed. This was my team and my issue."

Determined not to repeat his mistakes, Hill took a more assertive and studied approach as he brought on new team members. Not only did he demand the right technical skills and experience, but also he judged whether the candidates' competencies, behaviors, and values meshed with the culture of the team and the organization. Prospective members learned the norms of the team before coming on board.

Things changed dramatically. Since those early days, the team's performance, and that of the company, improved substantially. Perhaps equally important, the team began having the fun that Hill feels is critical. As one member put it, "We are a lot more fun and loose than we've ever been. We genuinely like each other. The level of trust is off the charts, and now the group feels like it's a *team* running the business."

6

Give Your Leadership Team the Support It Needs to Succeed

When Lou Gerstner took the reins of IBM in 1993, he quickly determined that if Big Blue was to regain its market dominance, it had to transform itself from a behemoth of towering functional silos into a flatter, matrix-driven company. That, he realized, would require reshaping the top leadership—his senior team as well as the teams that oversaw the various business units.

The structure he inherited was plagued by organizational barriers that slowed decision making. It also created artificial division and duplication that pitted individuals and business units against one another. To eliminate such hurdles, Gerstner knew that the behavior of IBM's executives and its senior teams would have to change. Rather than perpetuate the culture of personal heroics—in which executives focused on their own department or division, often to the detriment of other parts of the organization—the company needed executives who would orchestrate and enable rather than command and control.[1] So Gerstner set out to create a culture in which senior leaders worked through others, created strong teams, provided coaching, and strove to increase the capability not only of their own areas, but also of the larger organization.

The success of this huge, multiyear undertaking has been well documented not only in Gerstner's book and numerous articles but also in the company's performance: within a few years IBM's share price had soared, and it once again held a position of power and prominence in a highly competitive industry.

Many factors contributed to IBM's success. Among them was Gerstner's attention to providing a supportive context for leadership teams. As he created new teams to lead the company and its variety of divisions and business units, he carefully assessed his executive talent to find those leaders who best demonstrated the competencies needed for the new culture. Executives he found lacking were offered developmental opportunities and coaching. Measures were developed to chart progress, and leaders were rewarded, in part, based on their growth and development into the kinds of leaders he needed on his teams.

In short, IBM under Gerstner's leadership provided an important but frequently overlooked element of effective senior leadership teams—support systems.

Providing Senior Team Resources:
Why Even the Great Need Support

It seems that if there is any group in an organization that can get the support it needs, it is the senior leadership team. Such teams, after all, control the organization's resources and have all the authority they want over funding. Unlike a front-line team, a senior leadership team can simply demand anything it needs. Yet we found that senior teams lack basic support for effective teamwork. Most of the top teams we studied were much better at providing support resources for front-line teams than for themselves.

When it comes to having the necessary resources, senior leadership teams are often the cobbler's kids, lacking a decent pair of shoes. The reasons are twofold. First, senior leadership teams fail to recognize that they actually need such support, and second, as stewards of the company's resources, they often believe that they should not spend money on themselves. Parsimony becomes a frame of mind, and even though senior leaders typically are paid handsomely, they also feel a need to manage the perception that they are frugal with the organization's resources.

And of course they should be. When we talk about necessary resources, we are not talking about junkets to exclusive resorts or exotic locales. Nor are we referring to the excessive accoutrements that have become the legacy of many fallen executives. What we mean are those resources that smooth and facilitate the work of senior leadership teams. Our research has identified four types of support that are most critical:

- *Rewards.* The best senior leadership teams implement reward strategies that recognize and reinforce team members for delivering on the team's accountabilities.

- *Information.* Outstanding teams take action to acquire the data they need, in the form they need it for their special purposes—including measures that allow members to assess their performance as a team.

- *Education.* Leaders of great executive teams seek help in developing their teams' capabilities, in educating the members about aspects of the work on which they are not themselves experts, and providing outside technical expertise as needed.

- *Resources.* Senior leadership teams, like front-line teams, require the basic materials needed for collaborative work, including ample time, space, staff support, and mundane material resources. The best chief executives make sure that their teams have those resources.

Our research shows that these four support resources distinguish great senior teams from those that find collaborative work a struggle. Figure 6-1 shows the standing of the teams in our sample on the first three: rewards, information, and education. Outstanding senior executive teams, compared with mediocre and poor teams, do not skimp on support resources. First, members of outstanding leadership teams are much more likely than those in mediocre and struggling teams to be rewarded on the basis of team performance rather than solely on the basis of their individual contributions. Second, executives in outstanding teams are not shy about seeking additional education—in teamwork or in any other aspect of their leadership responsibilities—to hone their capability to make high-quality team decisions. Third, outstanding teams do not simply take what they get when it comes to information. They influence those who operate the information systems to be sure that they get the exact data they need, in a form and format that they can use, to assess and manage enterprise-affecting issues.

FIGURE 6-1

Effective senior leadership teams get more support

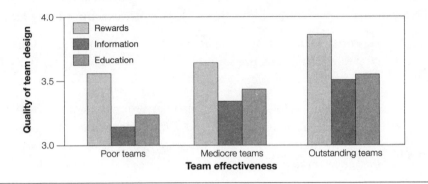

What about mundane material resources that support teamwork? Figure 6-2 shows one major difference between struggling teams—those that fail their constituencies and show few or no signs of getting better as teams or individuals—and the rest. The poorest teams in our sample were significantly underresourced. They were much less likely than mediocre and outstanding teams to give themselves the time and help they needed. Few of these underresourced teams were facing crises that made it impossible to get the resources needed to facilitate their work together. Instead, it was simply that their chief executives did not make leadership

FIGURE 6-2

Struggling senior leadership teams are underresourced

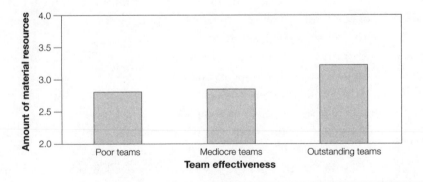

team resources a sufficient priority to pull them up from their downward trajectory of decreasing effectiveness.

In the pages that follow, we identify the most significant barriers that leaders need to overcome to properly support their executive teams, and through cases from our research we describe the actions that leaders can take to get in place the support systems that most powerfully facilitate team effectiveness.

Rewarding Senior Team Performance

One need only see where IBM's Gerstner put his money to realize the value he placed on team performance. Previously, executive bonuses had been based solely on individual performance. Within a year of Gerstner's arrival, a significant portion of every bonus was tied to organizational performance.[2] That alone was not unusual. Many organizations have moved toward some sort of variable pay strategy tied in part to the performance of the organization. But IBM took it a step further: executive pay was also linked to the development of key attributes and competencies that were necessary for executives to become effective team members. Another reward also was linked to acquiring those competencies: the chance to earn membership on Gerstner's Senior Leadership Group. The SLG, an important forum for senior executives, opened doors, provided information, and conferred status. Those who failed to adapt to the new behaviors or reverted to the old ones would have little chance of earning membership, or, if they were already members, eventually they would be removed.

IBM's approach is not unique. Many organizations have implemented compensation strategies to help foster and reinforce teamwork. Yet the idea of rewarding senior teams based on their unique contributions to organizational success is one with which many enterprises continue to struggle. How, chief executives ask, do you measure leadership team performance? How much weight should be placed on team versus individual rewards? Unfortunately, these questions are not well researched, because few senior leadership teams are measured on team performance. Performance within individual roles is well measured and well rewarded. Organization-level performance is increasingly well rewarded. But senior team effectiveness is not.

Moreover, the compensation of executive teams at the enterprise level of publicly traded businesses in the United States is controlled by the compensation committee of the board of directors. For a CEO, ensuring that the senior team is rewarded in a significant way for its effectiveness as a team therefore requires first educating, and then influencing, the firm's board.[3]

Might it be sufficient to tie collective rewards for the team to overall organizational performance such as revenue, profit, or share price? It is senior team members, after all, who make the decisions that have the greatest leverage on the success of the enterprise. That is a common reward strategy. But it poses risks, especially in large companies that have diverse businesses and geographies, where even members of the senior team are necessarily remote from the organizationwide results. For example, if a small minority of members is responsible, through functional or operational roles, for a major part of the organization's results, then other members may feel little responsibility for, impact on, or control of organizationwide performance.

We are not asserting that executive compensation should not be based on organizational performance. Rather, we note that, by itself, such a reward practice will not necessarily engender collaborative team behavior. Although organizational performance measures are easily available and appealingly quantitative, frequently they are too broad to accurately assess the performance of a senior team. Simply because a business is doing well does not mean that the team is doing well, and vice versa. Indeed, although shareholders may view the share price as a measure of senior team performance, that indicator may bear little relation to the behavior of the team. The organization's good (or poor) fortune may reflect market conditions or exogenous events more than it reflects the team's effectiveness.

On the other hand, paying individual members solely on the results over which they have direct control also can undermine a senior team. Individual incentives, especially when paid from a single funding pool and based on performance relative to peers on the team, can set team members against one another in seeking their own portions of the compensation pie. And that can induce team dynamics that damage the senior team's effectiveness.[4]

Effective team rewards should elicit and reinforce collaboration among members as they work together to achieve compelling team purposes. Perhaps the most effective reward approach for a senior leadership team, then, contains a long-term element tied to overall organizational performance, balanced with a smaller element that is closely linked to something strategically critical that the team members can influence or control (for example, changing the geographic mix for products and services or successfully managing a major acquisition).

Some senior teams we have studied have developed reward strategies that simultaneously reinforce both the leader's behavior as a team member and the team's performance overall. Under CEO Hill, for example, the Applebee's senior team members agreed to tie a portion of their bonuses to changing the climate of the team and to changing the culture of the company. The "Big Apple Metrics" program they created required members to put significant skin in the game for changing certain behaviors. It was the head of human resources who raised the concept. "Look," he told team members, "let's put some money at risk here and not make it just a mosquito bite if we don't get it. Let's make it hurt." The approach was straightforward. Members agreed to tie 5 percent of their total bonus opportunity to the improvement of their leadership styles and the work climate they created as a team. They measured their improvement through annual, highly calibrated assessments.

It was a profitable decision. In the first four years after the incentive plan was implemented, the team's work climate, dismal when it was first assessed, improved markedly. So did Applebee's performance, as Hill and team members continued to strengthen their collective focus. "The bottom line is the unbelievable difference in our business results since we started this process," noted one of the team members. "The correlation between team climate and bottom-line results is just about as positive as you could ever look at." From 2000 to 2003, Applebee's earnings per share outpaced those of the industry, increasing at more than twice the rate of its competitors. At the same time, its sales accelerated, while those of many of its competitors were decreasing. According to *Nation's Restaurant News,* Applebee's was at the time the tenth-largest restaurant chain in U.S. systemwide sales; in the casual dining segment, Applebee's was first in number of units, first in sales, and first in market share.[6] Team members took great pride in the fact that they hit both the business and the development goals set out in their Big Apple incentives. They also were quick to acknowledge the added satisfaction they gained from their continuing development as individual leaders and as a team.

Money, of course, is not the only way to motivate executive teams. As many leaders have found, simple recognition and symbolic actions can go a long way in reinforcing important team behaviors. It may be something as simple as public acknowledgment of a job particularly well done or a team toast with a bottle of fine champagne for successful completion of a challenging initiative. Or it may be something much bigger and more profound: in 2002, Sam Palmisano, who replaced Gerstner as IBM's chairman, chose to take a $7 million hit on his own compensation in order to better reward his team for its performance.

The most successful teams we have studied tend to use a combination of reward and recognition strategies that are linked to quantifiable but appropriate measures. AeroMexico's senior team, for example, used a number of performance indicators, including fleet and crew costs, pilot productivity, and market share. Although the overall goals of Unilever's Foodsolutions were set at the corporate level, Bevilacqua's team reviewed and approved—as a team, with each member getting an equal vote—performance targets for each of the company's sixty-seven countries. The team then measured its own performance in part by the performance in the various regions. Beyond these overall measures, both Barahona (AeroMexico) and Bevilacqua (Unilever) closely monitored the progress of the teams. Long after his leadership team became effective, Bevilacqua continued to check in at each meeting to determine how the senior team was developing and to identify key issues that might be impeding its progress. Even a few words of praise or correction from him made a big difference to team members.

In outstanding leadership teams, the CEOs and their teams found unique ways to identify accomplishments that are contributions of the team itself to organization purposes, signs that the team is doing well. We found no universally appropriate formula for doing that. Instead, teams identified the unique challenges they faced—their major shared tasks, most challenging roadblocks, must-win battles, or thorniest team problems—that were worth celebrating if they could be accomplished. Then they made significant and valued rewards, monetary or otherwise, contingent on their successes as teams in overcoming those challenges.

Information: Critical Data
When and How You Need Them

When it comes to getting the information they need to make critical decisions, it's often feast or famine (or both) for senior leadership teams. Many teams suffer from information overload: they are buried in reports and data that may or may not be critical to their work. Others find critical data unavailable to them when they are most needed. Why is getting the right information such a hurdle for senior teams?

One problem is that the same information systems serving the rest of the organization—built for other people and other purposes—often are the sources of data for the top team as well. But without intelligent intervention, those systems do not provide precisely what a leadership team needs to take care of its strategic, enterprise-affecting, forward-looking accountabilities. When Unilever merged its food services business with that of newly acquired Bestfoods, for example, Bevilacqua quickly found that he lacked crucial data on past performance. The problem: Unilever had always rolled its food service financials into the bigger commercial food business. As a result, for much of the first year his new team had almost no trustworthy data to use in assessing the effectiveness of its new operating model. IBM's top team faced a similar challenge. Despite its own technological prowess, it took the company several years to create a system that tracked market data in ways the team could really use. Gerstner says he was shocked by how little customer and competitive information was available. "There was no disciplined marketing intelligence capability. What market share data we had was highly questionable."[7]

For many senior teams, however, the issue is not a lack of information but rather an excess. The problem they face is accessing the information they need when they need it, in a form they can use effectively. The disorder of data can be just as debilitating as a lack of information. One of the most dramatic examples of this was the informational disarray of various U.S. intelligence services before the 9-11 terrorist attacks. According to the commission that studied the attacks, there was an abundance of information but it was not shared, analysis was never pooled across individuals and groups, handoffs of information between agencies were missed, and therefore effective operations could not be launched. "From details of this case," the commission wrote, "one can see how hard it is for the intelligence community to assemble enough of the puzzle pieces . . . to make some sense of them . . . We sympathize with the working-level officers, drowning in information and trying to decide what is important or what needs to be done."[8]

The same is true, unfortunately, for the senior leadership teams of many organizations. Decentralization of information services has fostered the adoption of different data processing programs in many parts of the enterprise, a problem that can be compounded by acquisitions or mergers with other entities. More often than not, these formerly independent entities rely on hardware and software that differ in fundamental ways from those of the organization that acquired or merged with them.

Given the complexity and cost associated with integrating large information systems, senior leaders often patch together their own system. They end up relying heavily on anecdotal information gathered informally through conversations that occur in the course of other work instead of systematic business intelligence. They depend on stories that team members gather within their own functional or operational areas. Or they seek out knowledgeable people to tell them what is happening when the need to know arises. One prominent business school's senior team actually systematized this process by assigning an individual team member to use her personal network to collect anecdotes from staff members who worked at competitor schools.

Some organizations have integrated information systems, but an integrated system alone does not guarantee that the data generated for the senior leadership team will be helpful in its work. All members of the senior team of the national pizza company we studied, for example, carried notebooks that contained week-by-week results of all the company's restaurants. Although these data may have been accurate, they did not provide the information the team really needed to make key strategic decisions to drive future performance. Instead, the weekly data sucked members into the past and into tactical minutiae.

Effectively managing information has long been a challenge for leaders. Henry Mintzberg noted as far back as 1975 that managers generally preferred stories, personal observations, telephone calls, and meetings over documents.[9] Technological changes in the past three decades notwithstanding, we, too, have often seen a preference for simple and unsystematic tools and unreliable reporting mechanisms over carefully selected and systematically analyzed data.

Many organizations are still playing catch-up both with the growing information demands they face and the evolving technology necessary to meet them. The best senior teams we have studied acknowledged the importance of capturing information in usable ways and made it a priority. In some cases, they decided to create entirely new systems for tracking and monitoring performance at a level and frequency that the leadership team could use. Other teams have found that merely rethinking the information they need or the form in which they receive it can go a long way in enhancing their efforts. A growing number of teams, for example, have embraced simple but effective real-time *performance dashboards:* constantly updated, well-designed displays of key performance indicators that appear as pop-ups on their personal computers. What it takes is for the team to recognize the need for such data and for the leader to authorize it.[10]

It is not sufficient for a senior team merely to receive data. Once in hand, the information must be analyzed before the team can draw out its implications and make constructive use of it. Some kinds of information, such as what is shown on performance dashboards, are useful mainly for tracking organizational operations or performance in real time. Making sense of such data is a straightforward task for senior teams. But what if the information is complex or ambiguous, such as data about the actions or intentions of customers, competitors, or regulators? That kind of information may be the most important of all, but interpreting and using it may be challenging.

Getting the greatest possible benefit from information requires both individual analysis and teamwork. *Data analysis* is a cognitive activity that requires a person to become deeply immersed in the numbers to identify the most significant patterns and themes. If you have ever strained to study a matrix of data projected onto a conference room screen, you know that it is not something a team does easily or well. By contrast, extracting the *meaning* from a dataset and teasing out its action implications is best done collaboratively: do those numbers mean what they seem to mean? Do they provide the complete picture? What's missing, and how can we get it? What should we do about what we're learning from these data?

Sometimes a CEO, CFO, or head of production will analyze a data-set and then make a specific action recommendation to the leadership team. Team discussion then is mainly about the pluses and minuses of the proposed action, and not what to make of the information. For crucial information, a better strategy is to ask a team member who is especially skilled in working with data to make the first pass through the numbers and report findings and interpretations to the team as a whole. The team then engages in a robust team discussion to assess the trustworthiness of the data, to identify the most significant aspects of the findings, and then explore what should be done about it.

We wish we could give you a positive example of a top team that op-erated in that way, but we do not have one. More common in the teams we studied is the suboptimal strategy of a senior team being shown a few pages of data followed by a free-for-all as members chime in with ideas about their implications. We can, however, offer a hypothetical case to il-lustrate how a good process might unfold.

Imagine that the SVP for sales has just completed her quarterly analysis of data on sales and revenue and is now showing a summary graphic. There is no noticeable trend: sales seem to be holding at about the same level as in previous quarters. But one team member raises a question: "The *variance* in sales across regions is getting larger," he says. "Why might that be?" That question is possible only because the team has specifically asked that sales reports include information about disper-sions as well as averages.

The question prompts a response from the senior vice president for Asia. "Competition in South Asia heated up last quarter," he says. "A new competitor went online and basically gave everything away to get off to a fast start. They'll pay for that next quarter."

"It's the opposite in North America," the vice president for the Amer-icas adds. "As you know all too well, we had big supply problems here the previous two quarters, but now that's behind us. We had a real spurt this quarter. It's probably just a one-time thing."

The CEO joins in. "So it's all likely to average out? There's nothing in particular we need to do at this point?"

As other team members start to nod in agreement, the chief counsel speaks up. "Not so fast. Maybe this increase in variance across regions is something we ought to look at more closely. Are there other data we could get that could confirm that there is nothing we ought to worry about—or that there is?"

Further discussion follows, and the team pieces together a nuanced understanding of sales trends—trends that, it turns out, do have modest implications for marketing strategy—as well as for the kinds of information the team wants to see at the end of the next quarter.

As we said, it's all hypothetical. In reality, many senior teams are remarkably reactive when it comes to analyzing even potentially consequential data, accepting without question or complaint whatever their information systems professionals give them, analyzing and interpreting those data on the fly if at all. The potential benefits of clean, appropriately analyzed, collectively interpreted data are not captured—and team members, in many cases, do not even realize that they are letting gold slip through their fingers.

Good use of informational support, then, requires having the highest-quality data, neither too much nor too little of it, in a form that makes it easy for the senior team to work with it. Excellent information support also requires a mix of individual and team work: individual analysis to prepare the information for the leadership team, and teamwork to assess it, interpret it, and draw out its action implications.

In sum, how your senior team gathers, organizes, and accesses information is best left to the information technology experts. What we can advise you, based on our observations and systematic research, is this: on senior leadership teams, it is vital to have information that is well organized and prepared for the specific analytic purposes of the team. The best decision-making leadership teams we have studied have spared no effort or expense in making sure that they have the data they need when they need it and in a form that makes it possible for them to use it.

Educating the Senior Team

Although senior teams often neglect the actions it takes to create a real information support system, generally they at least agree that information is a crucial resource. What they tend not to recognize is the value of educational support for their work. Most team members feel that they have adequate education and experience. Many have been through internal leadership development programs. Many also have done graduate work or postgraduate academic business programs. Not only do they feel they don't need another formal training program, but also, they will tell you, they don't have time for one. To take the whole team out of action for a two-day program, some say, would be a waste of money. It would be better to spend development funds lower in the organization where they could do some good.

Our research says otherwise. Even very senior, experienced, well-educated leaders have much to learn about what it takes to work well in teams. And those chief executives who take education seriously and invest in their team's development have better teams. Indeed, second to rewards, education about teamwork is the support resource that made the most difference between outstanding teams and all the rest.

Other researchers affirm the importance of the development of top leaders. A recent study by The Conference Board, for example, reported a growing gap between the demands on today's senior leaders and their development.[11] Only one-third of the respondents rated the capacity of their companies' leadership to meet the challenges of the business or to handle major change as good to excellent—down from 50 percent in 1997. At the same time, only 37 percent of those surveyed said that their organizations are effective when it comes to identifying future leaders, and fewer than half listed leadership development as a major priority for their top executives. As the report noted, given the growing complexity of organizations, within a few years "only teams of executives will be capable of creating and implementing winning strategies."[12]

Leaders of the most effective teams we studied not only have embraced the importance of ongoing development but also have made it a priority. They dedicate serious time and money to their teams' learning. We add, however, a significant qualification: many CEOs invest significant resources in leadership development for members of their senior teams but excuse themselves from participating. One of us participated in a major development program for the most senior leaders of a global financial institution. The course, which was extraordinarily expensive for the institution, involved weeks of offsite educational work for multiple cohorts of executives spread over almost a year. Literally every senior leader participated except one: the chief executive himself.

His stated reason for not participating: as much as he would like to join in, a highly demanding schedule made it impossible. The implicit message received by members of his leadership team: either (1) he thinks he already knows all this stuff ("But we know better"), or (2) he doesn't think it's very important ("Maybe human resources sold him a bill of goods"), or (3) both. Discussions overheard among participants during breaks in the program suggested that the consensus was option 3.

If you are going to invest in leadership development for your senior team, then make it leadership development for the senior team. You are the most important member of that team. To excuse yourself is inexcusable.

In contrast, when the educational assistance the team needs is of a more technical kind, chief executives are likely to arrange for it as soon as someone asks for it—or even to suggest that the team seek an outside expert. One nonprofit organization we studied, for example, had suffered through a succession of less-than-stellar chief financial officers. The senior leadership team was floundering as it tried to figure out how to extract the organization from a messy financial situation. Then one member said something along the lines of, "What we really need is someone like Sven to help us out." That comment was all it took. Sven Ehrstrom was a distinguished retired banker who served on the organization's board of directors. Soon he was meeting regularly with the senior team—not to solve their financial problems for them, but to help them learn what they needed to know to get the organization's finances stabilized and back on track.

That was a good use of a friendly resource who was eager to lend a hand (indeed, Ehrstrom was pleased to be asked to help with his expertise in addition to his checkbook). At other times a top team needs to go further afield to get the expertise it needs, as was the case for the leadership team of a health food company during the low-carbohydrate diet craze. Faced with significant customer concern about the ingredients of some of the company's products, the team members commissioned a nutritionist from a nearby teaching hospital to educate them. They sent her their questions and asked her to prepare a briefing about medical research on carbohydrates and obesity. They invited her to a senior team meeting and spent productive time quizzing her about the nuances of the findings and their implications. After hearing what she had to say, the team concluded that a major change in the company's mix of products would ill serve their customers in the long run.

Outstanding senior team leaders are willing to identify what their teams do not know or do not know how to do, and they invest time and money to provide the educational resources that make them smarter and more capable over time.

Small Acts of Support

Some of the support your team may need, such as information systems and leader development programs, can be costly or time intensive. Given such big-ticket needs, it is easy to overlook the many smaller, simpler forms of ongoing support that the best chief executives provide their senior teams. These small actions often require little or no expenditure but instead are generated through exceptional human capital: the insight and empathy of leaders. These leaders look beyond the traditional needs of their teams to those issues that may seem insignificant but turn out to generate a significant return on investment.

Consider, for example, Alan Jimson, new CEO of a global division of a large chemical company. His predecessor had employed a regional operating model; he rarely brought the team together, and never to work on joint issues. To say that team members "knew each other" was something of an exaggeration. Jimson changed the division's operating model, centralizing some key processes and launching some divisionwide initiatives. Aware of how precious was the time of his executive team, he traditionally started his global meetings with a working session over dinner and then continued with another working session through the end of the next day. The meetings were formal and highly structured, and invariably they succeeded in addressing all the items on the agenda. But despite the hard work, the team members failed to come together and to create initiatives that cut across the division, as Jimson had hoped.

After observing members' behavior at one meeting, Jimson had an inspiration: members really did not know one another well enough to develop the relationships needed for a cohesive team. Nor did they really trust their leader, at least not yet. He concluded that senior executives are unlikely to trust people whom they do not know. So he replaced the traditional evening work session with a leisurely cocktail hour followed by dinner. On that evening, there was no formal agenda, only casual conversation. Over a series of these get-togethers, members began to get to know each other and to build relationships. For the first time, they began to consult with each other between meetings. They developed and completed projects that were then delegated to subgroups. In Jimson's eyes, the members finally had crystallized as a team. Providing an informal, agenda-free evening was a small change in the group's resources, to be sure. Except for a bigger bar tab, it was not costly. Yet the results it generated for the team were large and lasting.

Anil Gavaskar, who ran a large division of a global manufacturing conglomerate, took the fine-dining approach to team building a bit further. He invited his expanded alignment team of the division's top sixty leaders to dinner at a spectacular villa whose ambience was rivaled only by the menu. But Gavaskar had all the chairs removed so that team members would have to mingle throughout the evening. In his view, the high levels of constant interaction that developed were vital at this time in the team's life, because there were many new members who had just come on board from a recent large acquisition. And Gavaskar knew that, left to their own devices and with traditional seating, they would spend the evening talking only to those people they already knew.

When Roger Enrico became president of Frito-Lay, Inc., he not only eliminated the chairs, but he also threw out the table with them. The problem was not really the furniture; it was the senior leadership team, which was far too formal for Enrico's aspirations for robust teamwork. "There was formal, structured communication—if you could even call it communication," he notes. "There was very little dialogue. The rule was, you didn't say anything in front of a senior leader that that person didn't already know you were going to say."

One of the first problems Enrico identified was the team's formal executive suite. "We had an executive wing lined in mahogany. It looked like a lawyer's office on Wall Street. We had a conference center that looked like the bridge of the starship *Enterprise* from the television series *Star Trek*. It was purposely designed to be a power conference room. So everyone who came into it was totally intimidated. It had a big, semicircular stone-covered table with huge chairs, and you looked like you were in Goldfinger's office [a reference to a James Bond movie villain] or something. So naturally there was just very little communication." The company also had detailed regulations about how decisions were to be made, minutes of top team meetings that reported who said what and who concurred, and even an official *Lexicon of Acronyms and Abbreviations*.

"This place used acronyms like the Pentagon—okay, more than the Pentagon," Enrico recalls. "It was ridiculous."

What he found most outrageous, however, was the impact of all this formality on the senior team. It restricted dialogue. It stifled teamwork. And it isolated people in their functional silos. "For the most part," Enrico says, "they were competent, even excellent people. But they weren't behaving like excellent people. There was almost no teamwork at the senior level, and therefore there wasn't very much below them either."

To transform the team, to help it find its direction, to make it a strong performer again, Enrico wanted to tear down the barricades of formality, create a sense of openness, and get the team members out of their silos and working together. His approach was as simple as it was successful. He threw away the decision-making regulations. He banned the use of acronyms. And he refused to enter the "Goldfinger" conference room. "You guys can do what you want," he told his team. "But I am not going in that room anymore." And he didn't. In fact, the conference room with its intimidating stone table was soon torn out, along with the rest of the executive wing, and replaced by smaller rooms, where, Enrico says, the team members could "sit around and actually talk."

"I wanted people talking to each other," he says. "I wanted to have anybody come to the team's meeting who would like to and say, 'Here's what I'm working on, I need your help.' Or, 'What do you guys think?' So that we were a resource rather than a rubber-stamping body." Roger Enrico's successes at creating leadership teams like the one at Frito-Lay eventually led to his appointment as CEO of PepsiCo, Inc.

The actions of Enrico and the other leaders may appear to be mere symbolism. In reality, they were the thoughtful actions of insightful leaders who understood that the settings in which a team meets shape members' ability to collaborate and, ultimately, their effectiveness as a team. Such small acts of support often create the space, the atmosphere—the time and the common ground—that senior leadership teams need if they are to develop productive working relationships.

The right resources, whether a multimillion-dollar information system or the simple removal of chairs from a dining room, are important to the success of any senior leadership team. Such acts are supporting elements—the times, places, and equipment the team needs to play its game effectively. You must create the specific resources your team needs in the context of its own unique challenges and opportunities. That is why your team's resource needs can be identified and provided only after you have established what game you are playing (your team's purpose) and how you're going to play it (its structure).

The Well-Supported Team

Here is a short checklist of the support systems that, our research suggests, most strongly facilitate great teamwork in senior leadership teams—as well as the continuing development of individual team members.

1. *Rewards.* Look carefully at the design of your team's rewards. Find a way to reward the team members for accomplishing the accountabilities you established with them as you crafted the team's purpose and structure. Putting significant team skin in the game—and attention to the team-level improvements that result—is a powerful influence on senior team performance.

2. *Information.* Talk with your team about what information—data, intelligence, analysis, creative ideas—is most needed to guide and inform its work in decision making. Seeking information can be a team task; identify the members who have the knack for gathering and summarizing information in a highly usable fashion, and turn them loose to tweak, or even to re-create, the executive team's information system.

3. *Education.* Take continuing education seriously. You have asked your team to embark on something that may be novel for many members, so providing them the training and educational resources they need—when they need them—can make the difference between a team that gets stuck in the starting gate and one that burns up the track.

4. *Support.* Look for opportunities to be creative in providing your team any other support—including time, settings, and mundane material resources—that can smooth team processes and build collective capabilities. Such simple actions, especially coming from you, the leader, can be powerful and constructive influences on senior team effectiveness.

7

Coach Your Team—
and Timing Is Everything

A t the end of a meeting, after intense discussion and tough decisions, Tony Lesston asked for a few more moments from his
clearly exhausted leadership team. "I just want to take some time
here to give my observations about how this team has been growing since
we started this whole thing," he said. He briefly described some of the
behaviors in the team that had improved since the members had begun
working together some months before, the norms he saw them consistently enforcing, and the few things they still did not do well despite trying hard: "Like me jumping on top of Hailey's comment without even
understanding her point, when we said we wouldn't do that." He then invited the team members to add their own comments and observations
about the team's work processes.

That was a powerful moment in the life of this team. The CEO took
deliberate steps to coach his team. He admitted his own violation of
group norms. He provided honest feedback and invited reflection on how
the team could work better together. These were skilled acts of team
coaching.

Senior leadership teams, like other teams, need expert help in learning how to become better at working together over time. Coaching such

teams is often more challenging than coaching front-line teams. High-spirited, independent-minded thoroughbreds are often convinced of the rightness of their ways and are not responsive to correction—even by the lead horse.

Compounding the difficulty of coaching a senior leadership team are complexities and pressures seldom faced by teams at lower levels—complexities such as the duality of individual roles versus team roles, the intense focus on and responsibility for enterprisewide results, and a wide range of highly demanding constituencies (e.g., the board, regulatory agencies, shareholders, key customers, partners, analysts, the community, and the rest of the organization), all clamoring for immediate attention. Meeting such demands often leaves little time, at least in the CEO's mind, to coach a leadership team.[1]

But if done well and at the right times, coaching is a powerful force in developing and sustaining a superb executive team. The outstanding executive teams we studied had available to them hands-on help in developing their team processes, whether from an outside expert, from their leader, or from team members themselves. As shown in figure 7-1, the poorest teams and the mediocre teams had only a modest level of coaching.

All teams found their leaders' actions in building the team to be helpful (see the bars to the far left in figure 7-1). But the outstanding teams had significantly more coaching, both from leaders and from one another,

FIGURE 7-1

Effective senior leadership teams have more helpful leaders, get more coaching from their leaders, and coach each other more

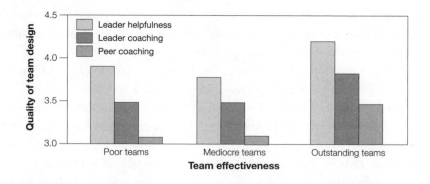

than did mediocre and struggling teams. The most significant influence on *peer coaching*—how much team members coached one another—was how much the team leader coached them. When you coach your team, the members gradually begin to intervene in their own processes in increasingly constructive ways. For teams whose design is solid, coaching can spawn a positive spiral of effective attention to improving members' collaborative decision-making processes.

What Team Coaching Is—and Isn't

A surprising finding from our research is that teams do not improve markedly even if all their members receive individual coaching to develop their personal capabilities. Individual coaching can indeed help executives become better leaders in their own right, but the team does not necessarily improve. Team development is not an additive function of individuals becoming more effective team players, but rather an entirely different capability. The reason for that is not immediately obvious. In essence, it is because the team itself is an entity separate from the individuals who constitute it. For the team to get better, that entity needs to be coached while members are actually carrying out their collaborative work.

By *team coaching,* we mean directly intervening in the process that the team members use to interact, in order to improve team effectiveness.[2] A good team coach holds up a mirror to reflect back to team members the collective behaviors that hinder and advance teamwork. In this way, the team can discuss team processes and agree on a new path forward. When members understand the kinds of actions that advance their work, the team can develop a template of sorts that can be applied to other situations. We found very few teams that were able to decode their successes and failures and learn from them without intervention from the leader or another team coach.

A case in point is the executive team of a global food ingredients company. The team's leader, Mike Massi, had recently conveyed the purpose of the team, and members had agreed on their shared accountabilities. They also had established a preliminary set of behavioral norms to be revisited as the team learned what did and did not work. Members were optimistic that this set of conversations and contracts would turn out to be a good investment, one that would pay off in real progress. And it appeared to work: members came out of a subsequent meeting a continent away from headquarters exhilarated by their newfound ability to dig into complex discussions of business strategy and generate ideas that drew on the full range of talents at the executive table.

At the next meeting, the team's coach—in this case, an external consultant working with the team—joined the meeting, as she did from time to time. Members commented with pride on the successful South American meeting and proposed following the same process that had felt so successful to them before. Massi's response was a firm no. "It would be a waste of time. There, we were talking about generating new initiatives. At this meeting, we have to review the proposals to integrate our software programs."

The coach intervened. She sensed the energy from the team about its forward progress and understood members' fear that they could lose their collective momentum if Massi reversed course now. She said to the team and to Massi, "It sounds as if the South American meeting was very successful. It may be helpful to take a few minutes to summarize what made it so, even if you do not decide to follow that procedure today." All eyes turned to Massi. After a momentary pause, Massi agreed, and the conversation proceeded.

One member said, "It was helpful to get all of the material in advance with enough time to read it." He quickly added, "As was done for this meeting, too."

Another said, "I agree. And the person in charge of leading each section of our agenda made it clear what he wanted from the group."

A third said, "I'd like to add that the biggest thing for me was that we took the time we needed on the important issues *and* made sure we all shared the same understanding."

When Massi added, "What was important to me was that I heard different ways to grow the business. I thought we had a good debate," team members laughed, recalling some animated discussions in South America.

As the discussion came to a close, the coach was silent. The team was silent. Everyone looked to Massi. He said, "The South American meeting was our most productive as a team. Until this discussion, I must admit I thought it was the topic, not the process we used, that made the meeting work. I think we should use what we just outlined for today's meeting." They did. And it worked for them again. And again.

The actions of the team's coach—in this case, an outsider—may seem simple. She did not offer to facilitate the meeting (something that would have risked creating unnecessary dependence on her). She did not suggest how to conduct the meeting (something that would have implied that the team had learned little from its own accomplishments). Rather, she created the conditions for the team to discover its own lessons from experience. And she created a moment for the team to capture what it had learned tacitly and make it explicit and usable for future work.

Effective team coaching addresses the task-related behavior of the team with the intent of helping it develop and sustain three things: (1) high levels of motivation for the team's collaborative work, (2) effective collective approaches to team tasks, and (3) the ability to identify and deploy all the considerable talent that team members bring to the table. High-quality team coaching is about the work that members must accomplish together. Behavior on the part of members that supports or impedes the three work processes just identified is fair game for a coaching intervention, whether the intervention corrects ineffective behavior or reinforces good teamwork.

The key to helpful coaching is to focus on the work and let the personal relationships in the team evolve as they will. You will see, as we have, that improvement in the ability of the team to accomplish important work together will, over time, naturally result in better relations among the members.[3]

It also is useful to note what team coaching is *not*. It is not about taking the team on treks to exotic locations. It is not about rope courses and trust circles. These activities may help the team bond, but they do not help it deliver on its accountabilities. In our view, coaching the team as it does its work behind the closed doors of the conference room is far more likely to generate long-term improvements in teamwork than climbing a mountain, crossing a desert, sailing boats, or driving race cars.

Team coaching can include a wide range of actions: clarifying team boundaries, creating or clarifying behavioral norms, calling out team members when they violate a norm (as Lesston did for his own behavior in our opening example), complimenting the team on the quality and depth of its discussion of a strategic issue, teaching members how to listen for the key concerns others are expressing, or even taking a break to reflect on how the team is doing.

Team coaching is entirely different from executive coaching. Executive coaching is one-on-one interaction aimed at developing the capabilities of individual managers. Both approaches have a place in helping leaders be more effective. However, individual coaching contributes to the leadership team only to the extent that it focuses on individual members' contributions to the team processes and to the execution of the team's accountabilities.

In our experience, typically there are two or three team members in any executive team who struggle with taking on an enterprise perspective rather than maintaining their traditional functional or operational orientation. These individuals may handle their individual leadership responsibilities very well and therefore are regarded by the leader as definite keepers. They are not derailers, but rather are leaders who are struggling a bit to make the transition to teamwork. These executives, we have observed, can benefit a great deal from individual coaching about their roles as members of executive teams.

CEO Priorities: The Leadership Team—or Not?

When we asked senior team members to describe the charge the CEO gave them when they joined the team, the response was similar across most of the organizations we studied. At best, the CEO outlined his expectations in vague terms and said little or nothing about the individual's role as an enterprise leader. It was rare for leaders to take the time to onboard their new direct reports. But when that happened, it made the transition easier, smoother, and more effective both for the teams and for the new members.

Beyond the preparation of individuals for their roles on the team is the ongoing observing, advising, correcting, reinforcing, reviewing, and shaping of team behavior. According to our research, coaching the team comes in a distant fourth when compared with the attention the leader gives to structuring the work of the team, coaching individuals, and, above all, attending to matters external to the leadership team. Figure 7-2 presents our findings about the relative amount of attention leaders give to each of these four activities. It shows how little attention team coaching gets in the face of the other demands on chief executives. This find-

FIGURE 7-2

How leaders apportion their attention

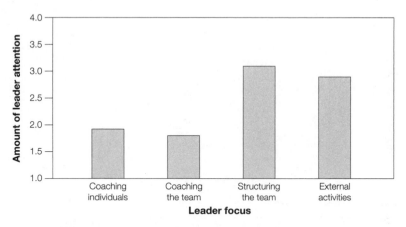

These scores are *relative* ranks; it is not possible to score high on all of them.

ing is ironic, because our research also shows that team coaching is invaluable in fostering and sustaining effective teamwork and performance.

Coaching individuals about their contribution to the team, coaching the team, and structuring the team and its processes are internally focused activities—attention paid to the leadership team *as a team*. We combined these three activities into an "internal focus" score and compared how much attention the chief executives of outstanding, mediocre, and poor teams gave to these internal activities compared to the amount of attention they paid to external activities. Figure 7-3 throws the pattern into stark relief: it was only the leaders of the most outstanding teams in our sample—the teams that served all their constituencies superbly and grew in capability over time—who had a true dual focus: they gave their teams the same focused attention that they gave to external matters.

When to Coach the Team

The timing of team coaching is critical. There are times in the life of a team when it is especially open to coaching, and times when any attempt

FIGURE 7-3

Leaders of outstanding senior leadership teams have a dual focus: Internal and external

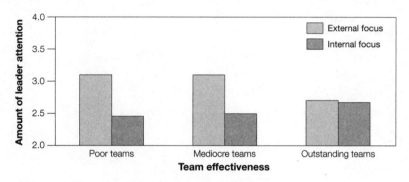

These scores are *relative* ranks; it is not possible to score high on all of them.

to make major changes in its trajectory is likely to be ignored. In Mike Massi's newly developing team, for example, the coach working with the team showed a highly refined sense of timing in recognizing that the team could effectively harvest lessons from the preceding team meeting now and that it would facilitate the work the team was about to begin. This example underlines our finding, in this and previous studies, that different aspects of team dynamics are better addressed at different times in the life of the team.[4] Figure 7-4 shows the times when a team is most open to coaching interventions, along with the kinds of interventions that are most helpful to it at those times.

FIGURE 7-4

The temporal appropriateness of different kinds of coaching

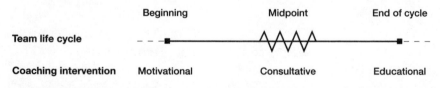

Source: Adapted from Hackman (2002). Used with permission.

As the figure shows, beginnings, calendar midpoints, and the ends of projects or task cycles provide special opportunities for team coaching. And three kinds of team coaching—motivational, consultative, and educational, respectively—are especially helpful to teams at each of those times.

Beginnings

The early stage in a team's life is the time to create energy and focus the team on its purpose.[5] Some organizations have established processes for launching teams and bringing members on board. Teams in such organizations tend to come together faster and with less effort than in organizations that don't have such processes. But even if your organization lacks well-designed procedures for launching teams, you can still learn from their example.

When we studied senior leadership at PepsiCo, Inc., for example, we found embedded in the organization some strong norms about how people should operate both as team leaders and as team members. Leaders who had risen through the organization's ranks knew the ropes by the time they became members of a senior team. A carefully scripted on-boarding process addressed the requirements of all team members before they joined the senior team. Senior leaders, too, knew exactly what they needed to do before the first team meeting to ensure that their team launches were successful.

Leaders' scripts included (1) identifying the core capabilities of each member, (2) articulating the team purpose, (3) establishing team boundaries by creating a sense of shared identity, emphasizing "we" and "our accountabilities," and (4) putting the norms and expectations on the table for the group to revise and ratify. Collectively, these elements established a positive trajectory for teams and made later coaching interventions immeasurably easier. After all, the clarity established in the room by this launch process made it straightforward to ask, "What's working for us in achieving our purpose? What's not? In what ways are we living up to and not living up to our own norms?"

A division president at one technology firm took a different approach but covered similar ground. This leader began work with the team by laying out the expectations early, telling members, "This is what I expect of you when you come to my meetings: do the prereading, come informed, and be ready to engage, because that's why these people are here for you.

I want you engaged. This is not, 'You take notes, you go home.' This is not a passive listening role. I want you in there duking it out, and if you think something's bullshit, I want you to raise your hand and say, 'Pardon me, we think that's bullshit.' If I'm engaged, and if it's worth my time, I figure it ought to be worth your time." Perhaps it is not surprising that under such supervision, the team turned around the division's flagging performance in a matter of months. Members took seriously the charge put to them, and responded with exactly the tough debate they had been asked for.

Unfortunately, most organizations lack a well-designed, institutionalized team launch process. Often leaders make the erroneous assumption that, once brought together, any group of experienced, talented executives should naturally work well as a team. Untested assumptions, it should be clear by now, are the bane of leadership teams.

But take care to put first things first. When we are asked to help a chief executive with a team that does not work, we often discover that the leader has overlooked the building blocks of an effective team: a shared understanding of its direction, the right number and the right people at the table, meaningful team tasks, and a constructive set of norms. Without this foundation teams will struggle, and any attempt at coaching will likely slide off like water on a duck's back.

Keep that core idea in mind: often the problems members have in working together are the direct result of a poor team design. If that is the state your team is in, go back and relaunch it, with special attention to the three essential conditions we have discussed in this book, before you attempt to coach it to greatness.

Midpoints

The next opportunity to make major alterations in the team's process does not come until members have logged significant experience working together, often midway through a team project. Big changes in how the team works are not likely to happen—or, if they are attempted, to take—until there is a natural break in the work. It is at temporal midpoints—halfway through a cycle, a meeting, or a project—that teams tend naturally to reorganize themselves and reorient their processes in preparation for the second half.

During such breaks, good leaders ask their teams to reflect on which approaches to the work are effective and which are misdirected, off base, or unconstructive. Some of the most effective coaching we have seen takes place during these downtimes.

Even the best teams tend to get caught up in the heat of battle, to get mired in inappropriate behavior and digressions. Letting them do so and then leading an after-battle assessment of the process may be the best way for the team to learn lessons that stick. It is at this point that you can pose questions such as, "How is it going?" "What's working?" "What do we wish we had or hadn't done?" "What shall we do differently for the next half?" We call this *consultative coaching*, as you and the team consult with each other about your observations and the changes they imply for how the team should operate henceforth.

On occasion, however, a more directive approach may be necessary, such as when the team is stuck, is having trouble staying on track, or may be about to experience a train wreck. Yuki Fujiyama, who runs a major business unit of a large financial services organization, found her team consumed by a heated debate about an unpopular cost-allocation process the CFO had introduced. Convinced that the team was on an unproductive tangent from which it was unlikely to recover, she stopped the debate cold, asserting that the team would spend no more of its time second-guessing its CFO.

Such pointed interventions let members know that they are significantly off track. They can be highly constructive, especially if you also take a moment to address why the behavior is problematic. Fujiyama took a serious risk that her team would read her actions as political support of a particular team member rather than as a statement about the kind of work she wanted to be the team's focus. It is better to explicitly state what you want and expect from the team than to allow members to draw their own (perhaps cynical) conclusions about why you act as you do.

Endgames

You can accelerate the development of your team's long-term capabilities if you take time at the ends of meetings, team tasks, and major accomplishments (or failures) to gather insights and reflect on lessons learned. Near the end of a task cycle—a project, a fiscal quarter, a met or unmet deadline—the focus of your coaching shifts from consultation to education: what can the team learn to help it grow even stronger for the next set of must-win battles? Again, timing is important because the need for coaching and direction must be balanced by the need to maintain momentum as a leadership team. The coach working with Massi's food ingredients team, mentioned earlier in this chapter, showed a fine sense of timing in addressing her educational role, helping the team glean concrete insights from its previous work to support moving forward on the current challenge. The conversation was not lengthy and belabored, but neither was it facile. The coach asked the team what had worked and what made those lessons relevant—or irrelevant—to the work they were beginning.

As a team matures, coaching increasingly becomes about helping the team learn from its own experiences. If you have been consistent in enforcing team norms, members will start to spontaneously provide their own insights into what the team is learning and increasingly will manage themselves.

Between Times

Coaching during the times between a team's key transition points—between the beginning and the midpoint, and between the midpoint and the end of a task cycle—should focus on quietly reinforcing good teamwork and, as needed, putting a stop to norm-breaking behaviors (recall how Lesston did this in the earlier example).

During these phases of a leadership team's work, the coach should attend to team norms: encouraging robust discussions and even disagreements, ensuring that members are listening to the positions of others, keeping the focus of critical comments on the issues and not on other members, and encouraging the team to wrap up its discussion and make a decision when an issue has been fully explored. Such coaching is an integral part of the everyday leadership of the team. It often comes at seemingly inconsequential moments, when noteworthy comments or observations are made, or when questions are posed that bring to light overlooked but critical team dynamics.

One of our colleagues worked with a team that was trying hard, but unsuccessfully, to come to a critical decision. Newer team members, she observed, did not speak up until at least two of the senior members had offered their opinions. When she pointed that out, the team explored for the first time why the younger members were hesitant to speak. Subsequently, seasoned members began eliciting the views of their newer colleagues earlier in the decision-making process.

In our observation, getting the timing right is a struggle for most leaders at some point in their careers. We sometimes have been surprised by the seeming inability of otherwise effective leaders to sense when to intervene and when to stand back and let team processes unfold. Perhaps we should not have been surprised: many chief executives have never had to coach a team as a group, and therefore they have not had much opportunity to learn about the importance of good timing in intervening in team processes. Indeed, in some cases the chief executive may not be the best person to have primary responsibility for team coaching, a possibility we explore next.

Who Should Coach a Senior Leadership Team?

There is no obvious or generally correct answer to this question. Some chief executives coach their teams personally. Others rely on particular team members. Still others seek outside help, whether from their own internal human resource experts or from external consultants.

We have observed team leaders who are successful in coaching their own teams. They have incorporated coaching as part of their repertoire of leadership skills, and they coach their teams naturally and unobtrusively, with acute sensitivity to what is happening in their organizations and on their teams.

We also have seen leaders exacerbate already dysfunctional team dynamics almost every time they make a coaching intervention that they intend to be helpful. We have watched as team members quietly but effectively mentor the other team members, but we also have seen team members pigeonholed into a coaching role and ultimately ignored. We have seen teams gel with the help of outside experts, but we also have seen them develop debilitating codependent relationships with consultants.

So who should coach the top team? Certainly it should be someone who has the capability to do so effectively and in a way that builds the team's self-managing capabilities. And that person, it turns out, more often than not is someone other than the chief executive. Let's look at some reasons.

First, even though you are the leader, you also are an integral part of the team, as caught up in the work as everyone else. And because you are heavily invested in the outcome, it is difficult to be objective about what you are seeing and experiencing. For Unilever's Bevilacqua, for example, it was difficult even to identify a number of the issues and dynamics that were undermining his team. He was too close to the action, he noted, too involved himself to step back and objectively observe what was happening and why—let alone craft solutions.

Second, you may not have well-honed team coaching skills. The leaders we have described in this chapter (Lesston, Massi, and Daniels) were successful in their coaching because they had a rare talent for observing and interpreting team processes. Although Massi must work at it (he admits to being a task-focused leader who likes to jump in immediately with observations, suggestions, and solutions), he has learned to be patient and listen carefully before stepping in to manage the process. Lesston and Daniels, in putting tough team issues on the table, demonstrated an attentiveness to internal team task processes that is crucial to outstanding senior leadership teams. Crucial—and rare. If you have doubts about your objectivity and about your coaching capabilities, it may be wise to seek outside coaching help for your team.

When to Go Outside

"A benevolent ghost who cuts through the crap"—that is how one leader described the way one of our respected colleagues enacted his role as an external team coach. Our colleague viewed the characterization as a compliment of the first order. It was a phrase spoken in appreciation of the gift of objectivity, describing someone whose interventions occasionally were pointed but usually were invisible.

Unilever's Bevilacqua also found it helpful to engage the services of an outside coach. After Bevilacqua's boss watched him struggle for some time to move his team forward, he suggested Bevilacqua get a coach: "I saw him losing impact. He was convincing himself that this struggling team was a problem he couldn't do much about, rather than of stepping back and aggressively attacking it."

It proved to be a wise decision. The coach, another colleague of ours, spent a great deal of time at Bevilacqua's side, especially during team meetings. Mostly, he observed and then fed back those observations, often over dinner or during a break. The consultant's observations captured team dynamics that Bevilacqua's close involvement with the team had kept him from noticing. He says of the consultant, "John has the ability to sit back and say, 'Look, you know, these were some of the things that seemed to be going on as you were dealing with that particular bit. But this may be what really was going on.' It is very hard for somebody who is leading a meeting to actually see it all objectively."

Looking back, Bevilacqua says, he views the outside coaching he and his team received as one of the critical ingredients of his team's success. Yet finding the right team coach or coaches can be far more difficult than simply selecting an executive coach for yourself or for certain members of your team. A senior team needs someone who understands the organization, who understands strategy, who understands team design, and who understands team dynamics—a rare combination in one individual. That's why it sometimes works well to use small teams to coach senior leadership teams. While one individual coaches the team leader about how to structure and lead the team, another focuses on team-level coaching, and others work with individual members to help them develop their capabilities for team self-management and ultimately for effective peer coaching.

Peer Coaching

Ideally, your aim as leader should be to help your senior leadership team become largely self-managing. In the early phases of a team's life, the leader must take primary responsibility for establishing and enforcing norms. In later stages, however, the team itself, helped by good coaching from the leader or from an outsider, can share that responsibility. Our research has shown that the most outstanding teams rely on a combination of the leader's coaching and subsequently developed peer coaching.

The timing for developing peer coaching varies from team to team, but once you have established your team's norms you can invite your team members to point out instances of violations, including your own, and to begin developing their capacity to self-correct. If you communicate your expectations that they begin doing that for straightforward norms (such as "Show up on time"), it is likely that they soon will develop and use additional self-management skills.

Perversely, sometimes it is wise to assign responsibility for policing a particular norm to the team member who most blatantly disregards it. After all, that person knows better than anyone else on the team what a violation looks like, and we often have seen such individuals take on the enforcement responsibility with good humor and much encouragement from colleagues.

Although leaders can never fully abdicate their own coaching responsibilities, they can act in ways that make room for and encourage the team—either certain members or the group as a whole—to take on ever-greater coaching responsibilities. Certainly, individual members can provide coaching in areas of their specific expertise. And occasionally, you will find a member or two with exceptional team coaching skills—individuals who can make sense of complex team dynamics and who are good at providing peers and even the chief executive with feedback as helpful as it is candid. Such individuals are extraordinarily valuable assets, and they should be encouraged to pitch in with coaching interventions whenever they see the need.

Recall Dave Levy, the pizza executive discussed in chapter 5 who helped team members stop perseverating on data about past performance. Levy, it turned out, was an exceptional coach. Upon joining the team he was struck by its lack of forethought and by an overemphasis on past performance. (In team meetings, you may recall, members plodded through thick notebooks that summarized the past performance of all the company's restaurants.) Levy could simply have accepted that as one of the requirements of membership on the senior team. Instead, he began working closely with the team leader to change the team's task process. He helped the leader reflect on how to elicit thoughtful, strategic discussion and how to discourage the team's relentless focus on the previous month's numbers. Levy's approach was subtle and effective. Not only did the team evolve and improve, but also, over time, he and his boss developed an exceptional working and personal relationship, and they continued to advise each other even after they were no longer working together.

Coaching by a team member often works best when the team leader has explicitly asked that person to take on coaching responsibilities for a specified period of time: "We should take some time now to look at how we're doing. Alejandra, I know you've done this before. Why don't you take us through it?" Alternatively, it may help to call on a member who is not deeply involved in the topic being addressed to serve as facilitator while the team works on that issue.

A cautionary note: there are limits to how much you should rely on any one team member to provide coaching. If overused, an individual can become typecast as the team coach and can be resented rather than respected as an equal participating member of the team. That risk is especially high, we have observed, if the individual is the senior leader from human resources. The natural tendency to look to HR for people matters can marginalize such an executive within the team, and that is not good for either the designated coach or the team as a whole. Moreover, when only one person provides team coaching, other members have little opportunity to develop their own coaching skills or develop a shared sense of responsibility for effective team processes.

A team member who serves as team coach, especially when she also coaches the leader, sometimes can become defensive and protective of the chief executive—in effect, an apologist for the leader's dysfunctions. Such was the case with Marcia Gliddens, a senior human resource executive and member of one team we studied. Gliddens was asked to coach her relatively immature and dysfunctional chief executive. This CEO was a chronic violator of team norms, ineffective at managing his own behavior, and incapable of personally coaching his senior team. Although Gliddens was a good coach and actually helped the CEO change some of his more egregious behaviors, over time she became defensive about his continued inappropriate behavior. In rationalizing his ongoing antics to the team, she not only slowed his development but also lost credibility among her peers as a coach for the team.

Prescriptions for Coaching Your Team

Here are four prescriptions, based on our studies of senior leadership teams, that can help you coach your team well, eventually developing it into a group whose members are willing and able to skillfully manage their own team processes.

1. *Do not skimp on coaching.* Although your team is likely to develop at least modest self-correcting capabilities over time,

the members are much more likely to do so when they have skilled and authoritative coaching from you or someone you designate.

2. *If team coaching is not in your repertoire, get help.* You must model the norms if the team is going to adopt them, but an experienced and expert coach, whether from inside or outside your organization, can help you with team coaching. An objective outsider can hold up a mirror to the team process and give you and the team room to focus on the vital, substantive issues in your work as a team.

3. *Take timing seriously. When* you offer coaching to a team powerfully affects the impact of your coaching interventions. Beginnings are a good time for orienting your team to its core purpose and motivating members to take on the challenging team accountabilities you and they have developed. Watch for natural breakpoints in the team's work, such as halfway to a deadline or right after a major project is completed. Use those times to assess with your team how the work is going and to identify any changes that may be called for in what you are doing or how you are doing it. And always, without fail, take a little time for a debriefing at the end of a project or task cycle. That is when you, individual members, and the team as a whole can reflect on what has been learned and draw out the implications for how you want to work together in the future.

4. *Pay attention to the coaching skills of your team members.* Any team member, or the team members combined, may have the main coaching talent in your team. Reinforce that talent, draw on it, and make those people your allies in attending to effective team work processes.

Whatever resources you draw upon to get your team the hands-on coaching it needs, remember that there are crucial actions that remain your responsibility as leader. Ultimately, it is you who must provide the clarity of purpose, establish the rules of engagement, bring the right people to the table, give them meaningful and important team tasks, provide the team with ample organizational support, and overall create the substantial commitment that is required for effective teamwork. Without those elements, your stable of thoroughbreds will blaze its own trail—or more likely, trails—and that may be counter to the course you are trying to run.

We reiterate these conditions—the essential and enabling conditions we have discussed throughout this book—because it is their presence that makes competent coaching of a leadership team possible. They provide the platform for effective teamwork. They minimize the number of process problems that arise in the team, and they increase the likelihood that competent coaching will result in robust and constructive discussions and team decision making.

How prepared are you for the challenge of designing, supporting, and coaching your senior leadership team? Do you have in your repertoire the leadership competencies that will serve you well in taking those steps to make your team great? If not, what are your options for developing them? We address these questions in chapter 8.

PART III

LEADING A
LEADERSHIP TEAM

We have covered a lot of ground in this book. We've described guidelines for deciding whether you need a senior leadership team, we've talked about strategies for designing such a team, we've explained what is required to coach senior teams well. We have summarized the material in the book as six conditions—three essentials and three enablers—that our research has shown to powerfully shape the likelihood that senior teams will become great. The best team leaders draw on the full range of their personal skills and styles to get those six conditions in place for their senior leadership teams, and to keep them there. No matter which strategies leaders use to build and coach their teams, competent senior team leadership always involves focused attention and effort, considerable intellectual and action skill, and the capability to compellingly articulate a vision for the top team.

This concluding part addresses the implications of these leadership requirements for chief executives themselves. We identify the cognitive, emotional, and behavioral capacities that creating a great senior team demands. We explore the implications of those demands for the development of senior leaders in organizations. And we end by highlighting those of our research findings that have the most significant implications for what it takes to make senior teams great.

8

Develop Your Own Team
Leadership Competencies

S ome seven decades ago, telecommunications executive Chester
Barnard wrote a book that turned out to be a classic in explaining
what executives must do to help their organizations succeed. The
title of the book, still in print, is *The Functions of the Executive*. We draw
your attention to the second word in that title. Barnard recognized that
getting people to work together to pursue organizational objectives depends on getting certain executive functions accomplished. What counts
is what you get done, and not your personality, pedigree, or position—or
even how you go about doing it.[1]

In writing this book we have benefited from decades of research on
the leadership of teams and organizations, as well as from our own studies
of senior executive teams. We find that Barnard's focus on functions has
held up remarkably well: success in leading executive teams depends not
nearly as much on a leader's style of acting as on what needs to be done
to foster effective performance. And because there are any number of ways
to get done what needs to be done, there is no need to specify the particular behaviors a senior team leader should exhibit in specific circumstances—a trap that snares many authors who write about leadership.

What are the critical functions that need to be fulfilled in making a senior leadership team great? As we have shown in the previous chapters, two general functions dominate all others.

1. *Getting the leadership team set up right.* This function includes making sure that the team is a real team, with clear membership, genuine interdependence, and reasonable stability over time. It involves specifying a clear and compelling direction or purpose for the team. It means choosing for your team the right number of the right members, people who will bring to the work the knowledge, skill, and competencies that are most needed. It involves creating specific team tasks and norms that are consistent with the team's overall purposes and account-abilities. And it means providing contextual support—arranging for the resources and support that can help the team perform superbly. Getting these conditions in place sets the stage for great leadership team performance, but it does not guarantee that your team members will take full advantage of the favorable circumstances you have created. For that, the second leadership function also must be fulfilled.

2. *Providing competent real-time team coaching.* This is what people usually have in mind when they talk about team leader-ship: hands-on guidance, coaching, and teaching as members work together. This second leadership function sometimes is handled by the chief executive, but it also can be done by members themselves or by a competent outsider. Even when well executed, however, these hands-on leadership activities cannot bring out greatness if the team was not set up right in the first place. A poor basic design dooms even superb real-time leadership.

Effective leadership of senior teams, then, requires that both of the critical functions be fulfilled. If the first function is the equivalent of get-ting electrical circuits properly wired, the second releases and manages the power that flows through those circuits. Both are necessary, but nei-ther, by itself, is sufficient.[2]

As we have noted throughout this book, the good news is that there is no one right way to accomplish these leadership functions. What is com-fortable for you may feel awkward to someone else. What is easy for that person may be hard for you. And what works well for you may backfire for one of your counterparts. Although you can learn from observing how other chief executives lead their teams, be cautious about any impulse to mimic the specific leadership styles of the best of them. You inevitably will be a pale copy of anyone you try to imitate. But you can be an interesting and effective one-of-a-kind if you rely on your own unique strengths and preferences in setting up and leading your executive team.

Some specific competencies can help you get the most from your own style of team leadership. By developing these competencies, you increase the likelihood that you will take care of those two critical team leadership functions efficiently and well. Absent these competencies, you run a greater risk of encountering problems in leading your senior team—for example, experiencing unexpected negative reactions to your well-intentioned initiatives or putting favorable conditions in place that come undone the minute you turn your attention to something else.

In the pages that follow, we draw on the experiences of the chief executives we have studied to identify and illustrate the competencies that are most helpful in leading executive teams. Note that we focus here on skills that we have found to be particularly relevant to senior team leadership; additional competencies, not discussed here, address other aspects of the chief executive's overall role.[3]

As shown in figure 8-1, there are four groups of competencies. The left column identifies those that are especially helpful for the first leadership function, getting the team set up right. The right column shows the competencies that help leaders fulfill the second function, leading the team

FIGURE 8-1

Key competencies for leadership of a senior team

	Team design	Hands-on leadership
Diagnostic	Organizational acuity Conceptual skill	Monitoring skill Empathy
Execution	Ability to decide Political skill	Ability to inspire Coaching skill

well in real time. Two subsets are identified for each column: diagnostic competencies (the top row) and execution competencies (the bottom row).

Diagnostic as well as execution competencies are needed. Just as physicians are not likely to provide competent treatment if they make a wrong diagnosis, senior team leaders risk taking unhelpful or counterproductive actions if they have a poor understanding of the leadership team and its performance situation. It also is true, however, that even an excellent diagnosis is of no use if the chief executive cannot help a senior team solve problems that are getting in its way or exploit emerging opportunities.

After describing and illustrating each of the competencies listed in figure 8-1, we invite you to assess your own standing on each of them. Then we explore alternative strategies you can use to strengthen those competencies on which you grade yourself lower than you would like.

Competencies for Team Design

Our research shows that team leaders need four competencies if they are to design excellent executive teams. Those competencies are organizational acuity, conceptual skill, the ability to make decisions, and political skill. Let's look at each of them in detail.

Organizational Acuity

When Lou Gerstner arrived at IBM in 1993, he did not know the computer business and did not yet have a vision for the company. Indeed, he actively rebuffed those who urged him to articulate a lofty corporate vision. "Don't ask me about my vision," he said, "because I don't have one. We're broke. We're going to fix that. Vision is not what is broke." What Gerstner had was an almost uncanny ability to sort through the ideas and issues that crossed his desk, distinguishing those that were substantive and important from those that were fluffy and distracting. He may not have known much about the computer business when he started, but his track record shows that he was a very fast learner.

The best leaders of executive teams have the same quality: a level of organizational astuteness that enables them to quickly understand how the organization and its leadership team operate and to prioritize the issues that most urgently require the team's attention. Consider the experience of Zoe Renfield, president of the innovation center in a large consulting firm. Traditionally, the center's mission had been to develop the capability of consultants worldwide, who in turn were responsible for strengthening the capabilities of the firm's clients. In recent years, however, the firm's overall strategy had gradually changed, with the semi-autonomous consulting practices now having much more responsibility than before for developing their own consultants. There was no organizationwide meeting to discuss the change, no transition plan, and no public announcement. It was, instead, the kind of gradual evolution that is common as corporations respond to changes in their competitive contexts.

As the changes began to unfold, Renfield quickly realized that they would have significant implications for the innovation center. "What made us unique in the firm—our developmental work with consultants—is not so unique any more," she told us. "As the practices do more and more of that work, we have to rethink our own purpose and contribution." She convened a series of meetings with her top management team to generate ideas about the implications of the broader change.

These discussions generated a new purpose for the center: to focus much more on research and development than previously and to become the thought leaders for the firm as a whole. "We'll generate the new ideas and push the frontiers of what the firm can contribute to its clients," she told us, "but the practice leaders will be the ones who train and develop their consultants in actually using those innovations." Because Renfield was quick to discern and make sense of the changes that were occurring outside her division, she was able to work with her senior team to rethink the innovation center's purpose before others even noticed that its historical mission was no longer either as unique or as strategically important as it had been.

Conceptual Skill

Ed Reilly and his leadership team at a chain of pizza restaurants were struggling to come up with a way of understanding their business that could guide their work to strengthen the brand. Nothing they generated quite fit the bill until one night Reilly awoke with a start from a deep sleep. He shook his wife awake. "I finally got it! We're in the *transportation* business. We transport pizzas to customers when they need them—that's what we do." It is probably just as well that history does not record his wife's reaction. But the idea was so powerful that, sooner or later, each member of Reilly's seven-member senior management team claimed to have personally had that reorienting insight.

For Reilly and his team, viewing the business as mainly transportation was a breakthrough idea. For most senior teams, developing a concept of the enterprise's core purpose is a gradual and incremental process. That is also true of conceptualizing the team's purpose. The move from identifying the interdependencies among team members to extracting the larger theme that makes for a compelling purpose requires great conceptual skill—and often more than one try. Recall the example of Bob Lee, the leader of Millennium Chemical, whose team relaunch we described in chapter 3. When Lee articulated a team purpose of growing the company "organically and through acquisition" he had not yet seen how he could identify the unique contribution that a small set of individuals, working interdependently, could make to the enterprise. The differences between what he had expected they would do and what they actually did provided the clues he needed to see how to conceptualize what he needed from the team.

Lee chose to relaunch his team to establish his newly conceptualized purpose; other leaders have responded to new realizations by holding clarifying conversations with the team. Whatever the process, developing a compact and powerful understanding of what the leadership team is about can spell the difference between a team that fragments and one that focuses intently on the handful of highest-leverage issues. Certainly all members of a senior team can contribute to the conceptualization of its work. But it is you, the chief executive, who have a special opportunity—and obligation—to guide that activity. And that requires at least a modicum of conceptual skill, the ability to gather in your mind the multiple relevant facts and ideas and then bring them together in a framework that others can understand and use.

When a leader cannot conceptualize the work of the team as an interdependent group, members are not likely to come together as a team to accomplish shared purposes. For example, Len Tesch, one CEO we studied, habitually defined his team's accountabilities (e.g., the team had shared responsibility for identifying trends in the market) and then just as habitually disaggregated those accountabilities into individual tasks: "You take Asia/Pacific, and you take Europe/Middle East/Africa," and so forth. The team members stitched together their contributions as best they could into a picture of global trends. But Tesch's chronic frustration with his team's inability to gel did not disappear until his trusted adviser helped him see how he could reconceptualize the work as a team task.

Ability to Decide

Many of those who view chief executives as people who mainly make decisions and take actions would be surprised by how much they vary in their readiness, willingness, and ability to do that. To make the call at the right time can be a challenge even for experienced chief executives. When a decision needs to be made about the composition or the agenda of the senior team, for example, some leaders move too quickly ("Let's just do it and get it behind us"), whereas others wait too long ("Let's hold off for a while and see whether we can get more answers to our questions before we act"). The best senior team leaders thread their way between these two temptations.

A leader's indecisiveness can destroy even a strong team, as illustrated by the experience of a large fast-food chain's top management team. The CEO, Ralph Reedy, was one of the brightest we have ever studied. He could analyze any issue from multiple perspectives, often generating fresh insights about problems that had been driving his team to frustration, and he could effortlessly spin out the long-term implications of various decision alternatives. The problem was that he was so good at analysis that he incapacitated himself—and rendered his senior team nearly impotent.

At one memorable meeting, the team had a long and difficult discussion about strategies for reversing a serious downturn in the firm's business. Then with Reedy's participation, members finally came to a decision about how they would move forward. They left the meeting feeling that it had been a difficult decision but the right one. Then, less than an hour later, everyone received an e-mail from Reedy saying that he had given the decision additional thought and they would need to revisit it at a subsequent meeting. It does not take many such episodes for members to conclude that their team meetings are a waste of time.[4]

Reedy had difficulty acting quickly and definitively. Leon Ferrer, the new chief executive of an information technology organization, had the opposite problem. Hired to turn around an organization whose performance had been spotty at best, the executive decided that the first thing he needed to do was to form a new team consisting of people he had chosen.

Within three months, Ferrer had replaced the chief operating officer, the head of infrastructure, and the head of networking with new hires from outside the organization. The problem was that these new individuals, although technically competent, had no local knowledge of the technical systems—knowledge that resided more in the heads of the departed team members than in technical manuals. In short order, systems began crashing, additional staff bolted, and Ferrer was barely able to hold on to his own job. Being too fast to decide can be as risky as being too slow—for the CEO as well as for the enterprise.

Wilhelm Tare, the chief executive of a metropolitan hospital, got it about right. In his first months at the hospital, Tare spent a great deal of time listening, watching, and learning. He identified a number of norms and practices that were impeding the work of the team he had inherited and that he believed were slowing improvements in the quality and efficiency of hospital services. When Tare eventually made his move, it was a big one: he fired the chief of surgery. This physician had the highest status and most power at the hospital but also was the person who symbolized and most vigorously enforced the norms that were slowing organizational improvements. Tare did not move too quickly, nor did he wait too long. His well-timed, decisive act opened up additional opportunities for constructive change at the hospital and, in the process, significantly strengthened its senior management team.

Whenever a significant leadership decision must be made, there always is some uncertainty. And when there is uncertainty there is anxiety. Is this the right decision? Have I consulted sufficiently with team members? Should I wait a little longer before deciding? Or have I already waited too long? Deciding too quickly and letting a decision go unmade can reduce your anxieties—but often at the cost of making a low-quality decision or losing the engagement of the leadership team. Developing competence in managing your personal anxiety, therefore, can significantly strengthen your ability both to get in place the organizational conditions for team effectiveness and to help your senior team make difficult organizational decisions.

Political Skill

Political behavior is sometimes viewed as backstage wheeling and dealing with little regard for the truth. That view is unhelpful for a senior team leader. Political activities almost always are essential for getting teams set up and supported well, and the best executives know how to achieve political ends without violating their personal ethical standards.

Only the most naïve of senior leaders would imagine that they can create the structures and systems that are needed for senior team effectiveness simply by sending a memo or making an announcement. Creating the optimal conditions takes careful preparation as well as a finely honed sensitivity to the timing of your actions and no small measure of skill in dealing with others.

Preparation, often overlooked, is real leadership work. It involves doing whatever you can to expand and deepen your knowledge about the changes your enterprise most needs, sharing that vision with others, building a coalition that is ready to provide support, and then taking initiatives to align the interests of powerful and potentially skeptical people whose cooperation you need.

Doing all that can take time and require considerable patience. Alain Bernard, president of a large European automotive parts company, wanted to recompose his senior team. He felt that it was not appropriate for his predecessor, who now was chairman of the board of directors, to continue as a team member. The predecessor's skills were redundant with those of other members, and the new CEO did not want to deal with leftover issues from the preceding administration. He wanted instead to chart his own fresh course for moving the enterprise forward.

But Bernard did not immediately remove his predecessor from the top team. To do so, he told us, would have been viewed as disloyal by other senior executives—and loyalty was a highly valued aspect of the organization's culture. So Bernard waited. Only when he had established his own track record as chief executive, and in the process developed a cadre of team members who now felt loyal to him, did he make his move.

Sometimes the right time to make a significant move is never. That was the conclusion reached by Hein Grecht, chief executive of a governance body that supports the work of a number of Roman Catholic hospitals. Among the trade-offs managed by this senior team was how to help member hospitals provide high-quality medical care while simultaneously maintaining their financial viability—and do it all within a religious context that required providing services to some people who did not have the means to pay for them.

One member of the senior team was eighty-year-old Sister Beatrice, a member of the religious order that owned the health care system. Although Sister Beatrice's formal role did not warrant her being on the top team, she had, as the CEO put it, "a direct line to the Vatican." So he retained her as a member, and her presence helped ensure that the religious character of the enterprise was respected in the team's norms and practices. Although most of the team's work involved wrestling with the business challenges of providing cost-effective, high-quality medical care, each meeting started and ended with a prayer. Sister Beatrice's presence on the team, Grecht said, helped the rest of the members, including himself, stay focused on the reason they were in the hospital business at all.

To provide adequate support for their own teams, senior leaders often must deal with peers in other parts of the business. One of us recounted the story of Hank, a manager who headed the production operation of a medium-sized manufacturing concern. His team needed the active cooperation and support of the heads of maintenance and engineering, support that historically they had provided grudgingly if at all. It happened that Hank's organization was located near some mountainous back country where he and his managerial peers regularly went to hunt game. And Hank was the best-outfitted manager of them all; in the status hierarchy of the outdoors, he ranked much higher than his colleagues. One year, early in the deer season, he invited the heads of maintenance and engineering to join him for a couple of days of hunting. Around the campfire on that trip began a series of conversations that extended over most of a year and eventually resulted in a fundamental improvement in the quality of the relationships between his team and theirs.[5]

Hank exhibited considerable political skill in arranging for his team to get the support it needed. He could not have achieved it by relying only on his managerial authority, nor through regular organizational channels. Politically savvy leaders such as Hank exhibit persistence and initiative to engage and align the interests of others to secure resources or remove constraints on team processes. And if one strategy doesn't work, they think of others they might try, or about a better time to take an initiative, or about other persons or groups that might lend a hand. Senior leaders who have such skills and use them well with their colleagues can do a great deal to free their teams from obstacles that may be impeding their performance.

Competencies for Hands-on Team Leadership

Like team design, superb hands-on team leadership requires a repertoire of competencies: monitoring skill, empathy for others, the ability to inspire your team, and coaching skill. In the sections that follow we discuss these competencies in detail.

Monitoring Skill

Just as organizational acuity is a prerequisite for designing a senior leadership team, the capability to discern and make sense of what is going on within the team is a prerequisite for effective hands-on team leadership.

Unfortunately, senior team members often keep the chief executive from seeing those aspects of their interaction that the boss most needs to know. To protect themselves (or you), team members may put on a charade. They may make it appear, for example, that they are working together more harmoniously than they really are, or that they are on top of team issues that in fact are confounding and distressing them. Whatever the reason, the absence of good data about your team's internal dynamics can result in your being blindsided when things finally erupt, something that tends to happen at critical, stressful times when you most need competent, coordinated teamwork.

The ability to monitor team dynamics, therefore, is a key competence for leaders of senior teams, and developing this skill is well worth the investment of time and energy. Even senior leaders who have considerable monitoring competence usually can benefit from assistance in making sense of the internal dynamics of a team—a trusted observer. This is someone who is in a position to observe team dynamics, who is competent in interpreting them, and who can give you the straight, unvarnished story of what is going on in the team.

Although trusted observers often advise a leader during a time of private reflection, they also can be helpful during team discussions, especially in probing for feelings or perspectives that may make some members uncomfortable. A question as simple as, "Would it be helpful to hear Georgia's views about this?" often can bring to the table matters that otherwise would be kept out of sight.

Stacy King, the chief operating officer of a large multinational electronics company, served as a trusted observer for Arn Emory, the chief executive. Emory was stunned that members of his top team, the regional heads of the business, were not following through on a strategic initiative that the team itself had helped to develop: to focus on global rather than regional marketing of the firm's products. "Why do they not work *together* on this?" Emory asked.

King called Emory's attention to exchanges in team meetings that suggested that members were unwilling to publicly own up to their real views about implementing the new strategy. Armed with the diagnostic data King had provided, Emory intervened with the team to increase members' willingness to candidly share their views with one another—and with him.

King herself was a member of the organization's senior team. In other cases, the trusted observer is an internal or external consultant, someone who can help the chief executive monitor the team and in the process develop the leader's own monitoring competence. The risk, of course, is that the consultant will be drawn into doing more monitoring than competence building. That can be great for a consultant's job security or a leader's feeling of being well supported, but it is not useful for strengthening the chief executive's monitoring skill or the leadership team's self-management capabilities.

Structured tools also can help. In our own work with senior teams, we use the Team Diagnostic Survey (TDS), an instrument that provides an assessment of a team's strengths and weaknesses on the conditions for effectiveness that have been discussed throughout this book.[6] Although the TDS has been validated for use with senior leadership teams, it is only one of a large number of structured instruments that are available to help leaders and their teams monitor team dynamics.

All these tools—trusted observers, consultants, and structured instruments—can be valuable in helping you monitor the progress and dynamics of your senior team. They can supplement, but never entirely supplant, your own responsibility for attending to and tracking what is going on in the team. And, of course, the most powerful diagnostic instrument of all is the team itself. When all team members are contributing not only to their collective work but also to the ongoing assessment of how the team is functioning, then your team will achieve a level of maturity that can spur an ever-ascending spiral of learning and performance.

Empathy

How important is interpersonal sensitivity in senior management teams made up of hard-driving individual producers? Our research suggests that it is crucial: unless half or more of the team members scored high on this capability, the team was not likely to make it into the "outstanding" category. How about the team leader? Is there a special need for chief executives to be able to empathize with the feelings of their team members?

An exchange among members of the senior team at a Latin American textile company is instructive. Team members had a complaint that is common in leadership teams: "We don't trust one another." When asked for an example, one member explained that he could not count on others to attend to, let alone care about, matters that concerned him. In his view, the team members were looking only at their own patches, and not at those being tended by others or at the whole garden. As the team began discussing the status of a major project that would affect all members, it looked as if the trust issue was going to surface again.

Janet Fieri, who was responsible for the project being reviewed, sat quietly for a while as other members complained about the project and characterized it as being "in trouble." Eventually Fieri could contain herself no longer and reported, with some emotion, that many of the things that her peers were saying needed to be done to get the project back on track already *had* been done. At that point, Madelina Guerrero, the CEO, intervened: "Janet, I completely understand your frustration. These kinds of things often happen for this kind of project, and we all need to understand that it may take several iterations before we get it right." It was a small thing, but in that brief comment Guerrero showed empathy for what Fieri was feeling—and did so in a way that both gave her a bit of support and signaled to other members that a little more patience and a little less blame might be appropriate.

Here's another example. During a leadership team meeting at a large financial services organization, Jann Wills, the human resources executive who had responsibility for planning the firm's holiday party, announced that it had become necessary to change the party's location. The senior vice president of customer services responded that the venue change would be a big problem for his people, and he showed signs of launching into a longer speech about the matter. Bernard Elias, the chief executive officer, did not let it happen. "Let's just let Jann handle this," he said. "It's his job, he's quite competent to deal with the change, and I'm sure he will help you resolve any concerns that you or your people may have." This mild intervention headed off what Elias sensed was going to be a large debate about a small issue. He showed empathy both with Jann Wills (who was about to come under attack) and with the customer services manager (who was going to have to communicate an unwelcome change to his people). At the same time, he protected the team's agenda for the day, which had zero time allocated for a debate about the location of the firm's holiday party.

The leaders of both of these senior teams exhibited empathy but in very different ways—Guerrero by sensing and responding to Fieri's feelings of frustration, and Elias by sensing and then heading off what was likely to be an exchange that would have been unpleasant and unnecessary. What do you predict would have happened if the leaders of these teams had not been empathic with the feelings of their members? In both cases, antagonisms likely would have been fueled, members would have marshaled additional evidence to show that their teammates could not be trusted, and the teams' capacity to work together would have been eroded, if only slightly. And with each additional episode of this kind, those small erosions gradually build into a larger pattern of mistrust and nondisclosure—the opposite of what is needed for real teamwork.

If empathy is helpful for small problems of the kind just described, it is essential for large problems that threaten a senior team's main purposes, such as dealing with a major collective failure, correcting chronically unacceptable performance by a team member, or implementing an organizational realignment that threatens the turf of one or more members. To be empathic as a leader does not mean that you provide false reassurance that such matters are not very consequential or that the big problems should be set aside to be dealt with offline. It means instead that you can sense members' feelings, accept them as real and understandable, and deal with them as an integral and necessary part of managing a senior team and its work.

Ability to Inspire

It goes without saying that chief executives are expected to have passion for their organizations and lofty aspirations for their future. Most chief executives care deeply about their enterprises. But having passion is insufficient; senior leaders also must get the others in their organizations to share it. Roger Enrico, while CEO of PepsiCo, once said that he spent 99 percent of his time trying to create a common vision for the company and get everyone aligned with it, using all the resources he could command, from language and symbols to decisions about agendas, rewards, and personnel.

That Enrico's message got through was evident in a conversation one of us had with a member of his leadership team whose main work was in the company's Frito-Lay division. That division manufactures and markets snacks including potato chips, not a product about which people get wildly excited. This team member couldn't wait to tell us about his recent vacation: "I went to Scotland to tour the potato fields there. It's been a really great year for potatoes." He then launched into an extended description of what it takes to grow a good potato and why the growing season is important in making great potato chips. His passion for his organization and what it does was infectious—and this from someone whose main responsibility at Frito-Lay was to manage the division's finances.

The contrast with a visit we had to a large computer company could not have been more stark. New electronic technologies are perhaps more inherently interesting to most people than potato chips, but you would never know it from a visit to this company's headquarters. Executives were busy with their jobs, and there was a lot of talk about finances, personnel, and all the other matters that are involved in running a large enterprise. But there was nothing about the company's products, not even about an innovative computer system that was soon to be brought to market. Leaving the headquarters complex at the end of the day, one consultant remarked, "If I didn't know the name of this company, I wouldn't even know they make computers!" Whatever vision the chief executive may have had for his company and its products had not gotten through to his leadership team nor, through it, to the rest of the organization.

What does it take for a chief executive to inspire a leadership team with a vision, to get members to focus intently and passionately on what is special about the enterprise? One popular image is that of a leader on a podium, revving up the troops with a rousing talk. That can help, and if you are an inspirational speaker you should of course take the pulpit whenever you have the chance. But what if you are neither comfortable nor particularly effective in giving talks that bring people to their feet?

There are many other ways to inspire, as was taught to his leadership team by Don Burr, the founder of People Express Airlines. Burr believed deeply in the power of inspirational leadership and was himself superb on the podium. "Nothing is more important than charismatic leadership," he told his senior managers at a training session one day. "And if you doubt that, just look at what Mike does with his team." That caught everyone's attention, because Mike, a pilot who ran the company's information technology group, was quiet and a little shy. "Mike doesn't stand up and make long speeches like I do," Burr explained. "But his understanding of our precepts and his deep commitment to our customers shines through in everything he says and does. He has his own special kind of charisma. And that's what I expect of you, to use your special gifts, whatever they may be, to inspire others to share your vision for our company."

The lesson Burr taught his team is especially germane as senior leadership teams become more demographically diverse. What might be called the "cheerleader model" of inspirational leadership is neither comfortable for nor well practiced by executives from some countries and cultures. In one large global firm, for example, Asian leaders were not winning slots on senior management teams. Why not? "They do not have the kind of passion that we need at the top," one executive explained. "Most of them are missing that important element of our leadership profile."[7]

Senior Asian executives objected to this characterization. The exchange went roughly as follows. "We have just as much passion as you do—we just show it differently." How? "By our dedication—our long hours, hard work, and long tenure with the company." But how do you inspire others? That's also an important part of being a senior leader here. "Being bubbly is not consistent with our culture." But if you are a senior leader, you have to inspire everybody, not just other Asians. How are you going to do that?

It seemed for a while as if the conversation had reached a stalemate. Then someone remembered Kimura-san, a senior Asian manager who did inspire his team members. And he did so without "jumping up and down and swearing a lot," which is how one Asian executive characterized the style of leadership to which he objected. Eventually, it was agreed that senior Asian managers had much to learn from Kimura-san—and also that each of them would similarly have to find his own unique way of providing teams the kind of inspirational leadership that Kimura-san brought to his.

Inspirational leadership is indeed an essential competence for the leaders of senior teams. But there is no one best way to provide it. The key is to identify which of your skills and styles can best be used to create in others the passion you feel for your work and then to hone and develop those resources as one core element in your personal repertoire of team leadership skills.

Coaching Skill

Senior leadership teams are often seriously undercoached, in part because few CEOs have much practice in shaping the interaction processes of a group of high-level executives. Yet coaching skill is essential if you want your leadership team to identify and enforce constructive norms, to conduct vigorous but focused discussions, and to learn from its work over time.

Two strategies for strengthening your coaching skills are first, to develop a repertoire of good questions to ask, and second, to hone your sense of timing. Good questions are a widely useful team coaching tool for several reasons. First, with a repertoire of good questions, a chief executive doesn't have to be the only expert on group process in the team. Asking questions about, for example, what the team sees as its strengths and weaknesses or what has helped and hurt its effectiveness allows you to draw on the coaching smarts of other members while at the same time using your authority to see that the team process gets the attention it needs.

Moreover, when working on a set of diagnostic questions, team members are engaged in an interdependent task, and that contributes to their experience of being a real team and prevents them from developing a dependency on their leader for all coaching. And questions kick a team into a reflective mode, which deepens their discussions and increases the chances that members will be open to learning something, both from their own reflections and from each other.

Conducting a good midcourse review or an endgame debrief, for example, is largely a function of insisting that the team take the time to reflect and then asking members questions about their successes ("What made it such a success?") and disappointments ("What should we do differently next time?"). Most of the examples of effective coaching interventions we described in chapter 7 relied on questions of this nature. The coach working with Massi's team at the global food ingredients company, for example, helped the team leverage its successful experience in South America by asking, "What made that meeting so effective?" The team's collective work on that question allowed members to repeat what they had done well before. But keep one caution in mind: be careful not to ask questions in ways that suggest you already know the right answer. If team members are each guessing in turn and waiting for the leader's nod or headshake, that is a sign that it would be better to pose a more open-ended question.

Taking advantage of midpoints and endgames as opportunities for constructive coaching underlines the importance of a second element of coaching skill: good timing. Timing can be a difficult high-wire act. Sometimes you will be so immersed in the substantive work of your team that an opening for coaching will pass by unnoticed—and when you do notice, it is too late to do anything. Other times you will see your team start to slip off track and feel a strong inclination to step in immediately to redirect the team's course. Suggesting that a team reexamine its focus is an appropriate intervention, but teams are not always open and ready for such coaching. Although there are predictable times in a team's life when members are open to reflection, right in the middle of intense work is not among them. So at times you will need to suppress your impulse to intervene immediately and instead wait for a better moment.

Rooney Anand, chief executive of Greene King—one of the United Kingdom's most successful brewing and pub companies—told us that he still struggles with the issue of timing. There are times when he would like nothing more than to jump in and offer an insight, comment, solution, or other intervention. But he has recognized that such moments can take the team off course. "My passion and desire to sort problems out, to rectify things, kicks in," he says. "But as a result of my behavior, the team becomes cranky or shuts down."

So, as he describes it, Anand resists the urge to offer suggestions during ongoing discussions, particularly if the team has built momentum. Rather, he scribbles notes and offers feedback as part of his debrief after the meeting.[8] Experimenting with the right times to offer reflections about team processes, as Anand is doing, can be an excellent strategy for learning how to tune your coaching actions to those times when your team is ready and able to take advantage of them.

How Do You Stand on the Team Leader Competencies?

Now that you have reviewed the key competencies for senior team leadership and have seen ways that other leaders exhibit (or fail to exhibit) them, we invite you to take a moment to reflect on your own competency profile. Following is a self-test that can help you do that. We ask first about design competencies, and then about hands-on leadership competencies. Score yourself on each skill as follows:

5 = A core competency of mine. I rely on this in my leadership work and am confident it is well established in my repertoire.

4 = A strength; could use some additional attention.

3 = Not sure. I see signs that I have it and use it, and other signs that I do not.

2 = A relative weakness of mine. I rarely use it and am not confident that I am effective when I do.

1 = I do not use this competency and am pessimistic about becoming able to do so.

Strengthening Your Competency Portfolio

Quite a bit is known about training procedures that can help people develop new skills or hone existing ones. We know that leaders cannot master skills by reading books, listening to lectures, or doing case analyses. Instead, to develop leadership competencies almost always involves intensive practice, detailed feedback, and reiteration. Given these requirements, what are some realistic options for effectively rounding out your set of team leadership competencies?

Here are three general strategies for expanding your competencies: (1) seek personal coaching to develop certain competencies; (2) rely on other members of your senior team to help provide certain competencies; and (3) learn from experimentation and experience.

Team Leadership Competency Self-Assessment

Design Competencies

_____ Organizational acuity   _____ Ability to decide

_____ Conceptual skill   _____ Political skill

Average assessment for design competencies _____

Hands-on Leadership Competencies

_____ Monitoring skill   _____ Ability to inspire

_____ Empathy   _____ Coaching skill

Average assessment for hands-on leadership competencies _____

- Which are your strongest competencies? Which are most in need of further development?

- Looking now at your average grade for the two sets, are you relatively higher on design competencies or on hands-on leadership competencies?

- How do you stand on the *diagnostic* competencies (the left column in each set) relative to the *execution* competencies (the right column in each set)?

- All things considered, which competencies appear to present the highest points of leverage for further developing yourself as an executive team leader?

Personal Coaching

Like training in medical diagnosis, developing team diagnostic skills requires considerable practice in cognitively moving back and forth between conceptual frameworks (such as the set of conditions for effectiveness described in this book) and specific cases (such as examples of senior leadership teams that perform especially well or especially poorly) and comparing the similarities and discrepancies between the two.

Development of execution skills, on the other hand, generally requires observing highly skilled practitioners in action, followed by practice and feedback in doing what the positive models do, but in your own way and using your own style. Learning diagnostic and execution skills, therefore, is necessarily personalized. It is the kind of thing for which a competent personal coach can work wonders with a motivated senior leader. It also is labor intensive, time consuming, and at times expensive.

Personal coaching may be best focused on those aspects of your competency repertoire for which you are unsure of your standing and for which your assessments are not extremely low. A good coach, given knowledge of the competency you want to develop and an opportunity to observe you in action, can help you clarify your strengths and learning opportunities through detailed behavioral feedback. Moreover, a coach can describe instances in which you displayed a skill effectively or missed an opportunity to do so. Focus personal coaching on those competencies that you assessed as a 2, 3, or 4 on your self-test.

Sharing Leadership and Relying on Others

Sharing team leadership involves inviting certain members of the senior team to take on particular leadership functions on behalf of the team. The authority dynamics of senior teams seldom allow for emergent leadership of the kind seen in more egalitarian teams elsewhere in the organization. Therefore, you may need to explicitly invite members to share in the leadership of the team, because some may feel that spontaneously taking leadership initiative would be a usurpation of your legitimate authority.

We suggest you rely on others to supply those competencies that are your major points of weakness—those that you seldom or never exercise and have little desire or optimism about developing. Imagine, for example, that you are not particularly good at monitoring team dynamics and have little interest in developing that skill. That particular competency, as we have noted, is one that can be drawn from the leadership team itself. Similarly, we noted that the team's conceptual ability can help hone and clarify a team's understanding of its shared purposes. Experienced senior team leaders stay on the alert for times and circumstances when their own leadership can be supplemented by that of members of the team.

Learning from Experimentation

If personalized competency training is not on your near-term agenda, what alternatives are available for developing yourself as a senior team leader? One option is to learn from experience, exploiting learning opportunities wherever and whenever you find them in your daily work.

Ideally, senior team leaders behave in ways that foster continuous learning, both their own and that of team members, thereby helping a team and its members become increasingly capable. To learn continuously, however, requires that senior leaders move beyond well-practiced leadership habits and well-learned personal models of what makes for a great leadership team. What's needed is active experimentation with new and unfamiliar leadership strategies, and whenever there is experimentation expect that there also will be failure. More often than not, trying out a new grip or swing in golf or tennis results in worsened performance for a while. But these experiments also generate learning that cannot be had otherwise. The same is true for experimentation with leadership strategies and skills.

In fact, error and failure always provide more opportunities for learning than do success and achievement, because failures generate data that you can mine for insight into how you might improve your assumptions or your mental model of team leadership. Indeed, the bigger the failure, the greater the learning opportunity. To learn from failure requires that you ask questions that arouse anxiety (for example, about the validity of your deeply held assumptions or about personal flaws in your diagnosis or execution abilities). Learning from failure also requires that you gather data that can help answer those questions and then adapt your mental models and your behavior. These activities are not natural or comfortable acts, and they are especially unnatural for successful people who have limited experience in learning how to learn from error and failure.

Therefore, leading a senior team well requires a considerable degree of emotional maturity in dealing with your own anxieties as well as those of others. Emotionally mature leaders are willing and able to move toward anxiety-arousing events in the interest of learning about them rather than moving away to reduce anxieties as quickly as possible. Sometimes you may even need to take actions that temporarily raise anxieties, including your own, to lay the groundwork for subsequent learning or change.

Moreover, effective team leaders can inhibit impulses to act (for example, to correct an emerging problem or to exploit a sudden opportunity) until more data have appeared or until the team becomes open to the contemplated intervention. It takes a good measure of emotional maturity to resist the impulse to get things taken care of sooner rather than later, and to find ways to deal with your anxieties and emotions that neither deny their reality nor allow them to dominate your behavior.

Unlike the more cognitive and behavioral competencies we have discussed in this chapter, becoming more emotionally mature may be better viewed as a long-term developmental task than as something you can learn in a leadership course. Such learning cannot take place in the abstract or by analysis of someone else's failure. Instead, it involves working on real problems in safe environments with the explicit encouragement and support of others.

Only to the extent that you actively seek out such settings are you likely to develop the habit of continuous learning and, in doing that, provide a model for members of your senior team to pursue their own continuous learning. Once that begins to happen, the team itself becomes an additional valuable resource for accomplishing key leadership functions. Indeed, one of the best things about a great leadership team is that when the chief executive slips, something that inevitably happens, the other members of the team are there to take up the slack—and even, when necessary, to nudge the boss back onto the high ground.

9

What It Takes
to Make Them Great

In this concluding chapter, we distill and highlight those of our research findings that have the greatest implications for the actions of those who lead teams of leaders.

You May Not Need a Team

Teams at the top are something like audio amplifiers: whatever passes through comes out louder. Senior leadership teams that are well designed and well supported can achieve amazing synergy and agility—like Mozart in surround sound. The work of well-designed senior teams can surpass anything that can be achieved in a traditional organization where leaders' separate contributions are coordinated and controlled by a chief executive. Senior teams that go bad—badly designed ones—on the other hand, generate head-splitting static. Even if they do not spawn organizational fiascos, as sometimes happens, they move ahead slowly, erratically, and with much backtracking. The enterprises they lead are easily outperformed by smoothly functioning traditionally led organizations.

The question, then, is not whether organizations with teams at the top perform better or worse than those led by chief executives who have no real teams. Sometimes they are better, and other times they are worse. The question is whether your organization needs a senior leadership team—and, if it does, whether you can structure and support it so that it has the best possible chance of success.

If you look at almost any organization, you will see several kinds of leadership teams: those that exist mainly for exchanging information, those that the chief executive consults before making consequential decisions, those used for coordinating initiatives and operations, and those that make decisions about vital organizational issues. Informational and consultative teams require much less attention to their design, support, and leadership than do those responsible for coordinating the work of the organization and especially those that make decisions of great strategic consequence.

Because the stakes are high for coordination and decision-making teams, chief executives should be conservative about using them. The drawbacks of poorly functioning informational or consultative teams are modest. But a poorly functioning coordination team can create operational disasters. And a decision-making team that leads the organization on a grossly ill-advised course can threaten the viability of the enterprise. Indeed, you should form these latter two types of teams only if you can point to the tangible benefits they can create for the organization—and only if you can structure, support, and lead them well.

Even so, it is not necessary to get everything about the senior team perfect from the start. It is true that you should not proceed with creating a senior team unless you can establish the three essential conditions: a real team, a compelling direction, and the right people. Those conditions provide the foundation for further improving the team's prospects by gradually strengthening the three enabling conditions: a solid structure, a supportive context, and expert coaching. But it is asking too much of a chief executive, who may be launching his first senior leadership team, to get all six conditions firmly in place on the first try. It's like changing a tire: you tighten a few lug nuts, then work on the others, and then return to the first ones to firm them up.

Give a Top Team Vital Work

The agendas of the senior teams we studied never ceased to amaze us. Members were the most senior leaders of the entire enterprise, their time was extraordinarily valuable, and sometimes individuals would literally travel halfway around the world to attend a leadership team meeting. Yet what was addressed in those meetings was sometimes so far removed from the organization's vital issues that we could do little except shake our heads. (But, really, what *should* be done about those snowblowers, storage boxes, and banquet menus?)

If you are going to have a senior leadership team, it must be a real team that has real work. This means that everyone knows for sure who is on the team, members are kept together long enough to learn how to work well together, and the team has large tasks that are consequential for the enterprise as a whole.

There are a couple of major challenges in creating meaningful work for a senior leadership team. For one thing, it is harder to define the work of leading a large, complex enterprise than it is to define front-line organizational tasks such as making a product or providing a service. For example, how is a senior leadership team to know how well it is doing? Knowledge of results is a critical feature of well-designed work, but it can be maddeningly difficult to obtain reliable, trustworthy data about the performance of leadership teams that make long-term, strategic decisions. It is essential, therefore, for the team to spend time on the seemingly simple question, "How will we know how well our work turned out?"

A second challenge in designing work for a senior leadership team derives from the fact that the members come from different parts of the organization; serving on the senior team is no one's sole job. This means that all members will feel pulled in two directions: running their own parts of the enterprise, and contributing to leading the enterprise as a whole. Complaints about that fact of senior team life are common and sometimes vigorously expressed: "So which one of my two jobs do you want me to do?" a team member may ask. "Tell me, and I'll do it. But at least be clear about what you expect." The response of one chief executive: "I expect both. It's your job." There is an analogy here between work and family life. What does your family want—for you to be a wage-earner, a spouse, or a parent? Members of senior leadership teams must learn to manage simultaneously the two components of their executive leadership positions. To do one but not the other is equivalent to doing half the job.

The obligation of chief executives is to make sure that both components are worthy of the time, talent, and energy of the enterprise's most valuable executives. If you want the work of your leadership team to have the same priority as members' individual responsibilities, then it is essential that the work you give the team be vital to the organization, and not trivial or time-wasting.

Clarity Is Everything

It's not sufficient for the senior leadership team to have real work; it also must be crystal clear to members what the ultimate purpose of the work is. Our research shows that most members of senior teams recognize that their work as a team is highly consequential. They also understand that accomplishing it will be a challenge. The problem is that the challenge they actually experience often involves trying to figure out what the team is supposed to be doing.

Achieving clarity of purpose for a senior team is far from a trivial matter. The leadership responsibilities of CEOs can exceed the capabilities of even highly talented and energetic executives. Sharing those responsibilities with a senior team can be enormously helpful, perhaps even essential for some multidivision global corporations. But obtaining the benefits of a leadership team requires that executive responsibilities be clearly partitioned among the CEO, the other senior leaders of the enterprise, and the leadership team. Unless that is done rigorously and systematically, some team members may end up confused about the main purpose of the team. For most of the teams we studied, members described their team work as having more challenge than clarity. But for the most outstanding teams, the level of clarity about purpose was just as high as the level of challenge members experienced in working together.

One of the most common confusions we observed was between the purpose of the senior leadership team and the objectives of the organization as a whole. It is true that a senior team's work is shaped by the organization's overall strategy. There is no possibility of coming up with a compelling direction for a senior leadership team if the strategy of the enterprise is fuzzy and ambiguous. But the senior team is not the organization; it is a small group whose members work together to provide organizational leadership. The best chief executives recognize this difference and think carefully about how to set directions for their teams that leverage the full range of members' capabilities in the service of the enterprise's overall strategic objectives.

Achieving clarity about team direction need not—should not—be the exclusive province of the chief executive. If you actively involve team members in honing the team's purposes, it almost always generates ideas and insights that otherwise would have escaped notice. Once a team's main purpose has been set (provisionally, because it always is open for further refinement), the best chief executives then give the team a great deal of latitude to figure out the best way to accomplish their work as a team. There is no point in having a top team that merely executes the boss's directives; that would grossly underutilize members' capabilities and the team's potential. But make no mistake about who has the ultimate responsibility for setting the direction of the team: it is the chief executive.

Consider, for example, the difference between a chamber music group (such as a string quartet) and a full-size symphony orchestra. Both have a score that was created by a composer. The score sets the overall direction for both types of ensembles. But members of the string quartet work collaboratively to determine how best to interpret and render what the composer has written. The symphony orchestra, in contrast, has a conductor who dictates all the details of how the music is to be interpreted and played. Senior leadership teams should be more like string quartets—playing the score created by the chief executive—than like a symphony orchestra that is micromanaged by its conductor.

Derailers Can Kill a Senior Team

Some senior executives have much to contribute to an enterprise but cannot make those contributions as part of a team. Whether that inability is due to an absence of team skills or a disinclination of these individuals to work collaboratively with others, the team and the organization almost always are better off without them as senior team members.

The best chief executives work persistently with such individuals to make sure that they understand that participation in the senior leadership team is an essential part of their job. And they coach difficult members individually to help them develop the skills they need to contribute constructively to the team's work. Chief executives often are happily surprised by their success in helping someone whom others see as a team derailer become a valuable and valued team member.

Sometimes, however, the senior team leader must come to terms with the reality that it is not going to work out and recompose the team to exclude such individuals—in the words of one CEO, to "redraw the boundaries of the team" with the derailer on the outside. Because the individual still is a senior leader of the enterprise, someone whose contributions are important to its success, the derailer cannot simply be turned out to pasture to wander around. Instead, the chief executive must find ways to keep the individual closely involved in the team's work, although as a nonmember. Input is sought from the person and is brought into the senior team's deliberations. Team decisions are communicated promptly and fully. But the derailer no longer has the opportunity to slow, divert, or halt the interdependent work of the senior leadership team.

A word of caution here. It is a fact of group life that members tend to load their negative feelings onto the person who is most different from the majority. So if a senior team has only one person of a different race, gender, age, or some other obvious identifying characteristic, that person may come to be viewed as a "problem member." This situation is especially likely if the person also expresses unconventional views in team discussions—something he may well do, because his background or perspective differs from that of the majority. So care is required to avoid the trap of identifying someone who merely is different as a derailer, the one who is responsible for the team's problems. Wise senior executives recognize that such individuals can be extremely valuable resources for the team. They cut them from the group only reluctantly and after a good deal of exploration and coaching with both the individual and the team as a whole.

Team Norms Are Crucial

Of all the factors that we assessed in our research, the one that makes the biggest difference in how well a senior leadership team performs is the clarity of the behavioral norms that guide members' interaction. Team norms provide guardrails to lessen the chances that behavior will get off track; they also serve as something of a centerline, identifying the behaviors that members most seek and value in their interactions.

Teams with norms that foster competent teamwork (see chapter 5 for examples from our research) perform much better than those whose norms undermine collaboration (for example, a norm that encourages members to defend the views of their home organizations) or teams that have no shared expectations at all about appropriate member behavior.

As is the case for team purposes, the best team norms are few in number and clear in implication. If a team has seventeen behavioral norms, it might as well have none. No one, especially not the chief executive, can keep seventeen behavioral guidelines in mind. The same is true for norms that are abstract, such as, "Everyone should be constructive." What does it mean to be a constructive team member? There is no general answer to that question, because it depends on the particular needs of this particular team in this particular context at this particular time of its life.

What a leadership team needs, then, is a way to create norms about behavior that are uniquely helpful to this team. It ultimately is the chief executive's responsibility to do that. You may choose to set team norms entirely on your own, especially if your team is not yet mature or if you have compelling reasons for establishing certain norms with which members may initially disagree. In most cases, however, you probably will choose to involve team members in setting norms. An especially good time to do so is when a team is launched or relaunched with new members or onto a new track. You might set aside part of one meeting to raise with members the following two questions:

1. What are the one or two things we must always do as we work together if we are to become a great senior leadership team?

2. What are the one or two things we must never do, behaviors that keep us from using the full range of members' knowledge, skill, and experience?

A vigorous discussion is almost certain to ensue, one that is likely to generate a short, specific list of norms that all members had a say in defining and therefore understand and are willing to enforce.

Initiatives to establish team norms are likely to founder, however, when the membership or basic purpose of the team is unsettled. We cannot decide how we should work together if it is not clear who "we" are or what our purpose is. So the chances of a team coming up with norms of behavior that facilitate its work are low if the three essential conditions—a real team, a compelling purpose, and the right people—are not in place. Behavioral norms are a key feature of effective senior teams, but they cannot be erected on shifting sands.

Outstanding Leaders Give Serious Attention to the Senior Team

Our assessments of how the leaders of senior teams spend their time showed that they give most of their attention to team structure and context and the least attention to hands-on coaching of the team. This is not surprising, given that many people who arrive at the top of their organizations got there by paying close attention to the demands and opportunities in the organization's external environment and then structuring and leading their parts of the enterprise to meet those demands and to exploit emerging opportunities.

Our findings show that senior leaders' attention to the context of their teams is well warranted: the best of them do not skimp on the support and resources that their teams need. These leaders make sure that team successes are recognized and rewarded, and they arrange for the other support—from information and education to mundane material resources—that can facilitate the team's work. A senior team whose members are rewarded solely on the basis of their individual accomplishments, for example, or that attempts to carry out its work unsupported and on the cheap, is almost certain to experience roadblocks and diversions.

Too much emphasis on structural features and contextual support, however, can create difficulties. We found that the more attention a chief executive gives to coaching her senior leadership team, the better it performs; but the less mindful of her team and the more emphasis she places on working the external context, the less well the team performs. Would a CEO attend a board meeting without first taking the time to prepare, to lobby board members for backing on key initiatives, and to ensure the quality of staff preparations? Yet that level of thoughtful preparation and attention is not always tendered to the senior team and its work. There is a perverse reality here: the external activities that command most of the time and attention of chief executives extract a significant cost in the effectiveness of the leadership team. The most outstanding teams in our research were those whose leaders gave the same degree of thoughtful attention to their teams that they extended to external matters.

Many chief executives are not particularly skilled or experienced in hands-on team coaching, and that may be one reason they tend to focus on external matters with which they almost always are experienced and comfortable. There are numerous strategies for obtaining expert coaching when the chief executive is unwilling or unable to provide it. One is to invite members to share in facilitating team processes. Possibilities include an external consultant—who, in addition to coaching the team, works with the chief executive to develop her own coaching skills—or a senior organization member, not on the top team, who is an experienced and expert team coach. Another strategy is to invite a consultant to work with members to develop their skills in coaching one another and the team as a whole. This strategy has much to recommend it, because the amount of peer coaching is one of most telling signs of how well a leadership team is working; the more of it, the better.

Whatever strategy the chief executive uses, the objective is the same: to make plenty of competent coaching available to the senior team. How that coaching is best provided varies from team to team and from leader to leader.

Leading Senior Teams Is a Learned Skill

It is straightforward to specify what the leader of a senior team needs to know about top team effectiveness, and to identify the skills he needs so that he can use that knowledge in strengthening the senior leadership of the organization. Indeed, those topics are mainly what this book is about.

The challenge is how to help chief executives, who already have well-practiced habits of leadership, develop new ways of leading that are attuned to the special demands of leading senior teams. This is not something that can be taught in any traditional sense of the term. Indeed, chief executives can read this and other books and learn important lessons from them. They can attend executive seminars and retreats to expand their understanding of what it takes to create and support a superb team at the top. But ultimately, learning about senior team leadership involves unlearning some strategies that previously have served the leader well and developing new habits of thought and action that initially may be as uncomfortable as they are unfamiliar.

Those activities require settings for learning that challenge a leader's existing behavioral models and provide support from others in exploring alternative team leadership strategies. It is not a matter of being taught; instead, it is about putting yourself into situations in which you can learn. But where should you begin? What team leadership competencies should be highest on your personal learning agenda?

One way to address this question is to return to the self-test offered in chapter 8. Did you find that you were relatively stronger in the competencies involved in designing a team, or in providing hands-on leadership? Are you more skilled in diagnosing what is going on in a team, or in executing actions to strengthen the team? The answers to these questions can point you to the specific competencies that you may want to consider developing.

Here's another question, one that only you can answer: will you and your senior team benefit more from expanding the range of team leadership competencies you have, or in developing greater depth in those few competencies that are most critical for leading your senior team? Another way to approach this question is to consider what kind of support you would need in your work as a senior team leader and how comfortable you would be in seeking such support. A chief executive whose competencies reside mainly in one area, such as designing a team well, may need to invite others to share in other aspects of team leadership, such as the hands-on coaching of the team. By contrast, a chief executive who has a wide range of competencies may have wonderful versatility but may need to seek help from others for specific issues that require well-honed leadership skills.

There are no right answers to the questions we've posed. But they need to be addressed, because learning team leadership skills always requires a considerable investment of time and energy. You cannot obtain such learning merely by attending a seminar or two. Instead, it requires ongoing engagement in settings that provide not only content knowledge but also the opportunity to experiment with new ways of leading, to obtain trustworthy feedback about the impact of those new behaviors, and to practice the ones that work until they become well established in your repertoire.

It is wise, therefore, to be thoughtful and deliberate in choosing settings for developing your team leadership skills. Only those leader development programs that explicitly take on the challenge of providing settings for learning, rather than courses to take, are likely to help you enter into a journey of never-ending learning about team leadership—and, in the process, provide a model for others on your top team to follow in pursuing their own continuous learning.

Making Leadership Teams Great

Chief executives would never take their competitive or regulatory environments as given. They would take action to create a more favorable context for their enterprises. But many of them take almost everything as given when it comes to the composition, structure, and support of their teams of senior leaders. They accept as members all of their direct reports. They perpetuate a traditional agenda-setting process that occupies the team with matters that are inconsequential for the success of the enterprise. They allow whatever team norms as happen to develop over time to persist unexamined and unchallenged. They accept without question existing reward and information systems, no matter how unsuited they are for supporting the work of the senior team.

Accepting as given too many existing features of the team and organization can generate frustrations for team leaders and members alike. Sometimes, for example, trying to make do with an unsatisfactory situation can result in endless wheel-spinning and little real progress. In such cases, the frustrated chief executive may take the reins and make the call even without the much-needed ideas and contributions of other senior leaders. Understandably, senior team members notice this and conclude that if something is really important, they are pretty much irrelevant. That further erodes their commitment to the team and its work, perpetuating a pattern of dysfunction that everyone dislikes but no one knows how to fix.

The main message of this book is that *it doesn't have to be that way*. Our research has identified six conditions that, when present, strongly increase the likelihood (but, of course, do not guarantee) that a senior team will evolve into an efficient and nimble task-performing unit, one that captures and uses every available bit of knowledge, expertise, and experience in addressing an enterprise's most important challenges and opportunities. Indeed, our research showed that nearly half of the natural variation in how well senior leadership teams perform is determined by the degree to which the six conditions discussed in this book are present.

These conditions—the three essentials and the three enablers—are as easy to remember as they are challenging to create and sustain. But our research shows that the challenge is well worth taking on, because these conditions powerfully increase the chances of having a great leadership team. The benefits of having the six conditions in place are not only that immediate business decisions get made sooner and better but also that the team itself becomes more capable over time. And team members enter on a path of continuous growth and learning—not only about their own functional specialties but also about what it takes to provide the highest-quality senior leadership throughout an organization.

Notes

Chapter 1

1. Details of the Foodsolutions case have been published in a case study (Spreier, 2007).

2. Quotations are drawn from Bevilacqua (2006).

3. There are dozens of studies by the media and by consulting and search firms chronicling the decline of executive tenure. The data cited here come from Booz Allen Hamilton's CEO succession study by Lucier, Kocourek and Habbel (2005) and *Globe and Mail* (Schachter, 2002).

4. See Bennis (1997).

5. Advocates and critics of coleadership include Heenan and Bennis (1999) and O'Toole, Galbraith, and Lawler (2002).

6. For a treatment of dominance hierarchies in nature, see Diehl (2000). For a related treatment of collaboration within species, see Boehm (2001).

7. Trivers (1985), 53–57.

8. Charan (2005).

9. Hambrick (1997) makes the case that corporate and strategic *coherence* are vital to the success of any organization. He shows that coherence is largely a function of the degree to which senior executives can think and act as a team.

10. The research on top management teams to date (e.g., Kilduff, Angelmar, and Mehra, 2000; Krishnan, Miller, and Judge, 1997; West and Schwenk, 1996; and Wiersema and Bantel, 1992) has relied largely on measures of firm performance—such as return on assets, bankruptcy, or number of new patents—as indexes of the effectiveness of the management of a firm. All these outcomes are influenced by many factors—and often much more powerful ones—and not only actions taken by

a leadership team. For example, external environmental conditions that are highly favorable can lead to high returns, and the departure of key scientists can cause patent
rates to suffer. Moreover, even when senior team actions directly affect organizational outcomes, it is difficult to predict precisely when changes in performance will
occur. Finally, neither patent rates nor bankruptcies nor return on assets represents a
relevant measure for public and not-for-profit entities.

11. We adapted our effectiveness scales from Wageman, Hackman, and Lehman
(2005).

12. There is a long tradition of addressing top management as an influence on
firm performance (e.g., Barnard, 1938; Gupta and Govindarajan, 1984; Hambrick and
Mason, 1984; and Szilagyi and Schweiger, 1984). Much of that research has focused on
the effects of the demographic characteristics of senior team members on organization-
level outcomes, arguing that strategic choices are influenced by the backgrounds and
preferences of the top managers in a firm. This "upper-echelon" perspective is quite
different from that of our research. The work in that tradition typically selects organization leaders at a certain hierarchical level and above—whether or not they are
named as members of the leadership team—and does not attempt either to define a
team at the top or to study the actual interactions of any decision-making team.

13. The instrument, called the Team Diagnostic Survey, has been tested for relia-
bility and validity in measuring team design, process, and leadership. For a complete
description of its contents and psychometric properties, see Wageman, Hackman,
and Lehman (2005).

14. Leaders' competencies were assessed using coded behavioral event interviews (BEIs). BEIs are a well-established method of determining executive competencies, and the BEI methodology has been validated in numerous studies (McClelland,
1998).

A BEI consists of a 3.5-hour interview in which the interviewee is asked to
tell four stories about recent work experiences in great detail. BEIs are taped and
transcribed for analysis. To ensure that previously formed impressions do not influence the interview process or data obtained, interviewers are blind to the performance of the interviewees (except for whatever information the interviewee reveals in
the interview). Interviewees are asked for two "high points" when they felt particularly effective, and for two "low points" when things were more difficult or when they
felt less effective. Interviewees are asked for the details of what they did, said, thought,
and felt as they went through these experiences.

These interviews are coded for evidence of a wide range of leadership competencies. The competencies are empirically derived, meaning that the behaviors described are actual behaviors seen in hundreds of competency models and thousands
of individuals. For a more detailed treatment of the competency assessment methodology, see Spencer, McClelland, and Spencer (1994).

15. For an in-depth treatment of the measures, statistical analyses, and findings of our research, see Wageman and Hackman (2008).

16. These conditions are identified and explored in depth for other kinds of
task-performing teams in Hackman (2002).

17. Real names are given for AeroMexico, Anglo American, Applebee's, British Petroleum, Citicorp, DaimlerChrysler, Forward Air, Frito-Lay, IBM, Kraft, Millennium Chemicals, Mobil Oil New Zealand, PepsiCo, People Express Airlines, Philips Electronics, Reuters, Roche Diagnostics Canada, Sainsbury, Shell, Standard & Poor's, Time Warner, Unilever, and people interviewed from those companies. All other company and personal names have been changed for confidentiality.

Chapter 2

1. For details about this research and its findings, see Allmendinger, Hackman, and Lehman (1996).

2. Gerstner (2003), 50–52.

3. Jon Katzenbach, author of "Making Teams Work at the Top" (1998), is tough on the senior executives he has studied. He says, "We observe very little team performance in the executive suite of most organizations." As with our observations of Mike Waters in this chapter, Katzenbach (1997a, b) points out that the lack of team discipline at the top of organizations is not inevitable, but rather is a function of common misconceptions or myths about strong leaders and collaborative teams.

4. Hackman and O'Connor (2004).

Chapter 3

1. See Hackman (2002) for a treatment of the challenges to consequentiality in team purposes.

2. One other source of confusion for a leadership team can be misalignments among organizational strategy and operating model and the design of executive jobs. It is beyond the scope of this book to advise about strategy and job design, but we have seen that the answers to two key questions can help a chief executive decide whether the organizational conditions are yet right for concentrating on redesigning the leadership team.

First, is the organization's operating model consistent with its strategy: does the organizational structure support or hinder the execution of the strategy? For example, one executive team that we studied struggled unsuccessfully for five years to achieve its strategy of becoming a major national player in the health care industry despite numerous initiatives and aggressive marketing. The problem: a decentralized operating model that continued to reinforce the firm's outdated regional approach to the market. Only after the team adopted a new operating model and restructured the business did it begin to get traction on its purpose as a team.

Second, is there a lack of alignment between individual executive roles and the organization's strategy? For example, if the top executives are uncertain about which senior executive is responsible for which decisions in the organization, then working together as an effective team is all but impossible.

3. See Ensley and Pearce (2001) for a description of how team dynamics can help create—or prevent—shared understandings of organizational strategy.

4. Peter Senge (1990) explores the relationship between establishing clear aspirations and managing the level of anxiety that such aspirations create. His work emphasizes the need to sustain what he calls "creative tension" rather than reduce anxiety, either for the leader or for organization members.

5. Hambrick and Siegel (1994) emphasize the role of the external organization environment in influencing the level of interdependence among senior leaders. Industry and market dynamism, for example, elevates the complexity and dispersion of information that senior leaders need to process. The cognitive demands of such complexity may be more than one individual can handle, creating the need for at least an information-sharing team at the top.

6. According to a Hewitt Associates survey (2006), 41 percent of baby boomers expect to retire within the next ten years. As these workers retire, they potentially will leave behind a gap in leadership talent (Bernhart, 2006; Rappaport et al., 2003; Wahl and Bogomolny, 2004). Moreover, demographic trends suggest that 50 percent of senior managers will retire in the next ten years, thereby creating an anticipated war for leadership talent and elevating the management of leadership succession to the enterprise level.

Chapter 4

1. For some decades, the focus of research into upper echelons has been the effects on organizational performance of compositional diversity—the range of functions, ages, tenure, and other personal characteristics represented on the team. Early studies suggested that certain forms of diversity helped and others hurt organizational performance, but a number of these initial findings have failed to be replicated in other studies. For a review and update of this stream of research, see Hambrick (2007).

2. For reviews of the research on how the presence of minorities can enhance group process and performance, see Nemeth and Staw (1989) and Hackman (1992). For an analysis of how excessive congeniality can impair the performance of decision-making teams, see Janis (1982).

3. Berg (2005) emphasizes the legitimate purpose that senior team members serve as representatives of their parts of the enterprise. He characterizes the job of CEOs as keeping members focused on "*both* their function or business areas as well as the overall corporate well-being and growth." That dual emphasis is a key tension for leadership teams, a tension that CEOs must actively manage and sustain rather than resolve by focusing only on one or the other.

4. Among the five major problems that CEOs report having with their top teams, Hambrick (2000) identified "inadequate capabilities of an individual executive." In only one case was the capability in question the individual's ability to deliver current performance. Rather, the problems were short-sightedness, poor credibility with other executives, and interpersonal deficiencies.

5. Team member competencies were assessed using coded behavioral event interviews (BEIs). See the endnotes of chapter 1 for a description of the competency assessment procedures we used.

6. For details of coding the behavioral signs of competencies in individual leaders, see Spencer and Spencer (1993).

7. Hill (2003) details the profound changes that occur not only in behavior but also in individuals' beliefs about themselves, their priorities, and their sources of self-esteem as they make the transition into a managerial role for the first time.

8. Argyris (2004) emphasizes that norms in organizations suppress the expression of feelings, especially negative ones, to the ultimate detriment of individual, group, and organizational learning.

9. Sutton (2007) identifies similar behavior as one part of his "asshole" test: after interacting with this person, do you feel belittled, humiliated, or oppressed? The individuals our experts identified as derailers generally would score very high on Sutton's "Are You a Certified Asshole?" self-test. Although Sutton's title is amusing, his fundamental point is not: individuals who display these behaviors are costly to an organization's ability to sustain innovation, collaboration, and performance.

10. Goodwin (2005).

Chapter 5

1. Studies of the impact of team size on the performance of teams elsewhere in the organization are unequivocal—larger teams perform worse—but the findings about top management teams are more varied. For example, Smith et al. (1994) find that having large top teams impairs their effectiveness, but Hambrick and D'Aveni (1996) found that failing firms were likely to have smaller teams. One difficulty with interpreting these seemingly conflicting findings is that in many cases the teams being studied are simply the number of direct reports to the CEO, and not bounded, decision-making bodies. The Senior Leadership Group at IBM described in this chapter suggests that very large leadership teams can be effective entities *for alignment functions*.

2. This treatment of team process problems as a function of team size is adapted from Hackman (2002).

3. See Gerstner (2003) for a description of how the CEO chose SLG members and why he encouraged membership in the group to change over time.

4. Research has confirmed that task design—in particular, combining smaller tasks and asking a team to complete them together, with real interchange of ideas and resources—enhances the motivation that team members derive from the work they do together and drives the degree to which members cooperate with and learn from one another. For a review of these findings, see Hackman and Oldham (1980) and Wageman (1995).

Chapter 6

1. Gerstner (2003), 74–75.

2. For a treatment of the role of reward systems in creating alignment between team performance and organizational strategy, see Lawler (1990).

3. Considerable research has examined the role and motives of boards of directors and CEOs alike in establishing compensation practices for senior leaders. Motivating teamwork is seldom mentioned. See Finkelstein and Hambrick (1988, 1989) for a treatment of the multiple influences on CEO compensation.

4. Siegel and Hambrick (2005) showed that the technological intensity of an industry generates a need for collaborative information processing and teamwork among senior executives and that this collaboration is diminished when large pay disparities exist. Their research showed that large differences in pay among senior leaders is harmful to their collaboration and ultimately to the ability of a firm to innovate and to perform over time.

5. Gerstner (2003).

6. *Nation's Restaurant News*, June 2002. Cited in Franchise Help, Inc., *Top market share dinnerhouse chains survey 2002*, 2.

7. Gerstner (2003), 190.

8. National Commission on Terrorist Attacks (2004), 355–365.

9. Mintzberg (1975).

10. Our research showed that in many cases it was other members of the team, and not the leader, who first identified the need for better-organized information resources and who then took on the task of getting the team its vital information. But it usually was the leader who created the focus on support systems that enabled members to raise and tackle these kinds of issues.

11. The Conference Board (2003).

12. Ibid., 12.

Chapter 7

1. More than thirty years ago, Mintzberg (1975) pointed out that one of the great "occupational hazards" of a chief executive's job is superficiality. The numerous and urgent demands on a CEO's time mean that she or he is driven to get things done quickly and move on, rather than probe, reflect, or get deeply involved. These pressures run powerfully counter to the role of leadership team coach.

2. Most research about coaching is found in the training literature and focuses almost entirely on individual skill acquisition (Fournies, 1978). Except for the many popular books and articles that extract lessons for team leaders from the experiences of athletic coaches, little has been published that specifically addresses the coaching of task-performing teams. For a treatment of the relationship between the quality of basic team design conditions and the impact of team coaching, see Wageman (2001).

3. Although interventions that address members' relationships and interaction can be engaging and have been shown to affect team members' attitudes, they do not improve team performance effectiveness (for reviews, see Kaplan, 1979; Salas, Rozell, Mullen, and Driskell, 1999; Tannenbaum, Beard, and Salas, 1992; and Woodman and Sherwood, 1980).

4. For a review of the research literature on team coaching that emphasizes the timing of coaching interventions, see Hackman and Wageman (2005).

5. The power and persistence of coaching at the launch of a team are shown by Ginnett's study (1993) of the behavior of airline flight-deck crews. Ginnett found that what happened in the first few minutes of a crew's time together carried forward through the crew's life. Crews led by captains who took the time in their preflight briefings to affirm the crew's purpose and norms of conduct fared better than those that received no briefing. Best of all were crews whose captains went beyond mere affirmation and actively elaborated the work context—identifying, commenting on, and engaging their crews in discussion of the unique circumstances of the trip that was about to begin.

Chapter 8

1. Barnard (1939). For a more recent use of the functional approach in analyzing what is required for effective team leadership, see Hackman and Walton (1986).

2. For details about the interaction between team design and hands-on leader behavior in shaping team effectiveness, see Hackman (2002, chapter 7) and Wageman (2001).

3. In our consultations with senior leadership teams, we always develop a competency model that is tailored to the particular leadership demands and opportunities of a given organization. We discuss here only those competencies that we have found to be helpful for leading senior teams in virtually all organizational settings.

4. Reedy's consultant eventually realized, to his dismay, that his own post-meeting conversations with Reedy apparently were prompting the chief executive to reopen and reconsider team decisions, and that led him to wonder whether he should perhaps avoid his client until some time had passed after team meetings. That impulse soon passed, and the consultant turned his attention to strategies for helping the client develop his capability to make decisions that would stay made.

5. See Hackman (2002), 136–138.

6. For a description of the instrument, see Wageman, Hackman, and Lehman (2005). A sample of the questions asked and the feedback provided can be viewed at https://research.wjh.harvard.edu/TDS or obtained directly from Hay Group.

7. See Hackman (1984), 32–35.

8. Quoted in Spreier, Fontaine, and Malloy (2006).

References

Allmendinger, J., J. R. Hackman, and E. V. Lehman. 1996. Life and work in symphony orchestras. *Musical Quarterly* 80: 194–219.

Argyris, C. 2004. *Reasons and rationalizations: The limits to organizational knowledge.* New York: Oxford University Press.

Barnard, C. I. 1938. *The functions of the executive.* Cambridge, MA: Harvard University Press.

Bennis, W. 1997. The secret of great groups. *Leader to Leader* 3 (Winter).

Berg, D. N. 2005. Senior executive teams: Not what you think. *Consulting Psychology Journal* 57: 107–117.

Bernhart, M. 2006. Preparing for a skills shortage, work intensification. *Employee Benefit News* (November): 1.

Bevilacqua, D. 2006. Leading the must-win battles journey. Speech delivered at International Institute for Management Development (IMD), Lausanne, Switzerland.

Boehm, C. 2001. *Hierarchy in the forest: The evolution of egalitarian behavior.* Cambridge, MA: Harvard University Press.

Charan, R. 2005. Ending the CEO succession crisis. *Harvard Business Review* (February): 1–10.

Conference Board, The. 2003. *Developing leaders for 2010.* New York: The Conference Board, Inc.

Diehl, M. W., ed. 2000. *Hierarchies in action: Cui bono?* Carbondale, IL: Center for Archaeological Investigations, Southern Illinois University.

Ensley, M. D., and C. L. Pearce. 2001. Shared cognition in top management teams: Implications for new venture performance. *Journal of Organizational Behavior* 22: 145–160.

227

Finkelstein, S., and D. C. Hambrick. 1988. Chief executive compensation: A synthesis and reconciliation. *Strategic Management Journal* 9: 543–558.

———. 1989. Chief executive compensation: A study of the intersection of markets and political processes. *Strategic Management Journal 10*: 121–134.

Fournies, F. F. 1978. *Coaching for improved work performance*. Bridgewater, NJ: Van Nostrand Reinhold.

Gerstner, L. V. 2003. *Who says elephants can't dance? How I turned around IBM*. New York: HarperCollins.

Ginnett, R. C. 1993. Crews as groups: Their formation and their leadership. In *Cockpit resource management*, ed. E. L. Wiener, B. G. Kanki, and R. L. Helmreich, 71–98. Orlando, FL: Academic Press.

Goodwin, D. K. 2005. *Team of rivals: The political genius of Abraham Lincoln*. New York: Simon and Schuster.

Gupta, A., and V. Govindarajan. 1984. Knowledge flows within multinational corporations. *Strategic Management Journal 21*: 473–496.

Habelian, J., and S. Finkelstein. 1993. Top management team size, CEO dominance, and firm performance: The moderating roles of environmental turbulence and discretion. *Academy of Management Journal* 36: 844–863.

Hackman, J. R. 1984. The transition that hasn't happened. In *New futures: The challenge of managing corporate cultures*, ed. J. R. Kimberly and R. E. Quinn, 29–59. Homewood, IL: Dow Jones-Irwin.

———. 1992. Group influences on individuals in organizations. In *Handbook of industrial and organizational psychology*, vol. 3, ed. M. D. Dunnette and L. M. Hough, 199–267. Palo Alto, CA: Consulting Psychologists Press.

———. 2002. *Leading teams: Setting the stage for great performances*. Boston: Harvard Business School Press.

Hackman, J. R., and G. R. Oldham. 1980. *Work redesign*. Reading, MA: Addison–Wesley.

Hackman, J. R., and M. O'Connor. 2004. *What makes for a great analytic team? Individual vs. team approaches to intelligence analysis*. Washington, DC: Intelligence Science Board, Office of the Director of Central Intelligence.

Hackman, J. R., and R. Wageman. 2005. A theory of team coaching. *Academy of Management Review* 30: 269–287.

Hackman, J. R., and R. E. Walton. 1986. Leading groups in organizations. In *Designing effective work groups*, ed. P. S. Goodman, 72–119. San Francisco: Jossey-Bass.

Hambrick, D. C. 1997. Corporate coherence and the top management team. In *Navigating change: How CEOs, top teams, and boards steer transformation*, ed. D. C. Hambrick, D. A. Nadler, and M. L. Tushman. Boston: Harvard Business School Press.

———. 2000. Fragmentation and other problems CEOs have with their top management teams. *California Management Review* 37: 110–131.

———. 2007. Upper echelons theory: An update. *Academy of Management Review* 32: 334–343.

Hambrick, D. C., and P. A. Mason. 1984. Upper echelons: The organization as a reflection of its top managers. *Academy of Management Review* 9: 193–206.

Hambrick, D. C., and P. A. Siegel. 1994. Interdependence within top management groups: Missing link in the debate about executive teamwork. Working paper, Columbia Business School.

Hambrick, D. C., and R. A. D'Aveni. 1996. Top team deterioration as part of the downward spiral of large corporate bankruptcies. *Management Science* 38: 1445–1466.

Heenan, D. A., and W. Bennis. 1999. *Co-Leaders: The power of great partnerships.* New York: Wiley.

Hewitt Associates. 2006. Three generations prepare for retirement. Retrieved 1/21/2007 from http://www.hewittassociates.com/Intl/NA/en-US/KnowledgeCenter/Articles Reports/ArticleDetail.aspx?cid=2790&tid=0.

Hill, L. A. 2003. *Becoming a manager: How new managers master the challenges of leadership.* Boston: Harvard Business School Press.

Janis, I. L. 1982. *Groupthink: Psychological studies of policy decisions and fiascoes,* 2nd ed. Boston: Houghton Mifflin.

Kaplan, R. E. 1979. The conspicuous absence of evidence that process consultation enhances task performance. *Journal of Applied Behavioral Science* 15: 346–360.

Katzenbach, J. R. 1997a. The myth of the top management team. *Harvard Business Review* (November–December): 82–91.

———. 1997b. *Teams at the top: Unleashing the potential of both teams and individual leaders.* Boston: Harvard Business School Press.

———. 1998. Making teams work at the top. *Leader to Leader* 7 (Winter): 32–38.

Kilduff, M., R. Angelmar, and A. Mehra. 2000. Top management-team diversity and firm performance: Examining the role of cognitions. *Organization Science* 11: 21–34.

Krishnan, H. A., A. Miller, and W. Q. Judge. 1997. Diversification and top management team complementarity: Is performance improved by merging similar or dissimilar teams? *Strategic Management Journal* 18: 361–374.

Lawler, E. E. 1990. *Strategic pay: Aligning organizational strategies and pay systems.* Hoboken, NJ: Jossey Bass.

Lucier, C., P. Kocourek, and R. W. Habbel. 2005. CEO succession 2005: The crest of the wave. *Strategy and Business* 43: 1–14.

McClelland, D. C. 1998. Identifying competencies with behavioral-event interviews. *Psychological Science* 9: 331–339.

Mintzberg, H. 1975. The manager's job: Folklore and fact. *Harvard Business Review* 53 (July–August): 49–61.

National Commission on Terrorist Attacks. 2004. *The 9/11 Commission report: Final report of the National Commission on Terrorist Attacks Upon the United States.* New York: W.W. Norton.

Nation's Restaurant News. 2002. Cited in Franchise Help, Inc., *Top market share dinnerhouse chains survey 2002:* 2.

Nemeth, C. J., and B. M. Staw. 1989. The tradeoffs of social control and innovation in groups and organizations. In *Advances in experimental social psychology,* vol. 22, ed. L. Berkowitz, 175–210. San Diego: Academic Press.

O'Toole, J., J. Galbraith, and E. E. Lawler. 2002. The promise and pitfalls of shared leadership. In *Shared leadership: Reframing the hows and whys of leadership,* ed. C. L. Pearce and J. A. Conger, 250–267. Thousand Oaks, CA: Sage.

Priem, R. L. 1990. Top management team group factors, consensus, and firm performance. *Strategic Management Journal* 11: 469–478.

Rappaport, A., E. Bancroft, and L. Okum. 2003. The aging workforce raises new talent management issues for employers. *Journal of Organizational Excellence* 23(1): 55–66

Rich, J. T., and J. A. Larson. 1984. Why some long-term incentives fail. *Compensation Review* 16: 26–37.

Salas, E., D. Rozell, B. Mullen, and J. E. Driskell. 1999. The effect of team building on performance: An integration. *Small Group Research* 30: 309–329.

Schachter, H. 2002. Chief executive officers and the revolving door syndrome. *Globe and Mail,* October 16, C10.

Senge, P. M. 1990. *The fifth discipline.* New York: Doubleday.

Siegel, P. A., and D. C. Hambrick. 2005. Pay disparities within top management groups: Evidence of harmful effects on performance of high-technology firms. *Organization Science* 16: 259–274.

Smith, K. G., K. A. Smith, J. D. Olian, and H. P. Sims Jr. 1994. Top management team demography and process: The role of social integration and communication. *Administrative Science Quarterly* 39: 412–438.

Spencer, L. M., D. C. McClelland, and S. M. Spencer. 1994. *Competency assessment methods: History and state of the art.* Boston: Hay/McBer Research Press.

Spencer, L. M., and S. M. Spencer. 1993. *Competence at work: Models for superior performance.* New York: Wiley.

Spreier, S. W. 2007. *The Unilever Foodsolutions journey: How a determined, sometimes dysfunctional team of executives came together to create a thriving global business.* Philadelphia: Hay Group.

Spreier, S. W., M. H. Fontaine, and R. L. Malloy. 2006. Leadership run amok: The destructive potential of overachievers. *Harvard Business Review* 84: 72–82.

Sutton, R. I. 2007. *The no-asshole rule: Building a civilized workplace and surviving one that isn't.* New York: Warner Business Books.

Szilagyi, A. D. Jr., and D. M. Schweiger. 1984. Matching managers to strategies: A review and suggested framework. *Academy of Management Review* 9: 626–637.

Tannenbaum, S. I., R. L. Beard, and E. Salas. 1992. Team building and its influence on team effectiveness: An examination of conceptual and empirical developments. In *Issues, theory, and research in industrial/organizational psychology,* ed. K. Kelley, 117–153. Amsterdam: Elsevier.

Trivers, R. 1985. *Social evolution.* Menlo Park, CA: Benjamin Cummings.

Wageman, R. 1995. Interdependence and team effectiveness. *Administrative Science Quarterly* 40: 145–180.

————. 2001. How leaders foster self-managing team effectiveness: Design choices versus hands-on coaching. *Organization Science* 12: 559–577.

Wageman, R., and J. R. Hackman. 2008. The design of senior leadership teams. Working paper, Harvard University.

Wageman, R., J. R. Hackman, and E. V. Lehman. 2005. The Team Diagnostic Survey: Development of an instrument. *Journal of Applied Behavioral Science* 41: 373–398.

Wahl, A., and L. Bogomolny. 2004. Leaders wanted. *Canadian Business* 77: 31, 35.

West, C.T., and C. R. Schwenk. 1996. Top management team strategic consensus, demographic homogeneity and firm performance: A report of resounding nonfindings. *Strategic Management Journal* 17: 571–576.

Wiersema, M.F., and K. A. Bantel. 1992. Top management team demography and corporate strategic change. *Academy of Management Journal* 35: 91–121.

Woodman, R. W., and J. J. Sherwood. 1980. The role of team development in organizational effectiveness: A critical review. *Psychological Bulletin* 88: 166–186.

Index

About the Authors

Ruth Wageman is Visiting Scholar in Psychology at Harvard University and Director of Research for Hay Group. She received her BA degree in psychology from Columbia College, and her PhD in organizational behavior from Harvard University. She returned to Columbia to teach at the Graduate School of Business, making her the first female alumna of Columbia College to return to the university as faculty. She then joined the faculty of the Amos Tuck School of Business, Dartmouth College, in 2000, and returned to Harvard in 2005.

Wageman's teaching, consulting, and research are focused on effective leadership and on identifying the organizational, group, and individual conditions that influence the effectiveness of task-performing teams. She has published numerous journal articles on a range of subjects in organizational behavior, especially about the antecedents and consequences of interdependence in task-performing teams and the effective leadership of teams. Her current research interests include the uses and misuses of power in teams, the design and leadership of effective senior management teams, and the theory and practice of leadership development.

Debra A. Nunes is Vice President at Hay Group's McClelland Center for Research and Innovation, where she leads the firm's international practice on executive team leadership. This practice engages in the study of senior leadership teams around the globe to identify the factors that contribute to senior teams' effectiveness in leading their organizations, and translates those findings into practical applications that executives can employ. Nunes works with large global companies, where she specializes in helping CEOs and heads of major business units execute their companies' strategy: integrating significant acquisitions, achieving organic growth, and expanding into markets. As part of this effort, she works with leaders to improve their personal leadership effectiveness and the capabilities of their leadership teams so that, individually and collectively, they can successfully meet the challenges associated with strategy execution and meet the demands of a changing marketplace.

Nunes's work with senior leadership teams spans more than two decades. She has worked with companies headquartered in Asia, the Pacific, Europe, Africa, and the Americas. She earned an MA degree in counseling and personnel at Western Michigan University and an MBA at Boston University.

James A. Burruss is one of the founding members and senior vice president of Hay Group's McClelland Center for Research and Innovation in Boston. Burruss earned his BA in psychology at New York University and PhD in clinical psychology and public practice at Harvard University, studying and working with the late Dr. David McClelland to understand human motivation and its impact on communities, teams, organizations, and societies. Burruss held a postdoctoral research fellowship for study in West Africa and a two-year postdoctoral fellowship at Harvard Medical School and was instrumental in developing a highly successful program for improving the academic performance of minority students at Harvard.

Burruss has applied his understanding of human motivation and performance over the past thirty years to helping organizations in both the private and public sectors around the world. His consulting experience has focused primarily on the role of leaders and leadership teams in creating high-performance organizations. His passion for transferring technology to and building the capability in other cultures has led him to work with organizations as diverse as the Ministry of Health in the Philippines, the Institute of Technology at Bandung in Indonesia, and local school teachers in Ghana, West Africa, in addition to coaching executives and executive teams in large multinational and regional companies in

India, Japan, New Zealand, Australia, Singapore, Sweden, France, Austria, Switzerland, Turkey, Spain, the United Kingdom, Zimbabwe, South Africa, Mexico, Brazil, and Canada.

J. Richard Hackman is Edgar Pierce Professor of Social and Organizational Psychology at Harvard University. He received his BA degree in mathematics from MacMurray College and his PhD in social psychology from the University of Illinois. He taught at Yale for twenty years and then moved to his present position at Harvard.

Hackman conducts research on many topics in social and organizational psychology, including team dynamics and performance, leadership effectiveness, and the design of self-managing teams and organizations. He is author of numerous articles and books, the most recent being *Leading Teams: Setting the Stage for Great Performances* (Harvard Business School Press, 2002). He has consulted to a variety of organizations about team effectiveness, leadership development, and the design of work. He also serves on the Intelligence Science Board of the Director of National Intelligence.

Hackman has received the Distinguished Scientific Contribution Award of the American Psychological Association's division on industrial and organizational psychology, and both the Distinguished Educator Award and the Distinguished Scholar Award of the Academy of Management. In 2004, *Leading Teams* won the Academy of Management's Terry Award for the most outstanding management book of the year.